No Longer Subjects of the British King

Journal of the American Revolution Books
Don N. Hagist, Series Editor

Journal of the American Revolution Books highlight the latest research on new or lesser-known topics of the revolutionary era. The *Journal of the American Revolution* is an online resource and annual volume that provides primary source-based educational articles by historians and experts in American Revolution studies.

A JOURNAL OF THE AMERICAN REVOLUTION BOOK

NO LONGER SUBJECTS

OF THE

BRITISH KING

THE POLITICAL TRANSFORMATION OF ROYAL SUBJECTS TO REPUBLICAN CITIZENS, 1774–1776

SHAWN DAVID MCGHEE

WESTHOLME
Yardley

For Jacquelyn, River, Dakota, and Kai

Westholme Publishing, LLC
904 Edgewood Road
Yardley, Pennsylvania 19067
Visit our Web site at www.westholmepublishing.com

ISBN: 978-1-59416-426-2
Also available as an eBook.

Printed in the United States of America.

CONTENTS

Illustrations

INTRODUCTION

"The Common Cause of America"

IN AUGUST 1777, THOMAS JEFFERSON NOTED A CURIOUS CHANGE that had taken place in the hearts and minds of George III's rebellious subjects. Writing to Benjamin Franklin, then serving as minister to France, Jefferson explained their countrymen had "deposited the monarchical and taken up the republican government with as much ease as would have attended their throwing off an old and putting on a new suit of clothes." In fact, not "a single throe," continued the Virginian, hindered "our political metamorphosis."[1] Though Jefferson exaggerated the ease of this transformation, he offered a sound analysis—a political metamorphosis had indeed taken place in British North America during the stormy 1770s. A resistance movement, which sought to restore harmony to the British Empire, had escalated into a struggle for independence. In other words, a crisis many Americans hoped to solve within the existing imperial framework found its solution outside the empire.

What caused this political metamorphosis? Why did American colonists, who once identified as "Your Majesty's faithful subjects," declare themselves no longer subjects of the British king?[2] Scholars of the early republic disagree over when a distinct American political community emerged from the ruins of the old order.³ Joseph Ellis recently argued that no national identity took hold among Americans until the implementation of the federal Constitution.⁴ Other historians remain convinced a national community formed decades later, either shortly before or after the carnage of the Civil War.⁵ Yet while exploring the origins of a permanent national identity remains a valuable scholarly pursuit, what is equally clear is that American Whigs forged a proto-national ethos well before the ratification of the Constitution and certainly prior to guns discharging at Fort Sumter. When did British subjects become American citizens? Put another way, at what point and by what process did the revolution create Americans?

The relationship between the metropole and mainland colonies had been deteriorating since the Stamp Act Crisis of 1765.⁶ Parliament's response to the Boston Tea Party, however, brought that relationship onto its most treacherous political terrain yet. The Coercive Acts of 1774 shut down Boston's port, revoked self-government to Massachusetts, allowed trials of royal officials to take place outside that colony, and opened unused buildings for billeting the king's soldiers.⁷ These laws created an atmosphere of panic and outrage that spread from New England to Georgia and even rippled across the Atlantic.⁸ And unlike the Stamp Act or the Townshend Acts of 1767, Parliament did not pass these latest measures to raise revenue—it designed them to punish Boston.⁹

For many alarmed subjects, the crisis at Boston became symbolic of colonial America's ongoing strife with Parliament. If Massachusetts could be crushed by the British boot, some colonists agonized, which colony might be next?¹⁰ South Carolina's Henry Laurens, after learning of Parliament's punitive acts, denounced those "extraordinary measures" as designed to compel "America to certain submissions." He gravely noted, "People will tell you, the Chastisement is intended only for Boston, but common sense informs me that in Boston all the colonies are to stand or fall."¹¹ Parliament hoped to crush that city, Laurens theorized, into a shameful obedience.¹² Massachusetts agitator Samuel Adams, for his part, reveled in his hometown's role as proverbial sacrificial lamb, boasting that while

Bostonians suffered in America's cause, "they glory in their sufferings."[13] Activists from Chesterfield County, Virginia, sent donations to "the unhappy inhabitants of Boston, whose case we look as our own." Those men and women, these Virginians claimed, suffered in "the Common Cause of America."[14]

Parliament charged Lieutenant General Thomas Gage, the commander in chief of His Majesty's Forces in North America, with enforcing the Coercive Acts. He recognized almost immediately the emotional connection mainland subjects had developed with that challenged seaport, explaining the "whole Continent . . . has embraced the Cause of the Town of Boston."[15] Virginia's George Washington also viewed this crisis as something more menacing than a local dispute. He thundered, "Americans will never be tax'd without their own consent," as "the cause of Boston . . . now is and ever will be considered as the cause of America."[16] The master of Mount Vernon reasoned Parliament had "no more right to put their hands into my pocket, without my consent, than I have to put my hands in your's, for money."[17] He then made a comparison that would have caused any Virginia gentleman to shudder, claiming Americans must defend their liberties or become "as tame, and abject Slaves, as the Blacks we Rule over with such arbitrary Sway."[18]

Alarmed colonists did not view Boston's plight as a mere abstraction; that town faced material scarcity that resulted in real human suffering.[19] During the Stamp Act and Townshend Acts crises, American subjects united to resist regulations that generally applied equally to each colony. Most joined in resistance over the principle rather than cost of taxation without representation.[20] The Coercive Acts aroused an even graver concern—Parliament intended to punish a specific colony, not equitably extract revenue from all. This logic escaped few, and Boston became a flashpoint for the Whig resistance movement.[21]

In this moment of profound crisis, city, town, and county leaders began passing resolutions that condemned the Coercive Acts and supported Boston. Many called for nonimportation of British wares and nonexportation of American resources to pressure Parliament into repealing its latest measures.[22] Some communities went further, advocating the suspension of wasteful leisure activities to publicly mourn both Massachusetts and America liberty.[23] These communities of suffering committed to self-denial so long as Boston suffered in the common cause. Alarmingly, local leaders advanced one final proposal that revealed the depths of their concerns: they called for a "Grand Continental Congress" to determine just how to relieve Boston and resolve imperial dissonance once and for all.[24] Heeding popular support for an American congress, each colony save Georgia sent delegates to assemble at Philadelphia in September 1774.

Once convened, the First Continental Congress completed a remarkable amount of work during its brief two months at Philadelphia. It crafted addresses to the people of Great Britain and Quebec, a memorial to the mainland colonies, a petition to the king, and itemized American rights and grievances.[25] Yet while each of these reveals something of the colonial mindset on the eve of revolution, the continental call to action lay in the Articles of Association, Congress's shrewdest initiative.[26]

Those supportive of the Articles of Association joined what contemporaries called the Continental Association. Congress reasoned that colonialwide commitment to the Association offered the most peaceful and effectual path to securing imperial harmony.[27] Channeling many of the main points from local resolutions passed that summer, the Association requested that colonists commit to nonimportation and nonconsumption of British merchandise and nonexportation of colonial goods.[28] Delegates aimed to weaponize economic pressure to redress colonial grievances, theorizing that once British manufacturers and merchants faced even a hint of financial hardship they would besiege Parliament.[29] And while most scholarship focuses almost exclusively on this economic aspect, the Association also asked supporters to abstain from certain cultural practices as well.[30] For example, it advised colonists to "discourage every species of extravagance," such as horse racing, cockfighting, theatergoing, and all other conspicuous displays of excess.[31] The Association also sought to end the practice of distributing scarves and gloves at funerals, a tradition many colonists felt connected them to their communities. These funerary gifts, according to some Americans, symbolized a material attachment to the deceased while signaling inclusion in a greater fellowship of mourning.[32] In order to enforce these austerity measures, the Association directed every county, city, and town to elect a Committee of Inspection and Observation. Congress empowered these local bodies to police their communities and publish so-called violators' names in local newspapers as "enemies of American liberty."[33]

No Longer Subjects of the British King argues that the Continental Association united American colonists through voluntary sacrifice, joining the many communities of suffering into a single pan-colonial resistance movement. Through the Association, Congress hoped to achieve imperial reconciliation and colonial moral regeneration. The first and most pressing objective involved getting the Coercive Acts repealed and American liberties settled on firm constitutional grounds. Yet Congress also sought to purify colonists from practices some Americans identified as corruptive in an effort to avoid the social decay many felt plagued Britain. As such, the Association directed American Whigs to forgo material and social excesses to restore liberty and an elusive ancient simplicity to the mainland colonies.

Geographically separated communities joined in solidarity with Boston and each other by committing to the Continental Association, transforming neighborhoods into militant zones of austerity, regulation, and sacrifice. In this hyperpoliticized environment, supporters monitored their neighbors, reported suspected violators, and censored literature critical of the resistance. Colonists who committed to self-denial quickly began to resent and ostracize those who refused to share the burden of suffering, viewing these outsiders as a subset with an incompatible worldview. One Massachusetts official captured this animosity when he described violators as villains who "sordidly preferred their private interest to the salvation of their suffering country."[34] This hardening division had the disquieting effect of fracturing communities into supporters of the common cause and their perceived enemies.

By adhering to the Continental Association and acknowledging the regulatory authority of local Committees of Inspection and Observation, Whig actors transferred sovereignty from king and Parliament to their national and local representatives. This political shift marked a profound psychological transformation for resistance actors. During this process, this work argues, many resistance actors exchanged their monarchical robes for republican clothes and British subjects metamorphized into American citizens.

No Longer Subjects of the British King focuses on uncovering when American Whigs determined their continued inclusion within the imperial architecture threatened their conceptions of liberty and empire. As national and local governments coordinated support for the Continental Association, curating American liberties and joining in self-denial emerged as primordial qualities that connected and sustained a pan-colonial political community. These newly established intellectual networks incubated an American ethos and ultimately the building blocks of a proto-American state, a federal republic in place of the old monarchy.

The Coercive Acts Crisis saw colonists take their first steps toward realizing a new identity as Americans. Chapter 1 traces the grassroots outrage over Parliament's measures at the town and county levels. Alarmed local leaders at once declared their support for Boston and asked their constituents to commit to nonimportation, nonexportation, and nonintercourse. They also called for a continental congress, sparking an intense debate among American subjects over who or what spoke on behalf of colonists. Chapter 2 follows colonial print media's narrative of delegates' journeys to and from Philadelphia. As recorded in the American press, localities feted these traveling congressmen upon their arrivals and departures, drawing readers into a narrative that stretched well beyond any single geographic center. The many social engagements delegates participated in during their time at Philadelphia helped shape strangers into an elite resistance fellowship and, through generous media coverage, Congress emerged as a symbol of national unity and director of a unified resistance movement.

Chapter 3 recovers the radicalism of the First Continental Congress. With virtually every decision, that assembly signaled its politics. Even mundane procedural determinations like where Congress convened or who recorded its minutes became politically charged. Each time, Congress catered to its radical faction. As that chapter reveals, the doctrine of self-preservation guided delegates' decisions and declarations, endangering imperial harmony from Congress's inception. Chapter 4 surveys the cultural context in which delegates drafted the Continental Association. It demonstrates that Congress infused that covenant with austerity measures inspired by classical virtue and Protestant dissent to achieve imperial reconciliation and inspire American moral regeneration.

The final chapter of *No Longer Subjects of the British King* examines Congress's enforcement mechanism, the Committees of Inspection and Observation, in conjunction with American print media. Printers reported most colonists as voluntarily complying with the Association while describing committeemen as virtuous sentinels tirelessly patrolling their zones of austerity. Combined, surviving letters and gazette coverage suggest an American political community forging through the shared burden of sacrifice. For these political actors, a jealous vigilance over liberty and a willingness to join in sacrifice, however short-lived, marked them as separate from the broader imperial community. Subjects no more, American Whigs transformed into citizens of a new republic.

One

The Genesis of a Pan-Colonial Political Community

BOSTON, A CITY MOST COLONISTS DESCRIBED AS "SUFFERING IN the common cause of America," became the psychological nexus through which an American political community developed.[1] When looking for the moment American subjects transformed into citizens, all proverbial roads of historical inquiry lead back to Boston.

As early as January 1774, thirty-eight-year-old John Adams received a letter congratulating him on the "Union of Sentiment of Spirit prevailing throughout the Continent." Boston's Tea Party, the letter revealed, had awoken and united resistance actors throughout British North America.[2] According to this account, American Whigs unconditionally supported Boston's destruction of the Honourable East India Company's tea. That same month, Samuel Adams, John's fifty-one-year-old cousin, claimed Boston suffered Parliament's wrath under the pretenses of destroying tea. But that seaport's actual crime, he theorized, lay in resisting a ministerial plot to enslave America. He next characterized Bostonians as "suffering the Vengeance of Administration in the Common Cause of America."[3] For the elder Adams, Boston had become the political front line of a constitutional crisis enveloping every mainland colony.

These Massachusetts Whigs, of course, might be written off as too biased to offer an objective interpretation of local events. They were not alone, however, in recognizing the existence of a "Union of Sentiment," or describing Boston as "suffering . . . in the Common Cause." In fact, these two observations reveal a remarkable grasp of the unfolding crisis: Americans created a union through self-imposed and self-regulated suffering. Months before colonial leadership stepped forward to coordinate a national resistance effort, communities supportive of Boston began implementing their own restrictions throughout British North America.

The destruction of 342 chests of East India Company tea in December 1773 enraged an already agitated king and ministry.[4] George III condemned Boston's breach of the peace and requested that Parliament determine how to better secure colonial dependence.[5] Outraged by Boston's insubordination, Prime Minister Lord Frederick North declared the contest between the metropole and her mainland colonies had arrived at a breaking point. The debate no longer hinged on whether or not Parliament could tax Americans, he warned, but whether Parliament had any authority over them at all.[6] "We must punish, control, or yield to them," North thundered.[7] Heeding the prime minister's call to action, Parliament moved swiftly to bring Boston to heel.

Parliament's Coercive Acts sought neither to regulate trade nor raise revenue. Instead, that assembly designed them to punish Boston.[8] The Port Act shut down Boston's commercial activity effective June 1, 1774. The Massachusetts Government Act altered that colony's charter, authorizing its governor to appoint civil officials and restrict town meetings to those he approved. The Administration of Justice Act allowed trials of royal officials to unfold outside the colony, denying subjects a jury of local peers. Finally, the Quartering Act mandated repurposing all unused local buildings for the king's troops.[9] These measures together enraged most British North Americans. Yet most colonists expressed true horror at the Massachusetts Government Act since it erased, in a stroke, the tradition of local government and home rule, striking at the core of colonial political identity.

When these retaliatory measures began washing ashore in the colonies in May 1774, subjects from New England to Georgia expressed their deepest sympathy for Boston. Most voiced concern that Parliament, emboldened by its subjugation of Massachusetts, next planned to enslave the rest of the colonies.[10] The prescient Henry Laurens predicted the ministry aimed to punish Boston to "terrify the other colonies into a compliance."[11] For alarmed observers, Parliament's vengeance threatened not only Boston, but all British America.

Local leaders reacted by drafting resolutions supportive of Boston, many pledging donations to that struggling port. Within these resolutions, resistance actors asked their constituents to commit to nonimportation and nonexportation, transforming many towns and counties into communities of suffering. Inhabitants of these spaces voluntarily committed to material sacrifice, offering the most pronounced outline yet of a pan-colonial ethos. Getting Parliament's latest measures repealed and securing local rule became, for these communities, the ultimate objective. Virginia's Edmund Pendleton, capturing the anxiety of the moment, claimed all recognized the attack on Boston as "a common Attack on American rights."[12] Whig actors began linking American liberty to the future of Boston, and a sense of alienation began separating those joined in self-denial from all others.[13]

Since most printers supported the common cause, Whigs received widespread political encouragement in the pages of American gazettes.[14] This supportive coverage helped unite distant but symbiotic communities into a single, pan-colonial resistance movement. At the same time, local leaders began agitating for a "Grand American Congress" to coordinate their isolated efforts into a broader continental movement.[15] Whig actors assumed synchronized resistance would maximize efficiency and prove more politically potent than multiple disconnected resistance communities.[16]

This chapter argues that commitment to self-denial awoke and united an American political consciousness in British North America. Enraged towns and counties embraced sacrifice to combat the Coercive Acts months before the First Continental Congress convened. Men and women suffering with Boston joined in public mourning, grieving for that city and American liberty by abstaining from certain commercial and social transactions. This sustained ritual became symbolic of colonial union, a rite of passage into an emerging community of sufferers. These colonists united through sacrifice to protect local identities, customs, and liberties. And the willingness to collectively endure difficulties for a common cause initiated the transformation of monarchical subjects into republican citizens. Once convened, Congress had a clear mandate to Americanize sacrifice that emanated from the streets, seaports, and hinterlands of the colonies. Grassroots resistance actors, then, first proposed and imposed self-denial as a means to relieve Boston. Consequently, this virtue became a principal quality of American political identity.

In order to trace the origins of union through sacrifice, this chapter first surveys the language of resistance employed by local leaders in the many town and county resolutions. It next explores colonial commitment to sacrifice at the local level. Some colonists offered their property, others refused their services, while some communities set aside days of fasting to mourn with Boston. Colonists unwilling to share this burden risked ostracization and even physical violence from the more militant members of their communities. Imperial traditionalists, those subjects who stood with king and Parliament, felt themselves threatened by majoritarian tyranny. From their view, Whig resistance represented sedition. The American press, however, reflected nearly propagandistic support for the Whig cause. Finally, this chapter contextualizes the frequent calls by alarmed observers for a Continental Congress, an assembly American Whigs hoped would nationalize the resistance movement and constitutionally secure American liberties.

It did not take long for observers well beyond Massachusetts to conclude the measures leveled at Boston threatened the liberty, property, and security of all American subjects. One alarmed observer claimed that while Parliament targeted Boston, anyone unable to see the Coercive Acts threatened every colony "must be blind indeed."[17] George Washington described Boston as suffering for all of America. Looking beyond Virginia, he theorized uniting with other colonies offered Americans their best protection from Parliament.[18] Washington also felt the ministry had made its objectives clear. "Is not the attack upon the liberty and property of the people of Boston," he queried, "a plain and self-evident proof of what they are aiming for?"[19] Others described Americans as caught between the Scylla and Charybdis, forced to either unite in suffering or be "devoured, one after another."[20] Parliament persecuted Boston, feared Henry Laurens, "for the Imputed sins of all the American Continent." If colonists refused to unite in resistance, he warned, American liberty and property "will indeed become all imaginary."[21] Another observer predicted that unified resistance would, "like an electric rod," shock Parliament into repealing the Coercive Acts. Each attack on Boston, the writer cautioned, struck at "the vitals of all America."[22] From the start of the crisis, many colonists considered the future of Massachusetts as predictive for all British North America.

Boston remained at the heart of the struggle, activating for many colonists a visceral fear. Parliament had stripped Massachusetts of its charter, trial by jury, right to assemble, ability to elect certain civic officials, and inclusion in the broader Atlantic economy.[23] Whigs felt this threatened the political identities of Massachusetts's subjects. Many Americans held a particular understanding of the English constitution rooted in a mythological history of colonial settlement. According to this view, the original settlers brought their political identities across the Atlantic, reshaped them while taming a dangerous wilderness, and memorialized them in colonial charters. Settlers earned these identities, this view held, at a tremendous cost of blood and treasure and embraced a tradition of passing them to their progeny inviolate. Colonial identities fused English rights with local customs and traditions, practices that varied by colony and even town.[24] For American Whigs, the Coercive Acts represented an assault on the political identities of every American subject.[25]

Beginning in the summer of 1774, many towns and counties began replacing traditional civic authority with local associations. Historian

Hermann Wellenreuther described these associations as "pre-parlia-mentary institutions designed to recapture delegated power and re-form what [colonists] thought corruption had deformed."[26] New Jersey governor William Franklin, recognizing this disintegration, complained he lacked the power to break up antigovernment gath-erings since the "chief part of the inhabitants incline to attend them."[27] Governor Sir James Wright of Georgia advised his fellow executives to return to England if they wished to avoid the mortifi-cation of "Committees and mobs" governing their colonies.[28] These committees and mobs that so alarmed Governors Franklin and Wright resulted mainly from local resolutions that communities passed in response to the Coercive Acts.

These resolutions recognized Boston as suffering in the common cause and expressed inhabitants' profound desire to secure English liberties and pass them on to posterity.[29] Most identified a colonial union dedicated to nonimportation, nonexportation, and noncon-sumption as the surest strategy for protecting this heritage of liberty. If colonists acted as "one man in every public measure" and adhered to the "resolves of the city and county where he resides," one com-mentator noted, they could salvage their rights.[30] What follows is a sampling of these resolutions by region that fleshes out remarkably consistent language.

New England resolutions made clear their support for Boston and called for a union through sacrifice to combat the Coercive Acts. Freemen of Cumberland County, Massachusetts, for example, warned that Parliament's measures not only endangered Boston, but "threatened all the colonies with ruin and destruction." Colonists must unite and suffer "many inconveniences," these men predicted, if they hoped to protect liberty.[31] Inhabitants of Rhode Island iden-tified Parliament's measures as an immediate threat to American lib-erty and property. Only "a firm and inviolable union of all the Colonies," these men surmised, could provide Americans security.[32] Connecticut's resolutions claimed for Americans the same liberties as subjects born "within the Realm of England," declaring Americans could only be taxed by their own consent. A union of colonies, the resolutions concluded, offered colonists the only path to guaranteeing American rights.[33]

As in New England, towns and counties in the mid-Atlantic region described Boston as suffering in the common cause and demanded that the next generation of colonists enjoy the rights of their fathers. To accomplish this, they called for a colonial union dedicated to sacrifice.[34] Residents of South Haven, New York, drafted resolutions declaring the Coercive Acts a direct attempt "to enslave the inhabitants of America, and put an end to all property." To parry this assault, they called for colonial union and nonimportation.[35] Freemen of Morris County, New Jersey, decried Parliament's punitive acts as destructive to American liberties. Colonists, they pleaded, must form a "union of colonies" and enforce nonimportation and nonconsumption.[36] In Lower Freehold, New Jersey, inhabitants urged colonies to unite or witness every province "share the same fate" as Boston. They, too, called for a colonial association to enforce nonimportation and nonexportation with Great Britain.[37]

Southern resolutions echoed the anxieties and proposed solutions circulating among their northern neighbors. To secure relief for Boston, inhabitants of Annapolis, Maryland, recommended breaking off all commercial exchange with Britain. These activists went further, threatening to break off trade with any town or colony that "decline[d] to come into similar resolutions."[38] Residents of Queen Anne County, Maryland, implored colonists to forge an American union to protect their constitutional rights. And like Annapolis, they urged subjects to stop commercial intercourse with Great Britain.[39] At Westmoreland County, Virginia, inhabitants denounced the Coercive Acts as an attack on natural justice, the English constitution, colonial charters, and local tradition. Like other alarmed communities, Westmoreland called for nonimportation, nonexportation, and a colonial union to "firmly unite to resist the common danger."[40]

Prince George County, Virginia, also pleaded for union and a commercial freeze with the metropole. This community, however, became the first to consider regulations beyond economic activity. Prince George's resolutions directed colonists to refrain from slaughtering sheep, stimulate domestic manufacturing, and forgo "every kind of luxury, dissipation, and extravagance." North of Prince George, Fauquier County's resolutions employed identical language a little more than a week later.[41] During this early stage, alarmed colonists expressed a willingness to sacrifice in solidarity with Boston by curtailing their commercial activity. Others advocated regulating certain social behaviors, as well, all in an attempt to protect liberties they felt Parliament had come to threaten.

Georgia, ill-prepared to join the resistance, also drafted resolutions supportive of Boston in August 1774.[42] Far more subdued than other resolves, it simply declared the Coercive Acts a "subversion of American rights."[43] St. John's Parish, the most radicalized community in Georgia, denounced these resolutions as weak and called for more animated language. The parishes of St. George, St. David, and St. Andrew, also uneasy with the timid response, agreed with St. John's assessment. St. John declared its commitment to Boston and desire to join a union of colonies and these several radical parishes met and adapted a new set of resolutions.[44] The *Georgia Gazette*, however, warned readers to ignore them altogether. These new resolutions, the paper quipped, represented the anger of a few men from fewer parishes. Georgia's divided confusion only worsened as the Coercive Acts Crisis deepened.[45]

Alarmed by Boston's perceived oppression, American Whigs adapted a common language of protest during the spring and summer of 1774. Virginia's Edmund Pendleton described Boston as suffering a "hostile invasion."[46] Americans needed a single Congress, he theorized, to relieve that port city and guarantee liberty.[47] Massachusetts assemblyman James Bowdoin claimed the spirit of resistance did not spread from colony to colony, but rather "burst forth in all of them spontaneously" once word of the Coercive Acts reached America. He predicted grassroots support for Boston would culminate in colonial union.[48] Virtually every resistance resolution expressed belief that the crisis at Boston held implications for every mainland colony. When communities committed to nonimportation, nonexportation, and nonconsumption, they joined in public mourning for Boston and American liberty. Local resolutions therefore testified to a commitment to sacrifice and revealed widespread desire for a centralized authority to unite localities.

Providence, Philadelphia, and Williamsburg actually set aside a day of mourning to observe the unhappy state of colonial affairs. On

June 1, the day the Port Act took effect, most businesses in Providence closed their doors and inhabitants darkened their windows and draped their homes in black.[49] The town took on the appearance and mood of a funeral procession. At Philadelphia, most colonists committed to a "solemn pause" in their commercial and social lives. Subjects closed their homes, officials muffled town bells, and ships at port lowered their flags to half-mast, each a recognized form of mourning.[50] Philadelphians "expressed their sympathy and concern" for those struggling at Boston.[51] Virginia's House of Burgesses also set aside June 1 as a "day of fasting, humiliation, and prayer." On that day, Peyton Randolph led his fellow burgesses from their meetinghouse to church to pray for Boston.[52] Governor John Murray, Fourth Earl of Dunmore, upon learning of this political theater, immediately dissolved the house. He viewed the burgesses' actions as a thinly veiled insult to the king.[53] Providence also set aside August 31 as another day for public mourning in recognition of the "gloomy Aspect of public Affairs."[54] Inhabitants of these towns joined in sacrifice for Boston by eschewing any commercial activity or festive engagement so long as Boston endured loss and suffering. These public determinations more broadly signaled inclusion in a self-imposed, pan-colonial mourning ritual.

Empathy for Boston's "suffering poor" inspired many communities and private individuals to donate money, food, and, in at least one instance, quality alcohol.[55] Newspapers provided plenty of space to report these initiatives, further propagandizing support for Boston to the reading public. Most resistance leaders included subscriptions for Boston in the very texts of their resolutions. In New Jersey, for example, Morris, Hunterdon, Monmouth, and Middlesex Counties each called for donations for that city's impoverished.[56] Philadelphia's resolutions also directed their committee to collect subscriptions "for the relief of such poor inhabitants" at Boston.[57] In Pennsylvania, Northampton County's resolves likewise requested donations for the "suffering inhabitants of Boston." They made clear each resident had an obligation to "contribute, according to his circumstances," to the aid of distant neighbors.[58] In Virginia, Norfolk County called for "the relief of the starving distressed poor in the blockaded town of

Boston," while James County summoned "money, corn, wheat, or any other commodity" to assist the cause.[59]

Bostonians, grateful for the support, appreciated the "Humanity, sympathy and affection expressed towards this distressed town." And Boston received plenty of material support.[60] Alexandria, Virginia, donated £350 for "that noble cause," while Virginia and Maryland both filled vessels with large quantities of flour and wheat and sent them to Boston.[61] Several towns in New Hampshire joined to provide Boston with cash, "eighty-four sheep, and 30 bushels of peas." In Massachusetts, Rehoboth and East Greenwich provided £14 and 112 sheep.[62] Marblehead sent twelve carts of fish and oil for "the sustenance of the Town of Boston," while Portsmouth donated £200 for the "suffering poor."[63] Hartford and Middleton of Connecticut gathered thousands of bushels of grain, while Rhode Island collected thousands of dollars "for the suffering inhabitants of this town."[64] New York City provided hundreds of barrels of flour, pork, and butter, while Marbletown, New York, offered twenty-one barrels of wheat and rye.[65] In New Jersey, Monmouth County delivered 1,200 bushels of rye and fifty barrels of rye flour, while Allentown and Freehold collected enough grain to fill a sloop.[66] By the end of August alone, Philadelphia residents had donated £4,000 to Boston.[67] Northampton, Virginia, collected 1,500 bushels of Indian corn.[68] South Carolina supporters sold 376 barrels of rice and sent the proceeds "to the sufferers" of Massachusetts; others from that colony simply sent rice directly to Massachusetts.[69] The above inventory is hardly exhaustive. American gazettes routinely published donations that poured into Boston. Thousands of bushels of grain, corn, and rice, hundreds of sheep, and vast sums of cash made their way into the city.[70] One observer proudly described the spirit of American resistance and sacrifice as "worthy of a Roman Bosum."[71] Another claimed Americans were "ready to sacrifice their interest, nay their lives" in defense of Boston and American liberty.[72] Boston's inhabitants, this observer offered, recognized Americans had united "in every measure of self-denial" to guard against "impending slavery."[73]

Individual actors also privately sent their property to alleviate Boston's misery. In Philadelphia, for example, Jeff Hand donated a "genteel Sum of Money" for the "use of the suffering poor of Boston."[74] New Jersey's Joseph Ellis generously provided $534, while schoolmaster Samuel Moody of Massachusetts, provided £5 to ease "the plight of the struggling poor."[75] One gentleman from New York provided £10 and "the best pipe of brandy in his distillery." He reasoned Virginia and the Carolinas had provided food but felt "such glorious sufferers for the common good ought to drink as well as eat."[76] This flood of donations illustrates the ways in which sacrifice connected colonists to Boston while drawing them into community with each other. Boston's committee, in recognition of this developing union through suffering, again expressed gratitude for the outpouring of support and sacrifice. The "firm attachment of all the colonies to the glorious cause of liberty," praised the committee, revealed Americans had united behind Boston's stand for liberty.[77]

Colonists expressed support by sacrificing more than just property. Many artisans, merchants, and laborers refused to provide goods and services they felt might contribute to Boston's continued oppression. Declining work, exchange, or wages came at the expense of the individual, so supporters denied themselves economic opportunity for political principles. Certainly others, feeling unbearable social pressure, followed suit to avoid social and commercial ostracism by their neighbors.[78] Colonists reading American gazettes, however, learned of a strengthening proto-national movement forming throughout British America.

Local committees at Boston and several neighboring towns directed constituents to withhold their labor, straw, and timber from the British Army. Committeemen cautioned locals to provide "but what mere humanity requires" for the soldiers' subsistence. Local leaders considered any assistance to the king's troops as conniving in the continued oppression of Boston.[79] When the army sought laborers to construct barracks, workers from New York "nobly rejected" the offer. Gazettes as far away as Georgia hailed the virtue of these men for refusing to help destroy the "liberties of their fellow countrymen."[80] Some New Yorkers voiced concern, however, that struggling Bostonians might not commit so firmly to self-denial as their workers had. To allay this charge, Boston's committee warned laborers and merchants alike that they risked their neighbors denouncing them as enemies should they advance the British cause.[81] Despite this warning, however, not all men bowed to local expectations.

In Rochester, New Hampshire, townsfolk suspected Stephen Wentworth of soliciting artificers to construct barracks at Boston and immediately alerted the town committee of their suspicions. In response, the committee sent member Nicolas Austin to interrogate Wentworth at his home. Once confronted, Wentworth confessed and felt "obliged on his knees" to publicly beg for forgiveness. Newspapers published and republished this exchange, broadcasting the reluctantly repentant Wentworth's betrayal and atonement.[82]

In another case, thousands of men gathered at Cambridge after learning two field pieces had gone missing. Colonists accused merchant Ebenezer Bradish of renting horses to assist in this undertaking. Bradish admitted he had rented a horse but claimed ignorance of the purpose. Had he known the renter's intentions, he testified, he would have canceled the transaction, "which has proved so disagreeable to my countrymen." He added, "I hope this will be satisfactory to the public."[83] It remains impossible to recover the private motivations behind Bradish's public address. If thousands of agitated men had indeed focused their ire on him, however, he may have found profound motivation in self-preservation.

Boston ironmonger Joseph Scott endured hundreds of angry neighbors who gathered round his home expressing "the greatest dissatisfaction at his conduct." Locals accused Scott of either selling or lending the British Army a small fortune's worth of weaponry.[84] Joseph Greenleaf explained to his brother-in-law, Massachusetts delegate Robert Treat Paine, the crowd had planned to rip Scott to pieces before local committeemen rescued him.[85] The fortunate Scott escaped with "no damage done to his person or property."[86] Locals considered the accusations leveled at Scott so egregious they nearly perpetrated violence on him without the safeguard of a trial. Incredibly, the Massachusetts Government Act, the Coercive Act that aroused some of the sharpest anger among Whigs, denied these subjects what they sought to withhold from Scott. While he evaded crowd violence, the ironworker became socially branded for allegedly placing his private interests above the public good.[87] Throughout the mainland colonies, a line of demarcation cleaved through towns, creating dichotomized communities of self-described supporters of American liberty and their inveterate enemies.

Some shipowners and merchants also sacrificed for the common cause. In New York, the *Massachusetts Spy* praised the "worthy citizens, who have to their immortal honour" refused to rent their vessels to transport British soldiers, ammunition, or field pieces. These shipowners, according to the report, proved unwilling to further oppress those Americans suffering in the common cause. The paper noted that had they helped Parliament's designs, the public would have instead heaped scorn and contempt upon them.[88] A similar scenario unfolded at Philadelphia when a local merchant refused General Thomas Gage's order for eight hundred blankets, claiming he could not stomach his wares aiding "an army sent against his country." The *Massachusetts Spy* lauded his virtue, encouraging all merchants to "follow the example of the worthy Gentleman."[89] This act of self-denial received press coverage as far away as Georgia.[90]

Some artisans politicized their services at the risk of alienating patrons. Again, whether they found motivation in principle, pressure, or disguised avarice is impossible to recover. But their public advertisements only added to the narrative of sacrifice. Samuel Waters of Sutton, Massachusetts, for example, sold skillfully crafted hoes. In an advertisement that ran for weeks, he described his patrons as "well Wishers to American Freedom." After this gratuitous nod to the prevailing political climate, he warned imperial traditionalists not to frequent his shop. He extended one exception, however, offering a single hoe to America's enemies if it helped dig a "Grave six Feet deep, to hide one or more of the Heads of those obnoxious Wretches."[91] Waters, according to his advertisement, imagined his community composed only of defenders of American liberty and hoped only to assist in burying its enemies.

Philip Freeman, a Boston glovemaker, also attempted to appeal to patrons' political persuasions. In another long-running advertisement, he wove together multiple themes already circulating in local resolutions, encouraging frugality, domestic manufacturing, and vigilance. As such, Freeman reminded Whigs that when colonists purchased American-made products, they "employ our own people, and keep a large Sum of Money here, which is annually sent to England for Gloves." He offered his wares to "all true Patriots" dedicated to the common cause.[92] Like the previous advertisement, whether or not Freeman offered a genuine appeal made little difference. The advertisement itself called on self-identifying patriots to favor American over British goods, a commercial distinction loaded with political implications.

Many observers felt colonists would need "god-like virtue" to secure American liberty through sustained self-denial.[93] These reports of sacrifice offered the reading public examples of virtue in which to aspire while bluntly exposing those who failed to live up to these expectations. The emerging resistance community formed around the triumvirate of political union, self-denial, and a propagandistic press. Yet while many colonists interpreted community and individual sacrifice as a unifying process, many realized that coordinated resistance offered the straightest path to salvation. Colonists most consistently identified a "grand American Congress" as the solution.[94]

Calls for a Continental Congress spread rapidly as Americans anticipated Parliament's response to the Boston Tea Party. As early as March 1774, a London observer predicted to an American correspondent the creation of a "general congress from your Colonies." He theorized colonists had two options: unite and enforce a nonimportation and nonexportation agreement or submit to British tyranny. He reasoned that if colonists committed to a commercial freeze for two years, Parliament would capitulate. The Londoner remained convinced, however, that the American Congress's directives would determine "the fall or rise of your country."[95] American agent Arthur Lee called on Americans to gather their wisest men "to save our liberties from shipwreck." He advocated for a general congress and a year-long boycott as a means to repeal the Coercive Acts.[96] Samuel Adams warned Parliament's current course could only lead to the "entire separation and independence of the Colonies."[97] Another Londoner warned a friend at New York of the grave danger

Parliament posed to American liberty. He advised Americans to "summon all the wisdom and firmness of the United Continent of America." In closing, he revealed the uncertainty of the time, explaining the ministry "would be glad to have my head . . . you will excuse me not writing my name—you know the hand."[98]

Days after word of the Port Act arrived in Boston in May 1774, concerned subjects gathered at Faneuil Hall to consider their options. After electing Samuel Adams moderator, they read Parliament's punitive directive and proposed inviting other colonies into a joint resolution stopping all trade with Britain until the Port Act's repeal. The proposal, likely at the suggestion of the calculating Adams, asked if neighboring colonies considered Boston as "suffering in the common cause of America."[99] Yet even before Boston's appeal reached Rhode Island, a town meeting in Providence declared Parliament's sanctions against Boston a threat to American liberty and called for "a Congress as soon as may be." Philadelphia also advocated for "a general Congress of Deputies from the different Colonies," while New York urged colonists to respond with a "virtuous and spirited union," or suffer endless oppression.[100] Colonists throughout the mainland colonies expressed immediate support for Boston at the start of the Coercive Acts Crisis. They expressed similar enthusiasm for a national Congress to synchronize American resistance.

Virginia's resistance leaders also called for an American Congress once they learned of the Boston Port Act. The House of Burgesses, in addition to setting aside a day of mourning, urged mainland colonists to act "as one Heart and one Mind" to defend "*American* rights [emphasis in original]."[101] After Governor Dunmore dissolved the burgesses, they declared themselves private men and met in an unofficial capacity.[102] Taking up residence in the Apollo, a large meeting room at Raleigh Tavern, the gathered subjects appointed Peyton Randolph moderator before crafting a response to Parliament's latest measure. After declaring loyalty to the king, they accused a wicked Parliament of designing to enslave Americans. They next condemned the Port Act as a blatant attempt to "destroy the constitutional liberty and rights of all *North America*." These subjects next advised colonists to consider the attack on Massachusetts an attack "on all of British America." Finally, they called for the creation of an American Congress to protect "the united interests of America." Flaunting their extraconstitutional status, those gathered signed off as the "eighty-nine Members of the late House of Burgesses."[103] While Boston's defiance surprised few in Parliament, Virginia's involvement elevated the latest conflict. The call for a Continental Congress signaled deep support for Massachusetts in the midst of a deepening imperial crisis.

Throughout the summer of 1774, colonies began selecting delegates to represent them in the proposed Continental Congress. The provincial assemblies of North Carolina, New Hampshire, New Jersey, Delaware, and Maryland convened without sanction of their governors while choosing their respective delegates. Encouraged by outside support and in defiance of the Massachusetts Government Act, Massachusetts did as well. The Bay Colony also recommended Congress convene in Philadelphia. Connecticut's Committee of Correspondence selected its delegates, while Virginia leaders held a convention. Historian Edmund Cody Burnett colorfully described New York as a "squirming mass of contending factions" incapable of reaching a consensus. Ambiguously and without further explanation, New York City delegates revealed that "proper persons, in seven wards" had selected five delegates for Congress. Only Pennsylvania saw its delegates elected by the regularly constituted legislature. Every colony save Georgia agreed to send delegates to Philadelphia.[104]

Georgia, despite its vulnerability to Indian attacks and dependence on Parliament's financial assistance to fund its government, still expressed support for Congress. Each parish sent delegates to Savannah in August 1774 to determine how to respond to the Coercive Acts despite Governor Wright declaring all such meetings unconstitutional and threatening to punish those who attended.[105] Defying the governor, delegates met anyway. After declaring the Coercive Acts unconstitutional and denying Parliament's right to tax colonists, they turned to electing representatives to the Continental Congress. Members from Savannah voted against sending delegates to Philadelphia. Members from St. John's Parish called for a second vote to send delegates to Congress, which also failed. Ultimately, no member of the First Continental Congress hailed from Georgia.[106]

Georgia remained deeply divided over joining the Continental Congress, with radical St. John and three other parishes openly supporting participation. St. John, described by Governor Wright as suffering from "Oliverian principles," most vocally supported the cause of Boston and Congress.[107] Its delegates made two more attempts at appointing members to convene at Philadelphia, but both failed to garner enough support. The radical parishes, acting outside of the colony's official provincial position, eventually elected Dr. Lyman Hall to Congress. Hall, recognizing he spoke for only four parishes rather than all of Georgia, declined the request to go to Philadelphia. Members of Congress, disturbed by the absence, expressed resentment of Georgia. Still firmly behind the cause, St. John sent £50 and two hundred barrels of rice to the suffering in Boston.[108] As late as September 12, 1774, New England papers were publishing accounts claiming Georgia had chosen its members for the First Continental Congress.[109] These reports proved false, but St. John did secure Hall's appointment for the Second Continental Congress.[110]

American Whigs and other sympathetic observers identified an American union as the only solution to the empire's problems. One South Carolinian synthesized the prevailing attitude when he declared "one great soul of harmony should animate this whole Continent, and dispose each one to consider an injury offered to any part as offered to himself."[111] According to a London observer, Parliament viewed Americans as too "attached to their private interests" to endure sustained sacrifice. Both Lords and Commons, he added, ridiculed colonists for their "high sounding declarations of patriotism." Americans could pressure Parliament into repeal, however, if they made a "sullen, united, and invincible stand."[112] Another Englishman described America as the only place "where public honesty and public virtue are to be found on earth." Every other nation, he continued, had devolved into slavery and servility. The idea of a Continental Congress, claimed this observer, "alarm your enemies more than anything else."[113]

Political commentator "Junius Americanus" warned General Gage to expect fierce resistance to the Coercive Acts from "every province-city-town-and county on the continent." He predicted that an American union dedicated to a commercial freeze would bring about repeal. If not, the pseudonymous essayist offered, the empire would descend into civil war and unleash "the accumulating rage of the whole continent."[114] Colonists from New England to Georgia joined in sacrifice for Boston, initiating a union through self-denial. This intercolonial participation in mourning began the transformation of British subjects into American citizens.

When word of the Coercive Acts washed up on colonial shores in May 1774, Boston received unwavering support from communities throughout British North America. Outraged subjects declared Boston suffering for American liberty and urged colonies to unite and sacrifice in the common cause. Town and county resolutions codified these pleas by committing their communities to self-denial. Resistance actors mobilized, not to forge new political identities, but rather to defend their existing ones. American Whigs identified two basic characteristics that qualified membership in their emerging political community: willingness to unite and willingness to sacrifice in defense of liberty.[115] Some colonists demonstrated these qualities by refusing wages, others by refusing goods and services if they furthered Boston's oppression. Still others donated material property to the men and women of Boston. In a few instances, whole towns shut down in mourning. All who supported Boston united through some form of sacrifice.

An observer from South Carolina demanded that Americans "make a willing sacrifice of our private interest to this glorious cause of infinite importance." He added, "By uniting we stand, by dividing we fall."[116] English migrant Nicholas Cresswell griped, "Nothing talked about but War with England." Committees, he gasped, had begun regulating colonial commerce, tarring and feathering violators, and burning property. He grew alarmed by the spreading militarization of communities throughout the colonies. "In short," the anxious traveler explained, "everything is ripe for rebellion."[117] Henry Laurens noted his countrymen needed "to be firm, frugal, and virtuous" and eschew "all trifling amusements." Americans must "prepare to stand the shock of living" in simplicity.[118] Laurens declared himself willing to forward his plantation's profits to those in need while he personally survived on what "virtue and [his] constitution will countenance."[119] George Washington felt Parliament would bend when Britain felt the economic squeeze of a unified nonimportation movement. Typically cautious, he remarked, "I hope that there is public virtue enough left among us to deny ourselves everything but the bare necessities of life to accomplish this end."[120] Most observers recognized the most desirable outcome, imperial harmony, required a degree of sacrifice and mourning throughout the colonies. In the very chambers of Parliament, Edmund Burke described the "present situation in America" as "a funeral" and the somberness of the moment escaped few. [121] As communities united through suffering, Americans called forth the Continental Congress, initiating the development of a pan-colonial political community. The leaders of that community began making their way to Philadelphia during the hot summer of 1774.

Two

The Formation of an Elite Resistance Fellowship

T O COORDINATE THE MANY GRASSROOTS RESPONSES TO THE Coercive Acts, colonists voiced deep support for a congress of representatives from each of the mainland colonies.[1] And when the First Continental Congress convened in September 1774, the hearts of most alarmed observers remained firmly in Boston. Their heads, however, shifted focus to the delegates' critical work in Philadelphia. Colonial support for Congress marked the next step in the political metamorphosis of America's white inhabitants from subjects to citizens.

This chapter argues that the First Continental Congress helped form two connected but separate political communities: the elite fellowship that took control of a unified resistance and the pan-colonial movement supportive of Congress's efforts to secure American liberty. The following pages first survey colonists' expectations of those

summoned to Philadelphia to mend the ailing empire. Press coverage
of delegates departing from home, arriving in Philadelphia, and returning to their respective provinces invited readers into a carefully
crafted triumphal drama, tightening the bonds of union between
them.[2] This chapter next explores the sociopolitical sinews that developed among Congress's representatives. Uncovering the festive atmosphere that reigned during their time at Philadelphia reveals the
succession of shared meals, toasts, and other rites of congeniality that
helped the upper echelons to form an elite resistance fellowship. Finally, these pages trace Congress's emergence as a symbol of political
unity, the connective tie that joined and synchronized grassroots resistance efforts throughout British North America. And though it remains impossible to recover how most colonists received and
processed press coverage, the surviving record reflects their performative sense of unanimity. Alarmed subjects performed union by calling for it, sacrificing in its name, and memorializing it in resolutions,
pamphlets, and papers. Delegates, the communities that feted them,
and printers who reported this celebratory atmosphere, crafted and
curated a narrative of political unity. As this chapter reveals, American resistance relied on political principle as much as performative
patriotism to achieve its objectives.

Even before American newspapers began publishing the Coercive
Acts in May and June of 1774, most observers felt Boston's latest act
of defiance guaranteed Parliament's retribution.[3] Clear-eyed subjects
called forth the Continental Congress to settle imperial differences
and prevent rash actors on either side of the Atlantic from exacer-
bating the empire's worsening troubles.[4] One Londoner advised
colonists to gather the political wise men of the continent to protect
colonial rights.[5] In a forgivable moment of hyperbole, another writer
proclaimed every American desired a Congress. Only through colonial union, he concluded, could Americans guarantee liberty and happiness.[6] Three major themes permeated colonial discourse on the
proposed Continental Congress: subjects envisioned it as a symbol
of colonial unity; expected it to embody America's collective wisdom;
and believed imperial salvation hinged on its efforts. Most observers
anticipated Congress's directives to broadcast as "the voice of all the
Colonies."[7]

In Massachusetts, constituents revealed the importance of a Congress to some recently elected officials. Bostonians, for example, advised an incoming General Court member that only "a firm and well constituted Union of the Colonies" could shield their constitution from its enemies. Therefore, they demanded he focus his political energies on helping create a Congress.[8] Worcester freemen expressed a similar view to a new member, describing the potential Continental Congress as a unifying agent.[9] One writer placed American union and colonial solidarity within a classical framework most colonists would have appreciated.[10] Why, he asked, did Greece fall to Philip of Macedon and afterward Rome? And why, he questioned, did Spain succumb to Carthage? "Because they contended for freedom *separately* [emphasis in original]," he lectured. And why, he continued, did the Swiss cantons successfully resist tyranny? "Because they wisely regarded the interest of *each* as the interest of *all* [emphasis in original]," he revealed.[11] On the eve of the American Revolution, alarmed subjects envisioned a colonial union and national congress as critical to securing liberty and imperial harmony. But what of the men burdened with coordinating this union? The potential delegates' character garnered significant attention in the months leading up to their convening in Philadelphia.

Most observers expected colonial leadership to appoint men of talent and virtue to Congress.[12] One pseudonymous writer predicted that assembly would house "the collected wisdom of America."[13] Philadelphia's Committee of Correspondence agreed, and urged potential representatives to "act with weight and authority."[14] New York City's committee also expected delegates to embody American virtue and asked that constituents grant them binding authority to speak for their respective colonies.[15] Pseudonymous observer "Anglo Americanus" cautioned against appointing self-interested men, reminding readers that only actors of "unquestionable zeal . . . in the common cause" could realize America's salvation.[16] As expressed by colonial newspapers, virtually every observer expected public-spirited men to take the reins of resistance.

After Congress assembled in September 1774, one Philadelphian proclaimed a more honorable assembly had not convened "since the days of the first Charles."[17] A Maryland observer described delegates as men chosen with the full confidence of their communities. Parliament's members possessed more land and wealth, he conceded, but America's representatives claimed more "honour, honesty, and publick spirit."[18] James Madison, a careful observer of the deepening crisis, pronounced his own faith in delegates' abilities. Americans ought to reserve their private opinions, the young Virginian confided to a friend, and heed Congress's collected "wisdom and judgment."[19] Some delegates received private letters surveying public opinion on Congress and its representatives. Abigail Greenleaf reported to her brother, Robert Treat Paine of Massachusetts, that the whole continent celebrated "their Choice of Patriots to compose this noble assembly."[20] Caesar Rodney of Delaware learned from his brother that Americans stood firmly behind the "united wisdom and virtue of the congress, in which we trust the fate of the colonies."[21] And according to Silas Deane, Connecticut's subjects considered the Continental Congress the most consequential assembly on the mainland. Every American, he claimed, "is intrusted to it and depends upon it."[22] As revealed by these commentators, many American Whigs held high expectations for Congress.

Most observers suspected the empire's future depended on Congress's performance. Massachusetts statesman James Bowdoin expected that assembly to forge a union and "work out Salvation" for all of the colonies.[23] Freemen of Marblehead, Massachusetts, also looked to that assemblage to bring about "the Salvation of American Liberty."[24] Philadelphia's Committee of Correspondence believed its actions would dictate the survival of American freedom.[25] Abigail Adams predicted the future of not only Massachusetts, but the empire, depended on Congress's efforts. Writing to her delegate husband, she reasoned, "The first of September [the loose meeting date for Congress to convene that summer], perhaps may be of as much importance to Great Britain as the Ides of March were to Caesar"[26] Adams interpreted Congress's convening as either the empire's rebirth or demise. Such widespread faith in Congress signaled the seriousness of the moment and the strengthening bonds of union among alarmed Americans.

Newspapers provided the public with a steady diet of support for Congress leading up to its convening. One Philadelphian, describing the degree to which that assemblage had taken hold of the American imagination, marveled, "The whole attention and conversation is wrapped up in Congress, [with] every mouth wishing them success." Colonists held delegates in great esteem, explained this commentator, and "ardently expect the salvation of America."[27] Solomon Drowne, a visiting medical student from Rhode Island, grew so preoccupied with Congress he wrote of nearly nothing else. After seeing delegates at their lodgings, he exclaimed to his father, "My blood thrilled thro' my Veins at the agreeable, Pleasant View of so many noble and sage Patriots, met in the great Cause of Liberty."[28] To his sister he confided he had sought them out to witness firsthand that "illustrious Band." But a story Drowne heard about Colonel George Washington really captivated him. After noting Washington's judgment and bravery, he gushed, "I heard he wished to God! the Liberties of America were to be determined by a single Combat between himself and G—e."[29] Attorney Joseph Reed, carefully observing the events unfolding in Philadelphia, summed up the spirit of the moment. The day before delegates convened, he recorded, "We are so taken up with Congress that we hardly think or talk of any thing else."[30] Even imperial traditionalist Samuel Seabury declared Congress "the object of Grand Continental Attention."[31] For most Americans, there was no bigger story during the summer of 1774 than the First Continental Congress.[32]

Not all observers, however, expressed such glowing support for the American assembly. Some grew concerned that allegiance to its directives might lead supporters to violently suppress dissent. One writer feared he might be "torn apart by the mob" should he not agree or consent to Whig dictates.[33] Others warned Congress against entertaining destructive nonimportation measures.[34] One prescient observer decried American resistance as "the beginnings of a rebellion." If left unchecked, he predicted, the empire faced something akin to the English Civil War, which subverted the English constitution and saw "the best blood of the nation spilled."[35] Despite these reservations, however, newspapers spent an impressive amount of ink supporting Congress and its delegates.

In paper after paper, printers invited readers to follow delegates from their home colonies to Philadelphia, making even their travels newsworthy. This was no small addition to the news cycle, as these reports heightened anticipation for Congress's convening. For example, readers learned New Hampshire's delegates arrived in Philadelphia on August 31, and "the Gentlemen Delegates from Connecticut are expected in Town this evening."[36] One paper reported Rhode Island's delegates, Thomas Arnold and Stephen Hopkins, along with the latter's wife, set sail for New York on August 27. Papers announced the Virginia delegation arriving in Philadelphia to "ringing bells" and "other marks of a most hearty welcome."[37] When only part of the South Carolina delegation entered that city in late August, press coverage assured readers the missing members were on schedule to arrive that same evening.[38] A circulating report described one North Carolina delegate as just hours outside of Philadelphia.[39] These updates related not only the importance of delegates' arrivals, but the urgency of the moment.

Festive events held in delegates' honor also helped strengthen the bonds of union between colonial readers. John Jay may have quietly slipped out of New York in late August, but a large crowd of "respectable Inhabitants" escorted fellow delegate Isaac Lowe and his wife to St. George's Ferry, feting the couple with music and "Loud Huzzas." After seeing Lowe off, the crowd returned to a local coffee house to "testify the like Respect" to the remaining New York delegates. When James Duane, Philip Livingston, and John Alsop boarded the ferry, Duane informed those gathered that he and his "Brother Delegates" expected Congress to restore American liberty. As the ferry began its southward journey, onlookers saluted the departing delegates "by several Pieces of Cannon, mounted on this joyous occasion." Some attendees marked "the Salvation of the Colonies from the Hour," signaling remarkable confidence in Congress. They next imbibed many "spirited Toasts" as celebratory cannon fire persisted throughout the evening. Animated celebrants volunteered to sacrifice their lives and property for "those worthy gentlemen of other Colonies" in Congress.[40]

After attending a grand celebration, the Massachusetts delegates set out for Philadelphia on August 10. A crowd of about thirty saw them off, wishing them safe passage. John Adams described the scene as "beyond all description affecting."[41] Adams, his cousin Samuel Adams, Robert Treat Paine, and Thomas Cushing had just started off to Congress, however, when a carriage horse suddenly became erratic, endangering the passengers. While the delegates waited for a replacement, a local colonel approached them and explained that "the Coachman must certainly have made a mistake and put in a Torry Horse."[42] By reporting, even in jest, the partisanship of a horse, this printer took for granted his readers' political persuasion. This instance also offers a glimpse into the Whig mind, as each celebrated actor and the authority figure in this scene supported the common cause. Only the animal supported king and Parliament.

Once delegates resumed travel, press accounts revealed a supportive crowd accompanied them roughly ten miles to neighboring Watertown. Upon arrival, local supporters joined the procession. Townsfolk honored the delegation with "an elegant Entertainment" before their visitors departed. The following day, readers learned New Hampshire's delegation passed through Boston escorted by 150 supportive men.[43] These processions signaled a hybridization of festivity and militancy championing the common cause. Similar anecdotes filled American newspapers from Massachusetts to Georgia, normalizing public support for Congress. By inviting Americans into a pan-colonial narrative, printers helped blur physical geography and join colonists in literary citizenry.[44]

When the Massachusetts delegation pulled into Hartford, Connecticut, inhabitants joyously greeted them before addressing the unhappy state of colonial affairs. That evening, delegates enjoyed a dinner in their honor before their morning departure.[45] A crowd again accompanied the procession six miles to nearby Wethersfield, where the travelers engaged in yet another round of entertainment. They parted "in great, good Humour" and continued toward New York. At the next town, another gathering, this time led by the sheriff and justice of the peace, greeted them. John Adams, deeply moved by the experience, recorded the moment in vivid detail: "As we came into Town, all the Bells . . . were sett to ringing, and the People Men, Women and Children, were crouding at the Doors and Windows as if it was to see a Coronation." He recorded inhabitants setting off about a dozen cannon salutes to honor the event. Congress, according to Adams, enjoyed support from every town his delegation passed through.[46] After this latest evening of feting, delegates set off again to join "the grand Congress."[47]

By following the delegates' movement and the celebratory atmosphere surrounding each arrival and departure in colonial newspapers, colonists became participants in an unfolding imperial drama.[48] The current crisis transcended any single town, county, or colony. Indeed, it ignored colonial geography altogether. It likewise transcended colonial linguistic barriers, most notably among German colonists, the largest ethnic minority in British North America.[49] Congress's supporters etched a proverbial line in the sand, marking themselves as vigilant defenders of liberty and all others as enemies. Despite the Whigs' confidence in Congress, however, its members arrived at Philadelphia strangers to one another. Engendering meaningful relationships, then, became a vital precondition for delegates before Congress could project a united front against perceived oppression.

When delegates finally began straggling into Philadelphia in August 1774, they were confronted with what John Adams described as "the violent heat" of that city.[50] In fact, schoolmasters suspended classes for nearly two weeks that summer because of scorching temperatures.[51] As Adams began studying his new colleagues, he grew alarmed at the daunting situation before delegates. "Fifty gentlemen meeting together," he fretted to his wife, "all strangers, are not acquainted with each other's language, ideas, views, [and] designs." These men, he wrote, arrived at Congress "jealous of each other— fearful, timid, skittish."[52] Writing his former law clerk, Adams gloomily described delegates as representing "a diversity of religions, educations, manners, interests . . . it would seem almost impossible to unite in one plan of conduct."[53] In his diary, he described delegates as deeply learned men conditioned to "guide his own province."[54] In other words, Congress consisted of leaders unfamiliar with the art of compromise and each other. Securing American liberties, however, required delegates to depend on and work closely with unknown characters.

Adams was not alone describing Congress as a collection of strangers convening to unite the colonies. William Bradford, a close confidant of James Madison, observed "a great concourse from all parts of the Continent" pooling into Philadelphia, which itself had become "another Cairo." Instead of "swarming with merchants," however, Bradford described the city as teeming with "politicians and statesmen."[55] A letter republished in the *Georgia Gazette* that September described Philadelphia as "full of Delegates and strangers."[56] Another writer urged Pennsylvanians to express enthusiasm for the cause so "foreign members of Congress" might realize Pennsylvania shared their same spirit of resistance.[57] Connecticut's Silas Deane recorded that the "city was full of people from abroad," while Pennsylvania's Joseph Galloway returned to Philadelphia to discover the "Temper of the Delegates," people he clearly knew little about.[58]

Connecticut delegates expressed happiness to learn "the whole Congress, and through them the whole continent," of one mind regarding the Coercive Acts. They explained to their governor, however, why the atmosphere of unfamiliarity foreshadowed trouble. Each colony had "modes of transacting publick business peculiar to itself," they cautioned, and each aimed to secure its own rights and interests. Delegates needed "time to become so acquainted with each one's situations and connexions," they theorized, before uniting the resistance.[59] In sum, observers described representatives as "strangers," or "foreign members," or "people from abroad," or, for Galloway, people so fundamentally unfamiliar that learning their "Temper" required careful observation.

How did these strangers grow to trust one another? Surveying delegates' social activities uncovers how they forged a united leadership that enabled them to harmonize the many resistance communities. During the dinner parties, social calls, and tavern visits in which they participated, many members developed a mutual respect, drawing them into an elite fellowship. And while some nurtured long-lasting relationships, most formed a specific form of friendship based on advancing the public good, a nod to the classical world.[60] Delegates' private correspondence reveals the important and understudied sociability that fashioned friends from strangers.

The classical world's statesmen exerted no small influence over eighteenth-century American elites, and few ancient writers loomed larger in their minds than Cicero.[61] Many colonists idolized his political virtue.[62] Indeed, before leaving for Philadelphia, John Adams ruminated on that Roman senator. Cicero, remembered Adams, denied himself every pleasure to ensure he faithfully served Rome. Adams characterized Cicero's behavior as worthy of study since it revealed all "that is great and good in Human Nature."[63] Virginia's elite, also entranced by that Roman's perceived selflessness, dubbed Richard Henry Lee the "Cicero of America."[64] Cicero interpreted friendship as a political alliance, a bond between virtuous men acting on behalf of the public good. Friendships collapsed, posited the senator, when one party's private ambitions took precedence over the needs of the commonwealth.[65] Many delegates imagined themselves joined in defense of shared constitutional birthrights, the Ciceronian variety of friendship.[66] And they spent plenty of time performing their public spiritedness in Philadelphia's taverns.

Taverns served a range of functions in eighteenth-century colonial America. In some communities, they doubled as a post office or offered traveling judges workspace when courthouses proved too expensive a tax burden for a given town. In addition, taverns hosted banquets, balls and weddings, served as marketplaces and meeting spaces, and became information hubs.[67] They also served as political arenas. As recognized by historian Peter Thompson, speaking in a tavern revealed "the true character of men and ideas" and offered citizens the opportunity to evaluate public actors.[68] Within Philadelphia's taverns, delegates ate, toasted, conversed, and gave speeches on the unfolding imperial crisis and these shared moments of sociability nurtured Ciceronian friendships among them. They acted out their politics before one another, performative exercises that expressed their dedication to the common cause.

Tracing some delegates to Philadelphia is essentially like drawing a line on a map through the taverns along the way. For example, Edmund Pendleton, Richard Henry Lee, and George Washington set out for Philadelphia on September 1, 1774. Over the next four days they visited three taverns, the final stop being Philadelphia's City Tavern, where they dined with local physician Dr. William Shippen.[69] As mentioned above, the Massachusetts delegates departed from Boston in mid-August. They also routinely visited taverns on their nearly three-week journey to Philadelphia. And though Adams at times felt overwhelmed by the frequent dining and drinking, he recognized it afforded him "the Acquaintance of many respectable People."[70] When they finally limped into Philadelphia on August 29, "dirty, dusty, and fatigued," they, too, settled at City Tavern, which Adams described as "the most genteel" public house in America. The exhausted travelers conversed with some of Philadelphia's principal men along with other recently arrived delegates. After roughly twenty days on the road, Adams recorded his delegation received a sincere "Welcome to the City of Philadelphia."[71]

Whether taking breakfast together, fraternizing at rented lodgings, or sharing libations in taverns, delegates' social engagements blended politics with pleasure. John Adams attended "so much business, so much ceremony, so much company, [and] so many visits," he remained busy nearly every conscious hour.[72] He reported to his wife he had imbibed no hard cider since joining Congress, feasting instead on "Phyladelphia Beer, and Porter" with the "Nobles of Pensylvania."[73] Connecticut's Silas Deane told his wife he intended "to dine out every day this week." Despite the indulgent appearance, Deane assured his wife, "it is hard work."[74] Delegates expended so much effort, according to Deane, that after each session they could do little else but eat, drink, and converse afterward.[75] Lingering political discussions no doubt spilled into the carousing Deane alluded to. These intimate moments allowed delegates to engage one another in performance politics.

One evening at City Tavern, Virginia's Richard Bland boasted to gathered delegates that he would have made it to Philadelphia had he been forced to walk. Rising to the occasion, fellow Virginian Benjamin Harrison claimed he would have attended Congress had it been held in Jericho.[76] These men performed their commitment to the cause, encouraging others to similarly express loyalty. The next afternoon, John Adams joined delegates from Delaware and Maryland, where they read newspapers, talked politics, and "drank punch."

This fraternizing continued at Philadelphia attorney Joseph Reed's home with the addition of some New Jersey delegates. Later that evening, this growing collection relocated to Pennsylvania delegate Thomas Mifflin's house, where Richard Henry Lee and others joined them. According to Adams, the group enjoyed a genteel supper and "drank sentiments till eleven o'clock." Lee had spent the afternoon drinking wine with John Dickinson before arriving and, as Adams remembered it, appeared "very high." Feeling the camaraderie (and likely the alcohol), delegates began offering toasts, each political salute bringing the spirited group closer together. Adams recorded one delegate shouting "Union to the Colonies," before delegates raised their glasses. "Unanimity to the Congress," yelled another member before the group lifted their next cup of spirits. One cried out "May Britain be wise, and America free," followed by, "A constitutional death to the Lords Bute, Mansfield, and North." Finally, another proclaimed, "May the result of the Congress answer the expectations of the people."[77] These early moments of fraternal festivity helped foster Ciceronian friendships among the delegates.

In a later October gathering, delegates again congregated at City Tavern for "a most elegant entertainment." As John Adams remembered it, an unnamed gentleman rose and offered, "May the sword of the parent never be stained with the blood of her children," after which the collection of men raised their glasses and joined in salute.[78] In colonial America, toasting communicated a sense of community among friends as well as strangers. A crowd signaled approval for a speaker's sentiments by joining the toast, thus drawing participants together through shared spirits and beliefs.[79] During these Philadelphia gatherings, celebratory gestures joined delegates into an elite resistance fellowship.[80] These men spent nearly two months socializing together, each festive interaction strengthening their bonds of union.

George Washington also kept an active social life while at Philadelphia, dining with fellow delegates, local attorneys, and even the colony's former governor. He spent at least ten evenings at City Tavern and virtually every other night fraternizing with others.[81] One exchange, however, indicates Washington's socializing had formed meaningful connections with former strangers.

While attending Congress, Washington received a letter from Robert Mackenzie, a former captain of Washington's Virginia regiment. Mackenzie, now a British lieutenant in the 43rd Regiment of Foot, disclosed to Washington his thoughts on the current state of imperial affairs. The Massachusetts rebellion, he explained, resulted from weak men who sought independence over reconciliation. Parliament would bring liberty and peace back to Boston, Mackenzie predicted, once Bostonians elected "abler Heads and better hearts." This slight against that colony's Whig leaders provoked a stern yet measured response from Washington.[82] After revealing his intention to write "with the freedom of a friend," he chided Mackenzie for siding with king and Parliament. The Coercive Acts, Washington lectured, violated "the most essential and valuable rights of mankind." The Virginia delegate explained he had "better opportunities of knowing the real sentiments" of that suffering colony since he knew their leaders intimately. No one in America, declared Washington, wished for independence. This last thought, however, came with a notable qualifier. Though reconciliation remained every mainland colonist's sincere wish, he claimed, none would resign a single liberty essential to the life of a freeman.[83]

Washington had no personal connection with the Massachusetts delegates before attending Congress. He learned their character and concerns while socializing in Philadelphia. In his exchange with Mackenzie, Washington defended men who were unknown to him less than a month earlier. Now he felt allegiance to Congress's elite fraternity, men joined in support of Boston and American liberty.

The press offered virtually nothing about the First Continental Congress during its time in Philadelphia. One critic described this informational omission as "that mysterious period of silence" that "kept the whole continent in suspense."[84] And what little news did trickle into the press offered nothing substantial. *Rivington's New York Gazetteer* described Congress's work as "profoundly secret."[85] Despite this secrecy, however, another paper claimed, "The greatest unanimity prevailed among the members of Congress."[86] And despite this perceived unanimity, a separate gazette reported delegates' failure "to agree on any one point."[87] One publication offered some old-fashioned hearsay, claiming, without evidence, every private and public conversation framed Congress as working tirelessly to defend liberty.[88] With the exception of conflicting or baseless claims, delegates' actions at Philadelphia escaped the press.

Part of this evidentiary blind spot likely revealed a politically calculated silence. During Congress's opening session, delegates agreed to "consider themselves under the strongest obligations of honour, to keep the proceedings secret."[89] And as noted by scholars Calvin Jillson and Rick Wilson, "Since there was more than a whiff of treason in the air," they intentionally concealed their efforts.[90] By keeping debates and divisions hidden from public scrutiny, delegates fostered a more candid political environment. Equally important, secrecy allowed Congress to maintain a carefully crafted veneer of unanimity. Nearly every delegate took this secrecy oath seriously. Though Thomas Cushing wished to share Congress's proceedings with his wife, he explained, "I am enjoined by secrecy, [and] must refrain."[91] John Adams composed a similar letter, disclosing to Abigail that Congress's work remained "a profound secret."[92] James Madison, hoping to remain abreast of the action at Philadelphia, thirsted for any news. The Virginian no doubt felt deflated when William Bradford, a college friend living in that city, explained Congress's deliberations remained "a profound secret and their doors open to no one." Bradford went further, claiming that even if Madison sat outside Carpenters' Hall, what transpired inside would still elude him.[93] While this silence denied the public basic information on congressional proceedings, social moments outside of Carpenters' Hall granted delegates unguarded access to one another.

Socializing not only afforded congressmen the chance to perform commitment to the cause. These festive gatherings allowed them to evaluate their colleagues' character and abilities. John Adams described his time in Philadelphia as a "perpetual round of feasting," which enabled him to describe New Jersey's William Livingston as a learned man and capable writer.[94] Richard Henry Lee impressed Adams as a deep thinker, while the other Virginians appeared "spirited and consistent." Adams described Caesar Rodney as "the oddest looking man in the world," being thin and pale with a face no larger than an apple. Yet Adams found "fire, spirit, wit, and humor" in him. John Dickinson appeared to Adams as "a shadow . . . pale as ashes," likely on the verge of death.[95] Yet he also struck Adams as a philosopher with an "excellent heart."[96] Samuel Adams also spent time with Dickinson and departed equally impressed with the Philadelphian. "He is a true Bostonian," wrote the elder Adams. Dickinson, he admired, cherished "the liberties of America."[97]

Silas Deane quietly assessed his colleagues as well. He characterized the Virginia delegates as "sociable, sensible, and spirited men" and walked away with "the highest idea of their principles and character."[98] Peyton Randolph struck him as dignified and noble, while Benjamin Harrison appeared less polished than the others. He declared Richard Bland an authority on Virginia history and marveled at Richard Henry Lee's unmatched oratorical abilities. George Washington, however, made the deepest impression on Deane. He recorded that Washington "offered to raise and arm and lead one thousand men himself at his own expense, for the defense of the country."[99] Deane revealed to his wife that he based each of his descriptions on "the knowledge I have of them in their public as well as their private conversation." He admitted that fraternizing brought a certain happiness that outweighed the "anxieties and troubles of such a journey."[100]

Caesar Rodney, another keen observer, described the Virginians as "sensible, fine fellows," and Massachusetts's delegates as moderates despite their fiery reputations. Delegations from South Carolina and Rhode Island, however, appeared to him the most radicalized at Congress. The quality of the members sent to the American assembly, he claimed, signaled how serious colonists considered the present crisis. Delegates' private correspondence while in Philadelphia reveals that social intimacy formed and strengthened connective bonds among them. Press coverage of a more public event, however, joined American subjects to Congress's elite fellowship. And while Philadelphia's elite socialized with delegates nearly every evening, Caesar Rodney explained city officials planned to honor Congress with a grand celebration. Rodney boasted, "It is intended to be the greatest intertainment that ever was made in this city."[101]

On September 16, delegates closed the day's congressional session and reconvened at City Tavern, where local representatives met and escorted them to the State House for an evening's entertainment. From there, notable clergymen, local elites, and numerous inhabitants greeted members of Congress.[102] Silas Deane estimated roughly "five hundred gentlemen sat down at once" for dinner and drinks. Congressmen suffered "no scarcity of good humor," Deane remembered, as spectators from every colony attended the event.[103] In his typical laconic fashion, Washington simply recorded he attended "an Entertainment" in honor of Congress.[104] Following dinner, delegates offered thirty-two toasts, each "accompanied by musick and a discharge of cannon," according to one account of the evening.

A widely reprinted account of this event itemized each toast. The earliest sentiments declared colonial loyalty to the king and queen. The next several echoed concerns reflected in the many town and county resolutions from that summer. For example, those gathered offered toasts to the "much injured town of Boston," promoting domestic arts and manufacturing and passing liberty "pure and untainted" to posterity. The crowd also raised its glasses to "Perpetual Union to the Colonies." Celebrants presented a toast each to Lord Chatham, Edmund Burke, Benjamin Franklin, John Hancock, and the "virtuous few" among Parliament. Finally, speakers toasted their sincere wish that the "[c]olonies faithfully execute what Congress shall wisely Resolve." When the libations concluded, attendees praised delegates for their efforts.[105] The crowd's adulation, claimed the article, proved colonists would support Congress's directives to secure liberty.[106] While in London, Benjamin Franklin received a letter from a friend detailing this event. Participants enjoyed a succession of "spirited toasts," the letter informed, including one to Dr. Franklin.[107] This event encapsulated resistance rhetoric, augmenting delegates' harmony and colonial union through performative politics. As American subjects increasingly focused on events unfolding at Philadelphia, Congress emerged as a symbol of colonial unity.

On Friday, October 26, 1774, Congress dissolved. And just as colonial papers covered delegates' movements to Philadelphia, the press reported their travels back to their respective colonies as well.

When the Massachusetts delegates returned to Boston, "Bells in Town were rung" in celebration.[108] One commentator claimed Bostonians unanimously pledged to "sacredly observe" Congress's recommendations.[109] When South Carolina's delegation arrived back in Charleston, constituents celebrated by collecting all available tea and setting it ablaze.[110] After approving Congress's directives, Pennsylvania's Provincial Congress thanked delegates for a "faithful Discharge" of their public responsibilities.[111] The Committee of Mechanics in New York expressed gratitude to Congress for producing such "wise, prudent, and spirited measures." It committed to supporting Congress's directives "to the utmost of our power and ability."[112] Virginia delegates enjoyed similar fanfare. Hundreds of colonists gathered at the capitol building in Williamsburg to congratulate Peyton Randolph and his colleagues for their efforts at Congress. Randolph, speaking on behalf of his delegation, thanked the crowd for their support.[113] The widespread public embrace of the delegates' efforts convinced one observer that Congress had created "the foundations of an American constitution." This writer concluded, "I almost wish to hear the triumphs and Jubilee in the year 1874."[114]

Not everyone, however, celebrated Congress's achievements. One critic, in a letter to Peyton Randolph, compared Congress to a vessel navigating a dangerous storm around an unfamiliar coastline. The writer determined "the ship is too crazy to afford hopes of riding out the storm; and the mariners are upon the point of mutiny." He condemned Randolph for exploiting popular passions and guiding delegates away from peace and compromise. Instead, this critic claimed that Randolph and Congress provoked a "violent inflammation" of a sensitive political environment. American subjects, he continued, placed their trust in Congress, "however unconstitutional and void of legal power and authority it might be." Yet Randolph and his colleagues offered supporters only "misconceived opinions and censures."[115] Despite clear concern, however, most press coverage firmly supported Congress. This carefully crafted political narrative aimed to normalize resistance and convince colonists of their own unanimity.

After Congress dissolved, some delegates remained in contact through shared commitment to the common cause. Robert Treat Paine of Massachusetts, for example, inquired about "all my freinds at Philadelphia," wishing them good health and spirits.[116] Paine likely made these friends during his weeks socializing in Pennsylvania's capital city. Richard Henry Lee, writing to Samuel Adams, described Virginians as united in the common cause. He then inquired, "How is Boston holding up? Are your people in good Spirits?"[117] These expressions of concern reveal the elites' shared struggle fostered Ciceronian friendships, companionships formed through routine private intimacy addressing public concerns. Silas Deane expressed similar sentiments to Patrick Henry, writing confidently, "One general Congress has brought the Colonies to be acquainted with each other, and I am in hopes another may effect a complete and perfect American Constitution, the only proper one, for Us, whither connected to Great Britain, or Not."[118]

After serving in Congress, Peyton Randolph referred to his fellow representatives as "my brother delegates" in one of his few surviving communications.[119] This inclusive description illustrates the bonds congressmen developed with one another during their stay in Philadelphia. Careful observers outside Congress also recognized the political dimensions of this fellowship. Joseph Reed recorded delegates parted "on terms of the utmost friendship" that "will have the most happy effect on cementing the union of Colonies, not only in ties of publick interest, but of private friendship."[120] Reed feared Parliament might design its response to Congress around a mistaken belief in the "disunion of the Colonies." He noted, contrary to this belief, delegates "parted with great affection and friendship." He then claimed "the spirit of the people has arisen" to support Congress's resolutions.[121]

Four years after the First Continental Congress completed its work, John Adams visited Benjamin Franklin in France. And though Franklin and Adams served together on the Second Continental Congress (not the first incarnation of that assembly), Adams's remarks about their meeting are worth noting. Adams recorded he and Franklin had developed "that kind of Friendship which is commonly felt between two members of the same public Assembly, who meet each other every day not only in public deliberations, but at private Breakfasts, dinners and Suppers" and other moments of social intimacy.[122] The First Continental Congress's delegates, who worked together, ate together, drank together, and conversed together, also formed the "kind of Friendship" described by Adams while at Philadelphia. Adams remembered colonies once exchanged "little communication or correspondence" and viewed subjects from other provinces as outsiders. Since uniting through Congress, however, Adams now described Americans as "intimately acquainted." Since the imperial crisis, they had "formed friendships that will never cease."[123] Delegates arrived at Philadelphia a collection of strangers suspicious of one another. They departed as members of an elite fellowship and participants in a united resistance community. Critically, the connective sociopolitical sinews that joined delegates together also helped determine the political machinations that unfolded within the chambers of Carpenters' Hall.

Three

The Radicalism of the
First Continental Congress

HISTORIANS HAVE GIVEN THE FIRST CONTINENTAL CONGRESS far less scholarly attention than its more famous 1775 incarnation.[1] This is not surprising, considering the Second Continental Congress declared independence from Great Britain, a watershed moment in American history. Likewise, the same Congress created the Continental Army and promoted Virginia's George Washington from provincial colonel to general of the new American forces. The Second Continental Congress is simply better known and fits more comfortably into the popular narratives that historian Gregory J. W. Urwin described as easily digestible "feel-good myths."[2] Whether quoting Thomas Jefferson's prose from the Declaration of Independence or recounting George Washington's humble acceptance of command of the Continental Army, popular American history in many respects begins with the 1775 assembly. And while some scholars focus on the First Continental Congress, their various interpretations hardly reach a consensus. The following historiographical sketch will make this clear.

Writing before curators collected and organized the records of the First Continental Congress, historian Herbert Friedenwald described that body as "purely revolutionary in its nature," a political "laboratory" that created a weak but obvious spirit of unity among the colonies.[3] Yet Worthington Chauncy Ford, who processed Congress's papers for the Library of Congress, characterized that assembly as "ill-defined," its actions "largely tentative." Dominated by conservatives, Ford claimed it dared not "take any radical step."[4] Edmund Cody Burnett similarly interpreted it as a "vaguely defined . . . idea of union among the colonies."[5] Yet he also described it as a stage rehearsal for national governance. Even here, though, Burnett mainly tipped his hat to the Second Continental Congress.[6] Jack Rakove pronounced colonists' creation of the First Continental Congress a daring step toward nationhood since it coordinated thirteen colonies under its direction. Still Rakove, like Burnett, reserved most of his praise for the 1775 Congress.[7] Rick Jillson and Calvin Wilson went so far as to describe the First Continental Congress as a "failed institution" that acted as more coordinating committee than legislative body.[8]

A fresh analysis is in order. When Parliament passed the Coercive Acts, it awoke some fundamental convictions about liberty and empire that had remained dormant among American subjects. Colonists thus summoned Congress to secure liberty and express their imperial vision. To do so, delegates itemized American rights and rallied colonists to sacrifice in order to secure them. Historians do not characterize men like Peyton Randolph, William Livingston, or John Jay as radical rabble rousers fanning the flames of imperial crisis; traditional narratives cast Samuel Adams and Patrick Henry as these agitators.[9] And scholars typically describe the latter two figures as outliers, true radicals tempered by their colleagues' sober deliberations.[10] Focusing on individual personalities rather than Congress's official positions, however, obscures that assemblage's radical nature.

This chapter argues that the First Continental Congress, from its inception, aimed to secure American liberty and identity more rigorously than imperial reconciliation. Some apparently trivial decisions, like selecting Congress's meeting place or choosing its secretary, signaled that body's intentions. Whether considering each colony's respective weight while voting, locating the origins of American liberty, or making any other in a range of critical decisions, Congress proved willing to take the radical road. And, as this chapter uncovers, delegates justified American resistance efforts with the doctrine of self-preservation. This declaration framed the Coercive Acts Crisis as a struggle for political survival and, with so much at stake, Congress claimed for Americans a right to defend liberty and identity at all costs and in virtually any form. These radical commitments joined American Whigs more closely, further entrenching them in a separate political community united around the common cause.

The Thursday before Congress convened, delegates gathered at City Tavern. A simple but symbolic decision required their immediate attention: Where would Congress conduct its business? Pennsylvania's Speaker of the House, Joseph Galloway, offered his colony's elegant State House.[11] Philadelphia's Carpenters' Association countered Galloway's political hospitality by offering Carpenters' Hall.[12] Delegates, for their part, agreed to tour both buildings the following Monday before making their selection.[13] Yet this decision, a simple matter of determining Congress's address, placed delegates at the center of Philadelphia's divided politics.

The State House hosted Pennsylvania's General Assembly. That building, according to one observer, offered spacious chambers and a library containing "all the laws of England" along with a respectable collection of "history and poetry." A wax bust of the colony's proprietor, William Penn, welcomed visitors in the front room. For many Pennsylvanians, the State House symbolized that colony's success, sophistication, and political leadership.[14]

Carpenters' Hall reflected Philadelphia's rapid expansion. Visiting medical student Solomon Drowne marveled, "You may judge how fast Philadelphia increases, from there having built in it, upwards of 470 Houses this year."[15] A pattern of remarkably steady work provided the Carpenters' Association, which formerly met at members' homes, enough capital to purchase its own meeting house in 1770.

By 1773, Carpenters' Hall boasted furnished rooms and some of the Library Company of Philadelphia's vast collection.[16] After touring the building, John Adams remembered the open entryway and the "excellent library."[17] Carpenters' Hall, however, offered much more than comfort and books.

After learning of the Coercive Acts, radical Philadelphians began gathering at Carpenters' Hall to condemn Parliament, turning the building into what historian Charles Peterson described as "the only available privately-owned meeting house in the city" that hosted "anti-government political sessions."[18] Charles Thomson, secretary of Philadelphia's Committee of Correspondence and a regular at these inflammatory sessions, emerged as a rival to conservative House Speaker Joseph Galloway.[19] This rivalry intensified when Galloway blocked Thomson's appointment to the First Continental Congress. Despite this savvy political maneuver, however, the Carpenters' Association continued supporting Thomson and his radical politics.[20]

These buildings represented Philadelphia's competing political camps, the State House embodying Galloway's pragmatic conservatism and Carpenters' Hall reflecting Thomson's outspoken radicalism. If Congress chose the State House, it would oblige imperial traditionalists. If delegates selected Carpenters' Hall, they would excite Philadelphia's artisans.[21] Whichever building Congress chose, however, was sure to signal certain political assumptions to observers of all persuasions.

On September 5, delegates toured Carpenters' Hall before their scheduled State House visit. However, South Carolina delegate Thomas Lynch called for a vote in favor of Carpenters' Hall before members even explored their other option. New York's James Duane reminded delegates that since Galloway, the host city's speaker, had offered the State House, Congress ought to grant him "a piece of respect which was due to him."[22] But, clearly, delegates had already engaged in some informal political intrigue. As early as August 30, John Adams recorded visits to both the State House and "Carpenters' Hall, where Congress is to sit."[23] How Adams learned of this is unclear. Silas Deane claimed his colleagues chose Carpenters' Hall since it remained "highly agreeable to the mechanics and citizens in general, but mortifying to the last degree to Mr. Galloway and his party."[24] New York's James Duane recorded a "great Majority" of Congress voted in favor of Lynch's choice.[25] By selecting Carpenters' Hall, Congress expressed its willingness to cater to the radical element of American politics. It also retained Philadelphia's best organized and most hostile anti-Parliament association firmly in Congress's corner.

Moments after delegates selected Carpenters' Hall, Lynch publicly credited one member with presiding "over a very respectable society, greatly to the advantage of America." He then announced support for Virginia's Peyton Randolph for chairman of Congress.[26] Delegates, apparently standing in a Philadelphia street, elected Randolph on the spot before naming their assembly "Congress" and the Virginian its "President."[27] Incredibly, Lynch wasted no time diving into his next maneuver.

Thomas Lynch turned his attention to appointing a secretary to record Congress's proceedings. A shocked Galloway recounted this moment in a letter to his conservative confidant, New Jersey governor William Franklin. The Pennsylvanian noted after selecting Carpenters' Hall, despite the availability of the State House, delegates "next proceeded to chuse a Secretary, and, to my Surprize Charles Thomson was unanimously elected."[28] Some New York and Pennsylvania delegates pushed back against this choice, John Jay specifically remarking Pennsylvania did not elect Thomson to Congress. Others countered, claiming any member burdened with secretarial duties could not fully participate in committee duties or floor debates, which would deny one colony a full participant. This argument convinced enough delegates to approve Thomson's appointment and they styled him "Secretary of Congress." Stung by this blindside, Galloway noted to Governor Franklin these two quick maneuvers, Congress's selection of Carpenters' Hall and Thomson, "were privately settled by an Interest made out of Doors."[29] Galloway's remark unveils his concern that partisans had made a political decision outside of the traditional arena where public decisions were typically debated and decided upon.

What historians have overlooked is just how Thomson's appointment shaped the public's perception of Congress's work. Thomson had played an active role in Philadelphia's resistance movement since the Stamp Act Crisis. By 1774, he had hoped to prevent colonial disunion and, as he divulged years later, "bring Pennsylvania's whole force undivided to make common cause with Boston."[30] His presence at Carpenters' Hall provided delegates a constant reminder of their host city's radical political element. Thomson's approach to recording Congress's minutes, however, created the illusion of unanimity among delegates, a sort of political sleight of hand.

How Thomson settled on his method for keeping Congress's journals is worth recounting. As he noted shortly before his own death in 1824, he arrived in Philadelphia to visit family when Congress summoned him to Carpenters' Hall. He honored the summons and, upon arrival, observed an assembly in "deep thought and solemn anxiety." President Randolph announced, "Congress desire the favour of you, sir, to take their minutes." Thomson accepted the assignment and immediately assumed the secretary's desk. He next witnessed a speech that inspired just how he would discharge the official duties of his new office.[31]

Shortly after Thomson sat, Virginia's Patrick Henry rose to address the assembly. Henry likened Congress's convening to when a man in serious trouble calls together his closest friends for their council. Once he received each man's advice, Henry lectured, the hypothetical troubled man would embrace the best plan and think "no more of the rejected schemes." Thomson recalled "this was very good instruction to me, with respect to taking the Minutes." What Congress agreed on, Thomson preserved in the journals. What it rejected, he "had nothing farther to do."[32] This approach resulted in Thomson recording what Congress did rather than what it debated, allowing the journals to project a veneer of unity among delegates. John Adams later complained bitterly about Thomson's refusal to capture debates in the journals. By leaving the record blank, Adams theorized, "the party in opposition" escaped later scrutiny and public backlash for their unwillingness to defend American liberty at all costs.[33]

Writing to the British House of Commons, Galloway, too, vented that Thomson's methods concealed debates and dissent. Yet Galloway's concerns ran opposite to those of Adams. The Pennsylvanian complained he and other delegates opposed certain resolutions only to find them recorded as unanimously approved in the minutes. Thomson recorded most settled actions as "Resolved, Unan." or "Resolved, N. C. D."[34] "N. C. D.," the abbreviated form of *nemine contradicente*, is Latin for "without dissent" or "without contradiction." Once published, Thomson's notes told the public of a harmonious Congress free of dissenting opinions. This manipulation, however, did not go unnoticed.

Shortly after *Journals of the Proceedings of Congress* became public, Anglican priest Thomas Bradbury Chandler responded with a blistering indictment of this maneuver by "artful leaders of Congress." He accused radicals of duping moderates into washing dissent from the official journals, allowing, according to Chandler, designing men to produce "uncommissioned and unauthorized" recommendations under the guise of unanimity. And these same recommendations, he cautioned, aimed to animate colonists into nothing less than open rebellion. To lend credence to his observations, the priest added that "certain anecdotes from Philadelphia" confirmed his suspicions.[35] This reference almost certainly alludes to some private conversations he engaged in with Galloway. During the summer of 1774, many local leaders considered colonial unity vital to getting the Coercive Acts repealed. Thomson, and by extension a majority of delegates, agreed to manipulate the *Journal* no doubt to carefully craft a narrative of unanimity and inspire deeper public support.

Once Congress elected its president and chose its secretary, each delegation read its credentials into the record.[36] These statements ranged from vague to quite specific in terms of the various colonies' expectations and grievances, but generally revolved around five mutually reinforcing categories. Most credentials authorized delegates to speak for their respective colonies, recognized the Coercive Acts as a constitutional crisis equally threatening to all colonies, aimed to redress American grievances through coordinated resistance, sought to secure colonial rights for posterity, and hoped to restore peace and mutual obligation to all parts of the empire. Boston's misery, many statements also agreed, embodied a shared threat that compelled an aggressive, synchronized response.

After delegations memorialized their resistance, New York's James Duane motioned to appoint a Committee of Rules and Conduct to outline congressional procedures. He acknowledged each delegation came from "Assemblies on the Continent" that had different sets of rules and expectations. He inadvertently opened a firestorm, however, that exposed many delegates' concerns over more than just legislative arcana. Some congressmen asked whether Congress's resolves were to be carried by a majority of colonies or a majority of delegates.[37] This question unleashed a political controversy that threatened to splinter Congress on its first day. Would Congress recognize colonies as political equals or weigh them according to their wealth, size, and population?

Thomson's journals reported Congress simply granted each colony one vote, at once leveling the large colonies with the small.[38] Yet as might be expected, the secretary's records only revealed part of the story. Recording the floor debates in his diary, John Adams characterized the method of voting as "a question of Great Importance."[39] Patrick Henry opined Parliament's latest measures had reduced American subjects "to a State of Nature," erasing distinctions between colonists. Immediately contradicting himself, however, Henry voiced concern that populated colonies risked a "great injustice" if they held no more weight than "a little Colony." Fellow Virginian Benjamin Harrison agreed, condemning equal representation as disrespectful to the larger colonies. Rhode Island's Samuel Ward challenged the outspoken Virginians, pleading for each colony to have an equal voice. When it came time to sacrifice for the common cause, he reminded, "The weaker Colony by such a sacrifice would suffer as much as the greatest."[40] Since Congress possessed no reliable data pertaining to the relative wealth and populations of the colonies, South Carolina's Christopher Gadsden admitted he could not "see any way of voting, but by Colonies."[41] But before delegates could settle this contentious issue, Congress received word of a "Bombardment of Boston" by the British Army that temporarily interrupted debate.[42]

Philadelphians signaled solidarity with their northern brethren after hearing of the alleged British attack. Silas Deane noted, "All the bells toll muffled, and the most unfeigned marks of sorrow appear on every countenance."[43] And though delegates eventually learned Boston had, in fact, not suffered an attack, the news helped them find common ground. They agreed "an Equal Representation was ever so just" and Congress granted each colony one vote.[44] This proved an important moment for the resistance. Rather than splintering over pride, property, and population, delegates found unity in purpose. Patrick Henry felt the current crisis had transformed colonists into Americans.[45]

Delegates next faced locating the origins of American liberty, many arguing that repeal of the Coercive Acts actually rested on this determination. Richard Henry Lee advanced that American rights balanced on a "fourfold foundation" of natural rights, the British Constitution, colonial charters, and common law. William Livingston, the poet-scholar from New Jersey, agreed, adding "it will not do for America to rest wholly on the laws of England."[46] John Jay concurred with Livingston, claiming natural rights provided the appropriate foundation. Jay theorized the original English settlers crossed the Atlantic Ocean and conquered a dangerous wilderness. Finding themselves in a state of nature, he lectured, they created governments to secure life, liberty, and property. Natural law, not princes or parliaments, granted these intrepid pioneers authority to construct governments for their security. Jay reminded his colleagues that these settlers voluntarily maintained allegiance to the king. And while these theoretical musings appear harmless, they exposed profound ideological differences among delegates and reveal further the radical nature of most of them.

James Duane, John Rutledge and, most forcefully, Joseph Galloway argued against rooting American liberty to natural law. Clearly uncomfortable with the position supported by Lee, Livingston, and Jay, Duane and Rutledge claimed natural law offered but "feeble support" for the colonial position. Their tepid dissent masked the actual reason for their opposition. Galloway provided a constitutional argument. "I have looked for our rights in the law of nature," he reasoned, "but could not find them." The liberties Americans cherished, he continued, existed exclusively "in a state of political society." He then connected the English Constitution to an intellectual heritage that stretched from the classical world to Magna Carta. In the end, American rights, he determined, originated from the British Constitution. A committed Anglo-imperialist, Galloway had dedicated himself to addressing the empire's shortcomings and modernizing the British Constitution.[47] These three imperial traditionalists, however, held a deeper fear of locating American rights in natural law.

Congress, to the dismay of Galloway and others, ultimately rested American rights upon the triumvirate of natural law, the English Constitution, and colonial charters, earning its radical element another clear victory.[48] Delegates rationalized that nature, not nobles, granted colonists the bounty of natural rights.[49] Resting colonial liberty on natural law, from a constitutional perspective, led Congress to a slippery slope. By taking this position, Congress declared Americans voluntary subjects of the British Empire. Congress's commitment to natural rights convinced Galloway that his opponents in that assembly "wished to throw off all subordination and connexion to Great Britain" and incite the "ignorant and vulgar to arms" to "establish American Independence."[50] Yet no delegate seriously pined for independence in September or October 1774. Even Samuel Adams, writing to Arthur Lee months after Congress dissolved, expected that body's efforts to "restore harmony to the British Empire."[51]

Some alarmed observers did articulate, however, that their attachment to the Crown did not outweigh their commitment to liberty. If relations between the metropole and colonies worsened, Samuel Adams and others quietly considered the grim alternative. Adams urged Americans to begin mastering the military arts in case the crisis descended into armed conflict.[52] Even moderate John Dickinson felt "Great Britain must relax, or inevitably involve herself in a civil war." He believed war between America and Britain would turn so violent that observers would characterize the "contentions between the Houses of York and Lancaster" and even the English Civil War as "gentle misfortunes" by comparison.[53] Yet despite these fiery missives, neither Adams nor Dickinson advocated for independence. If anything, these letters express the alarm and uncertainty they experienced during their time at Philadelphia. Congress's embrace of natural law, however, convinced some delegates that radicals conspired to engineer an independence movement. But Galloway condemned Congress's next move as nothing less than open treason.

On September 16, Paul Revere rode into Philadelphia with a dispatch for the Massachusetts delegation. The Bay Colony's leadership routinely coordinated news deliveries from Massachusetts to Carpenters' Hall to transport Boston's plight directly into the halls of Congress.[54] Galloway caught on to this scheme, blaming each conveniently timed intelligence express on the dark arts of Samuel Adams. The Pennsylvania speaker characterized Adams as one of the fanatical "republicans" who, while not brilliant, exceeded in both "popular intrigue" and coordinating his faction. He further described Adams as a man who ate little, drank less, yet was "indefatigable in pursuit of his objectives." Whatever Adams desired politically, noted Galloway, his cabal delivered directly to Philadelphia.[55] On that September day, Revere carried with him the Suffolk Resolves.

The Suffolk Resolves offered the most unapologetically aggressive defense of American liberty yet. And much to Galloway and Duane's consternation, a majority of delegates approved reading them into the record. Galloway and Duane condemned the "inflammatory resolves," the former declaring them "a complete declaration of war against Great Britain."[56] Mainly written by Massachusetts physician Joseph Warren, Suffolk's resolutions recounted colonists' "fugitive parents" fleeing relentless persecution from king and Parliament and settling a "savage and uncultivated" land with their own blood and treasure. Now Parliament, they claimed, sought to enslave these transplants' children, and the future of unborn millions depended on colonists' response to the "arbitrary will of a licentious minister." British North Americans, they lamented (with not a little hyperbole), currently suffered under "military executioners." Parliament had already mutilated one colonial charter, reminded the Resolves, and now lined American coastlines with warships to continue and expand upon its oppression. To secure American liberty, they urged colonists to unite in defiance of Parliament. Otherwise, posterity would condemn their inaction "until time itself had been absorbed into the abyss of eternity." To this end, the Suffolk Resolves proposed Americans master the military arts and ignore any provincial official holding office under the altered Massachusetts charter.[57]

Suffolk's leaders next navigated into even more dangerous political waters. While acknowledging George III as their rightful king, they claimed Americans owed allegiance first to "God, country, themselves, and posterity" and urged colonists to "defend and preserve" liberty by all lawful ways possible. They asked resistance actors to commit to nonimportation and nonconsumption of British goods and nonexportation of American resources to Britain and the British West Indies until king and Parliament restored colonial rights. Going beyond commercial concerns, the Resolves encouraged the development of domestic arts and manufacturing, signaling a growing unease with colonists' material dependence on the metropole. They then pledged to support whatever Congress recommended to redress colonial grievances. Coming to the brink of open treason, the Suffolk Resolves advised George III that colonists owed him conditional loyalty, self-preservation taking precedence over any other commitment.[58]

Galloway and a few others denounced the Suffolk Resolves, fearful they might encourage colonists to ignore Parliament's authority altogether.[59] Still, after a spirited debate, a frustrated Galloway recorded that the "republican faction in Congress" voted to support them. The Pennsylvanian privately believed delegates endorsed them more from fear than conviction, accusing Congress's violent faction of encouraging a mob to tar and feather anyone who dared vote against the resolves.[60] Yet despite these alleged threats, Galloway and Duane refused their support. Most delegates, however, endorsed the Suffolk Resolves. Galloway vented that by "this treasonable vote the foundation of military resistance throughout America was effectively laid."[61] Both Galloway and Duane demanded their written dissents recorded in Congress's journals. Denied this, they next asked Secretary Thomson to at least enter that two delegates voted against the Resolves. The majority struck down this subsequent appeal as well. Moved by this motion, John Adams described the day as "one of the happiest" of his life and came away convinced "America will support

. . . Massachusetts or perish with her."[62] Congress's *Journal* predictably recorded delegates' unanimous support for the Suffolk Resolves on September 18, 1774.[63] Thomson, and by extension the majority of Congress, preserved the veneer of political harmony during Congress's most radical step yet by again suppressing internal dissent.

Delegates, according to Samuel Adams, read Suffolk's resolutions "with great applause." From his perspective, their enthusiasm encapsulated "the spirit of the Congress."[64] In its official endorsement, Congress condemned Parliament's "unjust, cruel, and oppressive acts" while praising Suffolk's staunch commitment to liberty. Congress predicted a united resistance effort would overturn Parliament's ruinous policies and expressed hope that English subjects would elect wiser men to restore imperial harmony. Delegates ordered both the Suffolk Resolves and Congress's official endorsement released to the press.[65] The first official position of that assembly broadcast its radicalism to the public. Weeks later, Whitehall learned Congress had both endorsed the Resolves and published a blistering condemnation of Parliament.[66] These aggressive stances, while rallying Whigs, naturally terrified imperial traditionalists.

One commentator decried Congress's "extraordinary adoption" of the Suffolk Resolves, predicting it would result in the deaths of thousands of British subjects and the empire's collapse. Congress's reckless endorsement, this writer howled, suffocated any potential chance for imperial reconciliation. He suspected a faction had corrupted Congress and duped unwitting delegates into "adopting the most violent measures."[67] Upon learning of Congress's endorsement, eighty-four inhabitants of Rye, New York, publicly refused to support any resolutions designed to challenge the king. They declared themselves George III's peaceful subjects and condemned Congress's "hot and furious proceedings" as more likely to destroy the empire than remove any imaginary grievances.[68]

Shortly after Congress dissolved in October, a pamphlet addressed to "all reasonable Americans" explained that moderate men expected Congress to reflect America's "united wisdom" and compare to any "assembly of the greatest sages of antiquity." Instead, the author claimed weak or designing men had aligned themselves with "New England and other Presbyterian Republicans." The Suffolk Resolves, according to this writer, represented a clear attempt to create an independent government, and, shockingly, Congress's endorsement "was the first thing they did publish." The political situation, he cautioned, may yet bring the empire "upon the brink of a horrid civil war."[69] Though Congress enjoyed mostly positive press coverage, the broader political community divided over how to respond to the Coercive Acts. Loyalty to king and Parliament, for many American subjects, expressed commitment to tradition and empire. For others, resistance to perceived unconstitutional measures continued a proud heritage of Englishmen defending liberty from power.

On September 22, Congress directed colonial merchants to suspend all transactions with English agents until it determined how to apply enough economic pressure on English merchants and manufacturers to get the Coercive Acts repealed.[70] On September 27, Congress formally committed to nonimportation and nonconsumption of English and Irish goods, effective December 1, 1774.[71] Three days later, it recommended nonexportation of American resources to Britain, Ireland, and the British West Indies, beginning on September 10, 1775.[72]

This commercial freeze continued Congress's course in the radical direction. Galloway supported nonimportation, but feared nonexportation would "have tens of thousands of people thrown upon the cold hand of charity."[73] Delegate Thomas Cushing argued Britain had "drawn the sword against us," and nothing but American force could prevent Parliament from "sheathing it in our bowels." To avert this, Cushing voiced support for both nonimportation and nonexportation. Christopher Gadsden feared America would become "deluged in blood, if we don't act with spirit." Do not "let America look at this mountain," he cautioned, "and let it bring forth a mouse."[74] Galloway, concerned the republican element planned "a scheme of independence," skillfully steered debate back to restoring American liberty. It was at this point he revealed his Plan of Union, a design with which he hoped to secure colonial rights on solid constitutional principles and calm the empire.[75]

While Galloway shared other delegates' alarm over the Coercive Acts, he alone came to Congress with a proposal.[76] His Plan of Union provided a critical evaluation of the old empire and a model for an imperial future. Galloway concluded that the contours and limits of Parliament's authority and the range and application of colonial rule remained, at best, murky. Encouraged by Benjamin Franklin, Galloway hoped to address this murkiness and repair the empire.[77]

Though Galloway believed his plan appropriately addressed imperial troubles, he privately harbored little hope of it gaining traction with his fellow delegates. Writing to Richard Jackson, a friend and member of the House of Commons, Galloway expressed frustration at Parliament's failure to fix imperial weaknesses at the close of the French and Indian War, when Americans gloried in their attachment to the metropole. Instead of shoring up blatant deficiencies, Galloway vented, Parliament passed the Stamp Act in 1765. Americans reacted so violently to that tax, he claimed, because "they were not expressly represented" in Parliament. Galloway defended this defiance, reasoning an unaccountable legislature taxing American subjects with impunity "cannot be founded in Reason or Common Sense." In this scenario, the speaker wrote, colonists had no means to express their "Desires, Wants, and Necessities." Yet rather than fight the same ideological and constitutional battles during the present crisis, Galloway hoped both sides might consider taking "the other Ground." He called for political accommodation, blaming the current chaos and animosity on extremists from both sides of the Atlantic.[78]

Galloway's middle ground offered a fundamental reimagining of the British Empire, a vision he described as "the great outlines of the union."[79] Proposing his plan to Congress, he warned the present sense of disunion weakened the "fabrick of our civil polity" and threatened to bring about the "horrors of civil war." To create "the most perfect union," he called for an imperial Parliament made up of Britain's Lords and Commons with a unicameral American assembly.[80] The plan empowered colonies to select their own representatives to this new assembly. Galloway envisioned a president, which he expected to be an American appointed by the king, guiding this legislative body and further expected the American Congress to negotiate between Parliament and local legislatures. And while Galloway's model provided Parliament veto power over colonial law, it granted the American assembly no such authority over English policy. However, it did provide Americans a veto over Parliament's attempts at regulating colonial affairs.[81]

As Galloway predicted, Congress did not, in the end, embrace his vision. Delegates tabled and ultimately expunged the plan from the record. And while this erasure marked another victory for Congress's radical element, just why Galloway's plan slipped into archival oblivion remains less clear. Galloway blamed its failure on a conspiracy. Since moderates and conservatives alike acknowledged his vision's sophistication, he reasoned, radicals must have maneuvered to delay and ultimately disregard his imperial model.[82] Historian Robert Calhoun blamed its failure on Galloway's singular focus on the origins of American rights. Julian P. Boyd claimed it failed due to Galloway's "conservative mind," which left him with only "placid logic" to grapple with modernity's complexities.[83] These scholars focused on what they considered the shortcomings of Galloway's ideas. Neither focused on the political context, however. American subjects demanded that the First Continental Congress address an immediate political crisis while Galloway called for intricate renovations of Britain's imperial architecture. Many delegates already expected Parliament to ignore their work for fear it might legitimize Congress.[84] And on the off chance that Parliament found merit in Galloway's proposal, this changed focus all but guaranteed Congress would fail to quickly get the Coercive Acts repealed. Congress likely tabled the plan to focus on colonists' principal objectives, not repudiate Galloway's ideas. The moment required either the restoration of American liberty or something more extreme, something most delegates shuddered at the thought of. Yet during the summer leading up to the convening of Congress, many observers revealed their willingness to resort to more desperate measures if reconciliation failed.

As early as May 18, 1774, Samuel Adams described Bostonians as "impelled by the motives of self-preservation." He declared the Coercive Acts so barbarous that the "archives of Constantinople" held no comparable example. Adams cautioned "this town must and will look to their own safety."[85] An article published that same day in Philadelphia and reprinted afterward offered a similar argument. After acknowledging the advantages of belonging to the British Empire, the author chastised colonists for being "*passive* [emphasis in original] spectators" of Parliament's dangerous encroachments on American liberty. He condemned Parliament for stripping every American subject of life, liberty, and property over the vandalism of a few men (a clear reference to the Boston Tea Party). For too long, the writer decried, colonists had reacted to the "outrages committed by a *British* Parliament" on the "dearest birth-right of a *Briton*" with an embarrassing degree of moderation and gratitude. He declared "Self-preservation," that "first law of nature," took precedence over "any social or national obligations." Any individual who refused to fight for his liberties, the essayist warned, became "guilty of the worst kind of rebellion; he commits high treason against *God*."[86]

Colonists absorbed self-preservation so thoroughly that it found expression in private correspondence, circulated publications, and in many of the town and county resolutions from the summer of 1774. American resistance to Parliament inspired some to draw comparisons between themselves and those who gathered in opposition to Charles I or brought about the "abdication of that wretched runaway . . . James II."[87] Colonists volunteered to suffer in solidarity with Boston and sent delegates to Philadelphia with a mandate to coordinate a commercial freeze. For many colonists, the doctrine of self-preservation justified any additional form of resistance.

Connecticut's resolutions claimed for colonists the right to defend "their birthrights as freeborn Englishmen." After condemning the Coercive Acts and Parliament's attempts to tax American subjects, the authors determined it their fundamental duty to "maintain, defend and preserve, these our rights and liberties . . . entire and inviolate to the latest generations." They resolved to fulfill this commitment by any means necessary.[88] Virginia's Westmoreland County, after similarly decrying the Coercive Acts, urged for nonimportation and nonexportation "on the evident principle of self-preservation" to protect liberty and bring happiness to their "suffering countrymen" in Boston.[89] South Carolina's resolutions warned the Coercive Acts presented an existential threat to each colony. If Americans failed to resist this latest encroachment, the authors warned, they risked sweeping "even the shadow of liberty" from British North America. The "soundest principles of self-preservation" compelled South Carolina to support Boston.[90] Essex County, Virginia, also defended colonists' right to resist Parliament's recent measures by resorting to the doctrine of self-preservation, "that great law of nature."[91] And the Suffolk Resolves described above likewise vindicated their radical positions by appealing to "the principles of self-preservation."[92] For many observers, this doctrine represented the last line of defense for American liberty. And Congress ultimately founded its own resistance efforts on it.

On October 6, 1774, Paul Revere again delivered a dispatch from the Boston Committee of Correspondence reporting that the British Army had nearly completed fortifying that city. British regulars, it claimed, had begun treating colonists as "declared enemies." The committee pressed Congress for advice on whether Bostonians should escape the city or remain to "better serve the public cause."[93] Congress immediately halted debate on nonimportation and nonexportation to read the letter into its journals.[94] The following day Congress appointed Thomas Lynch, Edmund Pendleton, and Samuel Adams to a committee to draft a response to Lieutenant General Thomas Gage. Congress asked the committee to remind the general that every American considered Boston "as suffering in the common cause" and request he halt his fortification efforts. The committee next urged inhabitants to remain in place and directed Bostonians to hold "in detestation and abhorrence" any civic official appointed to office by Parliament's late measures. These men, Congress declared, represented the "wicked tools" of tyranny, men determined to destroy the fundamental rights that "God, nature, and compact" had granted America.[95] Samuel Adams wrote an early draft that Congress amended to limit his fiery rhetoric.[96] The final version, though less bombastic, still revealed Congress's willingness to resort to the doctrine of self-preservation in order to defend liberty.

The committee's address declared the Coercive Acts an attack on American rights and accused the British Army of violating private property and oppressing Boston's inhabitants. For the "preservation of their common rights," the letter advanced, colonists throughout British North America resolved to unite in opposition and entrusted the Continental Congress to act as "guardians of their rights and liberties." It then claimed Gage "cannot be a stranger to the sentiments of America," as every colonist condemned Parliament's measures. Finally, the address pleaded with General Gage to ease the people's minds and stop further fortification. Failure on these points, the response warned, "may involve us in the horrors of civil war."[97] Congress approved the address on October 11, legitimizing Boston's resistance on the basis of self-preservation.

Congress next appointed Richard Henry Lee, William Livingston, and John Jay to a committee to explain to English subjects why it was that Americans opposed the Coercive Acts. This "Address to the People of Great Britain" warmly greeted Britons across the Atlantic before accusing them of extreme negligence in electing members to Parliament. This negligence, claimed the address, resulted in a decay of virtue throughout the British Empire. It claimed that "no power on earth" reserved the right "to take our property without our consent," and declared Parliament's recent actions and taxation schemes "heresies in English politics." Parliament, the address warned, planned to enslave Americans and Canadians with British military power. Designing ministers, it claimed, sought to reduce even English subjects "to the same abject state." According to the address, Americans refused to allow Parliament to play "sport with the rights of Mankind." Colonists found themselves compelled, "by the over-ruling principles of self-preservation," to defend American liberty at all costs.[98] This address does not ring with the language of reconciliation. It offered a pointed critique of Parliament and chided English subjects for their silent complicity in prolonging imperial turmoil. Colonists, the address revealed, refused to assist in their own enslavement. "Place us in the same situation that we were at the close of the last war," delegates demanded, "and our former harmony will be restored." If the trend of the last several years persists, they warned, "we think it prudent to anticipate the consequences." Congress approved the address and ordered 120 copies printed for circulation on October 21, 1774.[99]

The same committee wrote a "Memorial to the Inhabitants of British America," calling for "a firm, united, and invariable observation" of Congress's directives.[100] Richard Henry Lee, the primary author, expressed his thoughts using funereal language, reminding Americans of their membership in a pan-colonial community of suffering. The memorial blamed Parliament's taxation attempts for the empire's recent troubles. Since the British imperial legislature operated beyond local control, the memorial explained, colonists rightfully considered these schemes unconstitutional and a threat to American security. It expressed outrage that an uncontrollable military commander exercised supreme control "in all the Civil Governments of America," and decried Boston's military occupation as a hostile invasion. While Parliament counted on American docility during its punishment of Massachusetts, the Memorial proclaimed all of British North America embraced Boston's cause as its own.[101]

According to this communication, colonists wished to sustain their "social band" with Britain, but Parliament's recklessness threatened to push the empire to "that fatal point" where Americans must "renounce every regard but that of self-preservation." It reminded colonists of their shared obligation to defend liberties their ancestors won at such cost. "Your own salvation, and that of your posterity," declared the address, "now depends on yourselves." It warned colonists they might suffer and experience "inconveniences," yet temporary hardship remained preferable to the "endless miseries" posterity might suffer should Americans surrender. These "most mournful events," the Memorial asserted, required each American to voluntarily suffer with Boston. It asked for "devotion of spirit, penitence of heart, and amendment of life, to humble your selves" to avoid a "final, ruinous, and infamous submission." The Memorial closed by calling on American subjects to join the community of suffering to thwart tyranny and avoid enslavement. Congress approved this appeal as well.[102]

On October 1, Congress appointed John Adams, Thomas Johnson, Richard Henry Lee, Patrick Henry, and John Rutledge to write a petition to George III. On October 17, Congress added Pennsylvania's John Dickinson (just recently elected to Congress) to the committee. The first draft, written primarily by Patrick Henry, failed to gain Congress's approval. According to Dickinson, the draft suffered from "a language of asperity" and offered little in the way of a "conciliatory disposition."[103] John Adams appreciated the spirit with which Henry had written his address, but felt the Virginian lacked "the Advantages of Education" to properly articulate the delicate task at hand.[104] Yet even the second draft, likely coauthored by Richard Henry Lee and Dickinson, bristled with radicalism.[105]

Congress offered no address to Parliament, a clear indication that a majority of delegates denied it held any authority over the colonies whatsoever. For many colonists, their political connection to Britain ran exclusively through the monarch. Lee and Dickinson, in the "Petition to the King," justified resistance with the doctrine of self-preservation. It informed George III that a "destructive system of administration" threatened to enslave Americans. Since colonists identified as Britons, the petition claimed, they naturally resisted Parliament's encroachments. The petition informed George III of a ministerial attack on Americans and identified "designing and dangerous men" in Parliament as common enemies of both king and colonists. It claimed members of Parliament, not American subjects, conspired to "dissolve the bonds of society." Colonists cut off commerce with Britain, it declared, to protect American liberty. The petition assured the king that Congress would instantly resume trade upon the repeal of the Coercive Acts. It argued Congress acted upon no other design than "the dread of impending destruction" brought about by Parliament's sustained attack on American rights. Colonists, it continued, desired peace, liberty, and a connection to Britain through the king. Compelled by "the force of accumulated injuries," and concerned for the "preservation of ourselves and posterity, the primary obligations of nature and society," Congress championed resistance.[106] This address, written under calm and deliberate circumstances, asked for reconciliation under radical conditions. Sent to the throne of majesty, it also reminded the king of Americans' voluntary connection to the empire. This embrace of sacrifice and self-preservation pushed colonists further from subjects and closer to citizens.

The Stamp Act and Townshend Acts sounded an alarm for many American subjects. The Coercive Acts, however, threatened their political identities, imperial vision, and status as freemen. Colonists' commitment to local control over local matters helped a proto-national identity emerge during this crisis. Americans, once mainly connected to one another through shared allegiance to the Crown, created new connections in their effort to retain local identities and liberties. This effort found unified expression in the First Continental Congress, and a majority of delegates committed to a radical approach to getting the Coercive Acts repealed. Radical considerations pushed Congress into Carpenters' Hall rather than the State House, a clear nod to the Carpenters' Association and its anti-Parliament leaders. Delegates' selection of Charles Thomson as secretary again catered to the radical element. Thomson brought a radical presence into the chambers of Congress and his secretarial methods fabricated political harmony among the delegates in Congress's official journals.

Congress most clearly projected its radicalism through its official positions. Delegates early on granted each colony equal weight while voting, which signaled they appreciated the sacrifice each delegation committed its constituents to endure. Congress also rested American liberty on its broadest base, natural law, which circumvented, in theory, colonists' dependence on king and Parliament. Congress's endorsement of the Suffolk Resolves and tabling of Galloway's Plan of Union pushed Congress further into the radical fold. Through these maneuvers, delegates exposed their unconditional commitment to defending liberty and their uninterest in a long-shot attempt at fixing the empire's broader deficiencies. Finally, resorting to the doctrine of self-preservation signaled Congress valued American liberty and identity over continued inclusion within the empire. Congress advised General Gage, subjects of England, inhabitants of British North America, and the king himself that the current crisis threatened colonial survival and self-preservation became colonists' fundamental objective. In a final effort to secure American liberties and achieve imperial reconciliation and colonial moral regeneration, delegates drafted the Articles of Association, the shrewdest and most radical step taken by the First Continental Congress.

Four

The Cultural Context of the
Continental Association

O N SEPTEMBER 6, 1774, MASSACHUSETTS DELEGATE THOMAS
Cushing requested that Congress open its sessions with prayer.
This motion immediately sparked a spirited debate among members
over whether or not Congress ought to offer "Reverence and Submission to the Supreme Being" like the Roman Senate, British Parliament, and many American assemblies had done before the present
convention.[1] John Jay voiced concern that, since delegates remained
divided religiously, Congress could not participate in the same religious service. Samuel Adams pushed back against Jay, claiming he
was "no bigot," and would listen to a prayer from any gentleman of
character who supported the common cause. Adams recounted that,
although he had arrived a stranger in Philadelphia, he discovered Anglican rector Jacob Duché fit those criteria and recommended the
reverend offer prayers before Congress.[2] Swayed by Adams, the delegates agreed and sought Duché's spiritual guidance.[3]

Duché accepted the invitation and delivered his first prayer on September 7, shortly after Congress had learned of the supposed bombardment of Boston.[4] After opening with part of the Church of England's morning service, Duché next read Psalm 35:

> Plead my cause, O Lord, with them that strive with me: fight against them that fight against me (Ps 35: 1). Take hold of shield and buckler, and stand up for mine help (Ps 35: 2). Draw out also thy spear, and stop the way against them that persecute me: say unto my soul, I am thy salvation (Ps 35: 3). Let them be confounded and put to shame that seek after my soul: let them be turned back and brought to confusion that devise my hurt (Ps 35: 4). . . . I humbled my soul with fasting; and my prayer returned into mine own bosom (Ps 35: 13). I behaved myself as though he had been my friend or brother: I bowed down heavily, as one that mourneth for his mother (Ps 35: 14). . . . Rescue my soul from their destruction, my darling from the lions (Ps 35: 17). . . . Let them shout for joy, and be glad, that favor my righteous cause (Ps 35: 27).[5]

This psalm's focus on struggle, sacrifice, mourning, and triumph struck members of Congress as particularly relevant. Silas Deane derived such inspiration from Duché's prayer that he described it as "worth riding one hundred miles to hear." He characterized the reverend's message as "accidentally extremely applicable."[6] Connecticut's Samuel Ward felt the rector had delivered "the most sublime, catholic, well-adapted prayers" he had ever heard.[7] James Duane believed it to be "one suitable to the occasion."[8] John Adams felt the same way and implored his wife to read it, marveling, "Heaven had ordained that Psalm to be read on that morning."[9] Yet as authentic as this occasion appears, Samuel Adams probably orchestrated it, recognizing the political utility of spirituality to the common cause.

Samuel Adams likely calculated that adding a prayer service might provide Congress with spiritual legitimacy. As noted by historian Martin J. Medhurst, radical delegates hoped the addition of an Anglican clergyman would encourage other Anglicans, from the pulpit to the pew, to share Whig political concerns.[10] Radicals outside of

Congress likewise hoped to garner Anglican support for the resistance effort. Massachusetts physician Joseph Warren, for example, received a private letter from Samuel Adams recounting both Duché's appointment and sermon. Warren felt the letter's contents so important that he ensured its publication in the *Boston Gazette*. The letter pointed out that some of the "warmest Friends" of the American cause belonged to the Church of England. And Jacob Duché, according to the statement, revealed himself to be a fierce defender of America's religious and civil liberties. In closing, Adams warned that "our enemies" would likely attempt to use religious prejudice to further partition colonists during the current crisis.[11]

A few nights after Duché recited Psalm 35, John Adams returned to his lodgings after a routine evening of fraternizing. Samuel Adams and Philadelphia attorney Joseph Reed visited the younger Adams in his room, where the three men continued "a very social, agreeable and communicative Evening." Reed claimed the two Massachusetts delegates "never were guilty of a more Masterly Stroke of Policy" than in getting Duché to offer prayers before Congress, as his appointment was certain to bolster the common cause.[12] This shrewd fusion of politics and religion again exposes some delegates' willingness to manipulate circumstances to help the resistance movement achieve its goals. And the political theater that led to Duché's appointment had the effect of bringing delegates together through a prayer that connected suffering with salvation, both of which the First Continental Congress would codify in the Articles of Association.

This chapter argues that Congress's Articles of Association simultaneously sought political reconciliation with the metropole and moral regeneration within the mainland colonies. While long recognized as a commercial freeze designed to pressure Parliament into repealing the Coercive Acts, few historians have considered the logic behind Congress's attempt to foster an environment that shunned a range of alleged debauched practices. Delegates hoped to restore civic harmony within the empire by committing colonists to material self-denial. They also sought to retrieve what some Whigs considered a lost sense of virtue in British North America by banning such traditions as horse racing, gambling, theater-going, and all other conspic-

uous displays of leisure and wasteful consumption. Congress expected this purge to reverse the moral decay many felt had so thoroughly corrupted England and retrieve for America a largely mythical
lifestyle of virtue, vigilance, and dignified simplicity.

American Whigs declared loyalty to Congress over king and Parliament by committing themselves to meet the American assembly's
objectives. They condemned those unwilling to support the Continental Association as enemies of America, casting them out of their
political community. Imperial traditionalists, for their part, remained
loyal to the empire's existing political institutions and refused to recognize what they viewed as an imposter government. For traditionalists, Whigs behaved more like licentious mobs than virtuous
patriots. This dichotomy exposed the political fracturing taking place
within communities throughout colonial America and furthered the
transformation of some British subjects to American citizens. This
divide is not representative of the partisan politics to which Americans are accustomed today. The combustible political environment
that existed by the eve of the American Revolution did not center
around which people would rule the government. Rather, the question became which government would rule the people.

Before this chapter examines the Articles of Association, it first
explores the intellectual and cultural environment within which Congress wrote those papers. It then briefly surveys the normative nature
of political resistance in early modern Britain before tracing the
reconceptualization of patriotism that materialized after 1763. Next,
this chapter reveals the ways in which classical virtue and Protestant
dissent shaped the language and expectations of the Continental Association. These pages next offer an examination of the Association's
goals and methods. Finally, this chapter compares how colonists of
various political stripes reacted to Congress's work so to highlight
the troubled nature of the empire during the final imperial crisis.

British subjects on both sides of the Atlantic had woven public resistance to perceived civic injustices into the very fabric of their political culture. Even before the crisis years following the French and
Indian War (1754–1763), the empire had experienced a series of jolts
to its system. Going back to the Stuart kings, alarmed subjects openly

challenged perceived infringements upon their liberties. Charles I's Forced Loan and collection of ship money beyond coastal regions and during peacetime (this was traditionally a tax levied only on seaport towns during times of war) struck at the heart of many subjects' understanding of property rights and threatened the hard-won legislative supremacy of Parliament. The protests and posturing in defense of English liberty and Parliament's integrity during Charles I's reign culminated with the English Civil War and that Stuart king's execution.[13] Within forty years, James II's so-called abuses of authority fomented a popular revolution that reverberated across the Atlantic Ocean, most notably in Massachusetts. In that colony, angry settlers forced Governor Sir Edmund Andros out of power and into prison after learning of the king's abdication.[14]

While studying the rich tradition of extrainstitutional resistance in British North America, historian Pauline Maier noted that nearly every instance of political upheaval resulted from local governments failing to adequately address local concerns. American colonists mobilized to keep foodstuffs available during the Boston Bread Riots of 1710, 1713, and 1729, thwart the enforcement of the White Pines Acts of 1722 and 1729, and rescue men from British naval impressment throughout much of the eighteenth century. As explained by Maier, American subjects did not intend for these moments of resistance to destroy or even limit governmental authority. They were, instead, popular expressions intended to remind elected officials of their constituents' concerns.[15]

Historians partly trace the genealogy of organized resistance in America during the crisis years to the Loyal Nine of Massachusetts, a group of radical artisans and shopkeepers who met to coordinate resistance against the Stamp Act. And even this group relied on more experienced actors to choreograph its street protests. For this political theater, the Nine recruited the North and South End mobs, two gangs that had for years participated in annual street fights on Guy Fawkes Day. Yet when the empire's political troubles deepened, the Loyal Nine saw their membership expand. This broader group styled itself the Sons of Liberty, a loose network of associations that permeated New England, the mid-Atlantic region and the southern colonies. As noted by historian John Ferling, a "thicket of associations" had been operating in British North America twenty years before Parliament passed the Townshend Acts.[16] Membership in these networks included a range of local actors, from men of modest means to those of great influence. In Virginia, for example, Richard Henry Lee organized the Westmoreland County Association in 1766, which included, among others, George Washington and leading men of the prominent Lee family.[17]

Historian T. H. Breen argued that American colonists were likely the first to weaponize consumer goods to solve political problems that remained beyond a constitutional solution.[18] And after 1763, most resistance actors in colonial America utilized economic pressure to realize their political goals. The Stamp Act Congress inspired colonists to organize an intercolonial nonimportation movement so as to force Parliament into repealing the Stamp Act of 1765.[19] And while the quick abrogation of that measure leaves open to debate the effectiveness of this early attempt at economic coercion, the Townshend Acts of 1767 again reignited colonial enthusiasm to refuse what Samuel Adams dubbed the "Baubles of Britain."[20] George Washington, writing his friend and mentor George Mason, voiced his guarded support for nonimportation during the Townshend Acts Crisis.[21] Since petitioning the king and remonstrating to Parliament had both failed to redress colonial grievances, Washington believed Americans might best secure liberty by "starving their [British] Trade and manufactures." If virtuous Americans universally joined in a nonimportation effort, the master of Mount Vernon conjectured, British goods could only be sold to "the non-associater." And, according to Washington, colonists ought to make these subjects "objects of publick reproach." While supportive of nonimportation, however, Washington expressed concern over whether Americans could successfully organize and sustain a uniform plan throughout the colonies.[22]

By 1770, with all duties but the modest tea tax repealed, the colonial coercive effort lost much of its force.[23] Samuel Adams, impressed by Whig resistance, marveled at the merchant class's "grand Tryal which pressed hard upon their private Interest."[24] He also remained among the vocal few, however, to warn of the fragile state of American liberty during the quiet after the Boston Massacre.[25] In 1773, Parliament adjusted the Tea Act to lower the tax while granting the struggling East India Company a monopoly on that commodity in colonial America. In protest, Boston's Sons of Liberty tossed 342 chests of tea from three vessels berthed at Griffin's Wharf into Boston Harbor.[26] South Carolina's Henry Laurens wondered how the destruction of the tea by those "Wily Cromwellians," or fanatical Puritans, might be received across the ocean.[27] By March, Parliament had passed the Coercive Acts. And by the summer of 1774, colonial resistance again took the form of nonimportation. Each of these boycotts required some degree of material sacrifice on the part of American subjects. During the crisis years, protest and prohibition complemented one another. Indeed, they became one and the same. And during this revealing process, colonists experienced the subtle but consequential transformation of a concept: What constituted a public expression of patriotism?

American subjects frequently defined, discussed, and encouraged patriotism. Before 1764, theorists typically characterized this quality as a subject's disinterested love of country.[28] Most observers felt disinterestedness helped distinguish "the patriot from the Traytor."[29] One commentator felt a true patriot's commitment to the public ranked superior to preferential attachments to both family and friends. Relatives and associates of the commonwealth, this writer offered, dedicated themselves exclusively to the public good. Patriotism, another essayist theorized, provided stability and glory to any civil society. True patriots, he declared, kept a "noble disinterested Love of the Public." Those who refused to dedicate their head, heart, and hands to their country or acted from selfish principles, he added, must be treated as "a Foe of Society."[30] These early treatises reminded subjects of their personal obligations to the public weal and the disastrous consequences of private avarice. The degree of patriotism in any society, according to these writers (and presumably their readers), predicted its continued survival or imminent decay.[31] For many observers, virtue united friends of the commonwealth and ostracized its internal enemies. But publicly practicing vigilance and love of country remained conceptual and rhetorical at best. By the 1760s, however, American subjects blended a material element into their understanding of patriotism that allowed colonists to parade their virtue.

When Prime Minister George Grenville guided the Sugar Act of 1764 through Parliament, it set off proverbial alarm bells for many colonists, particularly in the port cities of New England.[32] The act actually reduced the tax on sugar from six to three pence, as Parliament expected most subjects would rather pay the modest fee than risk the penalties of smuggling. Yet plenty of Americans profited from the illegal transport of foreign sugar, particularly from the Dutch and French West Indian islands. Naturally, those engaged in this illicit commerce stood to lose out on a once-profitable endeavor.[33] Other colonists, however, expressed concern for the power the act assumed for Parliament and the vice-admiralty court at Nova Scotia.[34] Simply put, the Sugar Act accorded Parliament the right to raise revenue in America without colonists' consent. It also determined that a foreign court possessed jurisdiction over cases involving maritime seizure and confiscation.[35] And while protest to the Sugar Act did not generate the type of outrage conjured up by the Stamp Act, colonists did push back against this perceived threat to American property and liberty in creative fashion.

In protest to the Sugar Act, one commentator urged Americans to demonstrate patriotism through action. Colonists could display virtue by "renouncing foreign Toys and Fripperies of Dress" and using only locally manufactured merchandise. Proudly adorning oneself with American made gloves, stockings, or any other domestic materials, the writer continued, showcased the "Marks of Patriotism."[36] This new addition to American resistance, linking patriotism to the production and consumption of American goods and the rejection of British commodities, enabled colonists to publicize their political principles and showcase virtue. Shortly after the passage of the Sugar Act, Grenville shepherded the Stamp Act through Parliament.[37] This direct tax again triggered widespread resistance that allowed Americans to broadcast their patriotism.

In response to the Stamp Act, New Jersey attorneys called a meeting at Perth Amboy and, after conferring with the colony's chief justice, decided against purchasing stamped paper.[38] They vowed to cease practicing law until Parliament repealed the Stamp Act, offering to sacrifice their private finances for the public good.[39] By refusing to consume British paper at their own expense, New Jersey attorneys joined patriotism with material sacrifice.

Students graduating from the College of New Jersey in 1765 also connected patriotism with self-denial while protesting the Stamp Act. Recognizing the state of "their suffering Country," each graduate dressed in homespun clothing. As reported in the *Pennsylvania Gazette*, these young men cast aside "those Articles of Superfluity and Luxury" in favor of locally produced wares, fusing protest and virtue.[40] This focus on material culture manifested something deeper than promoting domestic manufacturing or harming British industrialists. Such acts of public sacrifice allowed participants to flaunt their politics and inspire others to do the same in defense of American liberty.

As noted above, Americans again resorted to nonimportation in their effort to get the Townshend Acts repealed. And some newspapers still provided standard conceptual primers defining patriotism as a disinterested attachment to the state.[41] One writer urged Americans to emulate the selflessness of Cato during the latest nonimportation effort. That Roman senator, mused the author, defended Rome's liberty against the world's conquerors and "resigned his breath" when he no longer had a country to sacrifice for.[42] But other commentators continued to focus on material sacrifice, pleading with Americans to save their money in liberty's defense. Colonists, one contributor to the *Boston Evening Post* exclaimed, must "cloathe themselves with their own manufactures." America's daughters, he continued, ought to "nobly . . . exert themselves" in producing clothing from domestic wool to wean colonists off their industrial dependence on the metropole. By reducing "our superfluities," this observer concluded, subjects could enjoy the comfort and happiness provided by the natural bounty of America.[43]

In the same paper, another party reported that men and women who attended a ball in New London, Connecticut, "appeared dress'd in Apparel" made in that colony. Inhabitants at the same location

agreed to "discourage . . . expensive Entertainment" during the selection of militia officers and reduce the use of alcohol.[44] Surveying
imperial developments, George Mason explained to Washington that
Great Britain's traders and manufacturers would "quickly awaken"
if Americans joined an association that refused to import any item
Parliament taxed. "Our All is at Stake," Mason warned his fellow
Virginian. "[T]he little Conveniences and Comforts of Life," when
in competition with American liberties, "ought to be rejected not
with reluctance but with pleasure."[45] In less than a decade, the concept of patriotism transformed from abstract rhetoric into measura-
ble displays of self-denial.

In 1770, "Portius" explained that Americans could express virtue
by joining in a nonimportation agreement. He hoped towns and
counties would create committees "appointed by the voice of the people" vested with the appropriate authority to enforce this association's directives. Portius then reminded Americans that patriotism
required action not words. Flying liberty colors, wearing red liberty
caps, and erecting liberty poles, he quipped, protected American freedoms no better than "mere playthings for children."[46] Another pseudonymous observer chastised American merchants, particularly those
of New York, for catering to their own self-interest over the public
good. During this critical time, the writer proclaimed, the "powers
of Patriotism" must be drawn from the rest of the community. To
defend liberty, he reasoned, Americans must stop purchasing those
items "marked with such badges of slavery."[47]

In an essay deriding Whig resistance, "A Husbandman" resented
Whigs labeling men like himself as a "Great Enemy of his Country"
for preferring British manufactures to domestically produced goods.
He ridiculed describing as patriots those colonists who denied themselves and their families any luxury items. Next, he decried Americans who felt any "patriotic lady" must spend her time creating
homespun.[48] This ardent observer remained deeply unsettled by what
he felt was the appropriation of patriotism. The behaviors that troubled him, however, were clearly widespread enough for him to take
time articulating his disdain.

Following the passage of the Tea Act of 1773, a commentator
from Virginia urged colonists to stop purchasing that product,

"which is pregnant with Mischief to the Health and Liberty of the People of America."[49] Another writer going by "Hamden" (likely a reference to John Hampden, a Parliamentarian who resisted Charles I's tax schemes) also connected tea to moral corruption. He framed *amore patriae* as both a religious and moral duty for Americans and claimed that biblical figures such as Moses, Samuel, and Jesus possessed religious virtue in proportion to their public spirit. Building off this theological-civic connection, Hamden urged Americans to abstain from purchasing and consuming tea. That poisonous plant, he declared, contained something worse than death—"the seeds of Slavery." He reminded readers of their ancestors' unparalleled sacrifices to secure and pass liberty inviolate to the present generation and asked them to consider their own posterity during the present crisis.[50] This generation's actions, Hamden claimed, would determine the future of liberty in America. Patriotism, for these observers, necessarily incorporated material self-denial and birthed a new form of resistance that relied more on economic and social pressure than organized violence.

Commitment to material sacrifice and social simplicity became fundamental components in creating a pan-colonial political community in British North America. One essayist lectured on the fragility of civilized society, urging colonists to embrace virtue and frugality and resist avarice and luxury. The latter traits, he warned, ushered in "venality, effeminacy, dissension, and cowardice" into any community. Sparta and Rome remained proud and independent, he asserted, while adhering to "frugality, public spirit, valour, and moderation."[51] It was leisure and luxury, he explained, that brought ruin to those admired polities. John Hancock, addressing a crowd on the fourth anniversary of the Boston Massacre, defined patriotism as a quality that compelled people to "sacrifice everything" to assist those suffering for a public cause.[52] In this highly charged political environment, resistance actors expected Americans to perform self-denial within the discerning gaze of the public.

Alarmed Whigs sought to cure colonists of frivolous material indulgence as well as their addiction to what they considered debauched pastimes. These pursuits, many felt, diverted Americans

from meaningful civic and spiritual engagement and deepened colonial dependence on English manufactures and luxuries. Many saw
the results of this decadence and dependence in the perceived quick-
ening moral decay of British North America.[53] To redirect from this
perilous path, Whigs looked to a unique synthesis of the classical tradition and Protestant dissent. An idealized version of the classical
past inspired some to refashion colonial America as an interdepend-
ent community of material and cultural frugality guarded by a virtuous citizenry.[54] Protestant dissent merged a series of complex beliefs
into a politico-religious worldview informed largely by English com-
monwealthmen and real Whigs. Despite the conflicts and differences
within the components of this worldview, however, emerge some
principles to which American Whigs generally subscribed. Most advocated virtue and simplicity, agreeing that moral decay resulted
from corruption and luxury. They also fiercely supported consensual
government and the natural right to resistance.[55] Combined, both
classical virtue and Protestant dissent informed many colonists of desired behaviors that might regenerate private and political purity in
colonial America.

For many Britons, the classical tradition modeled ideal moral and
political behavior and overwhelmingly their examples derived from
ancient Greece and Rome.[56] The collapse of these revered civilizations
instructed colonists on what happened to societies that experienced
a rapid decline in public spirit. American subjects immersed in this
history connected their commonwealth's survival to its citizens' political virtue and Britain became, for many, a terrifying example of a
once-glorious empire in decline.[57] Riddled with what they viewed as
moral corruption and political deterioration, these observers considered the metropole a contemporary version of imperial Rome.[58] One
commentator observed that empires, like the human body, cycle
through birth, maturity, and decline. Luxury and its constant com-
panion, corruption, he cautioned, invited certain decay and paved
the way for the rise of an arbitrary prince. Americans ought to be
alarmed at the "present degeneracy of the people," he advised, but
"a small share of national virtue" may overcome such moral failure.[59]
"Lucius Publicola" offered a similar solution for America's predica-

ment. Britain, he claimed, had taken the road to ruin like Athens and Rome before it. Parliament's despotism resulted from "the degeneracy and corruption of the people," and curing it, he argued, could only be "wrought by the regeneracy of the people."[60] Virtue, according to an idealized reading of the ancient past, provided American subjects a chance to overcome the current crisis and retrieve ancient simplicity.[61] But how exactly did colonial Americans understand virtue?

For classical Greeks, virtue (*arete*) applied only to individual actions beneficial to the public good. Citizens who acted in ways useful to the greater community in war and politics publicly expressed their *arete*.[62] Romans, for their part, understood virtue as a combination of social, political, and philosophical ideals. Cicero described it as a form of fortitude that provided two main functions useful to the public: scorn of death and scorn of pain. This required civic courage, a type of bravery men might display on a battlefield, in their homes, or at the public square. And for Romans, like Greeks, this behavior did not apply to reckless actions. It applied only to selfless behaviors made on behalf of the state. Additionally, according to Cicero, virtue revealed itself in deed more than word.[63]

These instructions filtered, however imperfectly, into the minds of colonial Americans. Benjamin Franklin, echoing the Greek and Roman ideal, made certain to draw out that self-denial for its own sake did not constitute virtue. That coveted quality, he wrote, applied only to instances of sacrifice that advanced the public good.[64] Being a virtuous Roman, according to historian Catalina Balmaceda, involved fulfilling one's public role to benefit the community. Private bravery, for instance overcoming a fear of the dark, did not qualify as virtuous.[65] Contemporary American newspapers and imported tomes on ancient history informed colonists of the social value of disinterestedness and self-denial. And this political education reminded many inhabitants of their interdependence on one another.

Not unlike classical virtue in some ways, Protestant dissent broadly encouraged industriousness, virtue, and vigilance. In fact, some dissenters not only condemned leisure and indulgence as vices but blamed them for the fall of Rome. Those guided by this belief system promoted local industry, hopeful it would create sustainable colonial economies and create a self-sustaining American. They further anticipated the normalization of self-denial to rehabilitate colonial virtues and habits.[66] Yet equally important, dissenters advocated popular sovereignty and a God-given right to resistance. While these ideas resonated with American Whigs, however, they had become fringe beliefs at best in England.[67]

Jonathan Mayhew, among the most influential dissenters, encapsulated this worldview most forcefully.[68] John Adams declared Mayhew's wit superior to even "Swift or Franklin," and claimed his work "was read by every Body, celebrated by Friends, and abused by Enemies." According to Adams, Mayhew "Spread an Universal Alarm against the Authority of Parliament," warning that if the assembly could tax Americans it could establish the Church of England in the colonies and crush all other denominations. Mayhew, asserted Adams, helped bring about the "commencement of the Revolution."[69]

Jonathan Mayhew gained notoriety after publishing a deeply controversial pamphlet on the 101st anniversary of Charles I's execution. Instead of framing the king as a martyr, Mayhew condemned him for endangering liberty and vindicated those in Parliament who resisted Charles and ultimately condoned his beheading. As recognized by historian J. Patrick Mullins, no "New England clergyman had dared defend the regicide explicitly since Rev. John Cotton in 1651." Though Mayhew's first sermon argued that Protestant dissent secured British liberty by prohibiting further Catholic dynasties and ushering in the Hanoverian kings, many viewed his embrace of regicide as seditious. Still, Mayhew continued to support popular resistance throughout his career, most notably in his final sermon, "The Snare Broken." In this address, he again advised followers to remain vigilant of power's encroachment upon liberty and advocated immediate action against any threat to constitutional freedoms.[70] Like many other dissenters, Mayhew's unapologetic defense of civil and religious rights drew on John Trenchard and Thomas Gordon's *Cato's Letters*, Algernon Sidney's *Discourses Concerning Government*, Benjamin Hoadly's *Measures of Submission*, and John Locke's *Second Treatise of Government*, among others.[71]

These two worldviews, the classical tradition and Protestant dissent, informed many colonists and helped them rationalize and respond to their tumultuous times. Radical Samuel Adams felt sufferers in Boston, animated by self-preservation, had discovered "the Spirit of Rome or Sparta."[72] By this, he meant Bostonians had adapted to their circumstances and embraced the austerity forced upon them by the Coercive Acts. John Adams wrote to his wife that "Frugality, my Dear, Frugality," will bring about salvation. He also hoped that women would limit their expenditures and voluntarily embrace a Spartan lifestyle. "Let us Eat Potatoes . . . drink Water," and wear simple sheepskin to avoid submission to Parliament's tyranny, he proposed to his wife.[73] Abigail Adams responded by stating Americans might regain their inherited liberties by practicing the "primitive Simplicity and Manners" of their fathers instead of seeking leisure and comfort. Abigail Adams accepted laboring with her hands, she explained, since the occasion called for "all our industry and economy."[74]

Boston law clerk William Tudor encapsulated the spirit of the moment in a letter to his mentor and friend, John Adams:

> The Luxury and Corruption that has debauch'd and deprav'd all Ranks in great Britain has led them to treat public Virtue as a public Jest, and to consider the Love of one's Country as the most idle Reverie. But I hope this Country will soon demonstrate to that mistaken Nation, that Patriotism is not a Chimaera, and that Americans in full Vigour retain that heroic Virtue which once directed the Conduct of their Ancestors as well as ours.[75]

Tudor then recounted for Adams a conversation he had had with a Boston ship captain who remained unemployed due to the Boston Port Act. Tudor asked the man if he felt it time that colonists submitted to the Coercive Acts so that trade might finally resume. The captain answered in the negative, explaining he would survive on clams if he had to. And if they became scarce, the seaman declared, he would scour the woodlands for acorns before submitting to slavery. "What a Roman," Tudor exclaimed, expressing his confidence that Bostonians possessed "Spartan Virtue." Americans, he con-

cluded, had as much "Patriotism and Heroism [as] the most celebrated of the Grecian Republics."[76]

In the decade leading up to the summer of 1774, alarmed colonists
had already developed a framework of intellectual and political resistance that relied on unanimous commitment to material sacrifice.
During that same period, their understanding of patriotism had transformed from a conceptual focus on vigilance and character to meas-
urable public acts of material self-denial. By March 1774, American
Whigs added to this material dimension, asking supporters to forgo
conspicuous displays of leisure and happiness so long as Boston suffered in the common cause.[77] This plea invited colonists to perform
patriotism in public by committing to frugality and refraining from
certain social behaviors. Additionally, threatening to label neighbors
who refused to commit to sacrifice as "enemies of American liberties"
had already become commonplace when the First Continental Congress met in September 1774. In sum, much of what Congress ultimately recommended within the pages of the Articles of Association
had already been circulating in the resistance lexicon when that assembly finally convened. Resting silently within the lines of these recommendations is a fusion of classical virtue and Protestant dissent.

The Continental Association provided an assessment of colonial
society and its perceived moral decay and offered colonists solutions
on how they might salvage the American essence. When the Association is situated with classical virtue and Protestant dissent against
the background of normalized resistance and material patriotism,
Americans' participation in a joined rite of sacrifice not only makes
more sense, it stands as the only plausible path to salvation for a generation of Americans convinced the empire was sinking into the same
ruinous depths that had swallowed western Rome. The following
pages will offer a contextualized examination of the language, goals,
and methods of the Articles of Association. While the First Continental Congress supported the controversial Suffolk Resolves, outlined American rights and grievances, and petitioned the king in its
effort to get the Coercive Acts repealed, the actionable directives of
that assembly lie in the Continental Association. And though the document does not spell out an American creed per se, it became the

heart of a nationalized resistance effort and a covenant of sacrifice and endurance that built an American political community.

The opening lines of the Articles of Association recorded each delegation as authorized to represent the interests of its constituent colony in Congress. The remainder of that paragraph surveyed the crisis years from the Whig perspective.[78] After declaring loyalty to the king and a sincere attachment to the empire, the Association claimed Parliament had adopted "a ruinous system of colonial administration" at the close of the late war designed to "enslave these colonies and, with them, the British Empire." Parliament's actions, according to the Association, deprived colonists of consensual taxation and trial by jury, punished Massachusetts with the Coercive Acts, and threatened colonial security with the Quebec Act. The latter provoked Congress to offer a paranoid assessment fueled by religious and racial bigotry. Delegates feared it exposed Protestant subjects to the violent hostility of their French and Algonquin neighbors "whenever a wicked ministry shall chuse to direct them."[79]

For some delegates, Richard Henry Lee among them, the Quebec Act embodied the arbitrary authority exercised by king and Parliament. For others, that legislation represented a clear betrayal of George III's coronation oath, which committed him to enforcing English law and securing Protestant liberty.[80] In order to extricate British North America from its political difficulties, the next section of the Association laid out an American code of conduct over fourteen articles. Congress remained hopeful that if colonists followed this code, Americans could procure imperial reconciliation, secure American liberty, and restore colonial virtue.

Articles 1–4 directed favorably disposed Americans to strictly adhere to nonimportation and nonconsumption of British and Irish imports (including slaves) effective December 1, 1774, and, beginning September 10, 1775, nonexportation of American resources (save rice to Europe). Scholars typically view this commercial dimension as colonists' attempt at economic coercion, which placed a particular burden on American importers who bought and sold foreign goods.[81] And while this assessment is not incorrect, it is incomplete. The directive also expected nonimporters to forgo purchasing manufactured luxuries, including glass and medicines. This effectively changed not only consumption patterns, but the quality of life for supporters of the cause. And delegates equally expected exporters to voluntarily suffer hardship in defense of both Boston and American liberty should the Coercive Acts still be in effect the following September. Self-denial, from the Continental Association's opening directives, became a principle quality of the emerging American political community.

Articles 5, 6, 9, and 13 specifically directed ship captains, British merchants, and American vendors to honor Congress's directives. The Association warned captains and merchants against smuggling illicit goods and vendors against raising prices during potential moments of future material scarcity. Otherwise, offenders risked commercial and social ostracism from the American community.[82] The threat of losing financial viability and social inclusion, Congress expected, offered powerful incentives for colonists wary of adhering to its directives. Article 11 (explored below) outlined the broader punishment for those who dismissed the Association.

Article 7 asked that colonists dramatically reduce the slaughter of sheep to encourage local wool production and reduce American dependence on British textiles. It further directed those with an abundance of sheep to offer surplus chattel to their less fortunate neighbors at reasonable prices. Article 10 provided three options to vendors who placed orders with British merchants too late to cancel. They could choose to have their goods shipped back to England, stored until the repeal of the Coercive Acts (at their own risk), or sold at public auction to recover costs, all profits going to the sufferers at Boston.[83] Congress designed the Association to promote American agriculture and manufacturing, both potential engines of material independence.[84] Delegates hoped to organize a self-sustaining society and liberate Americans from England's perceived debauched influence. And while each of the above articles asked colonists to refrain from some form of commercial activity, article 8 focused on social behaviors and moral regeneration.

Although scholars recognize the commercial aspects of the Continental Association, the social concerns expressed by Congress have typically been glossed over with little attempt to rationalize how they fit into the logic of a nonimportation, nonconsumption, and nonexportation movement.[85] Yet when considering the Association as a code of conduct influenced by classical virtue and Protestant dissent, it is the boycott that suddenly fits into a broader scheme of industrial liberation and moral regeneration. If Congress could help correct these supposed deficiencies, some Americans believed, colonists might restore the primitive simplicity that Abigail Adams and others so longed to recover. To do this, the Continental Association's eighth article urged adherents to practice "frugality, economy, and industry," qualities considered virtuous in both the classical world and in line with Protestant ethics.[86] It next encouraged supporters to "discountenance and discourage every species of extravagance and dissipation."[87] The word "discountenance" has evolved in modern English to mean "discourage" or "disfavor." Yet for eighteenth-century subjects, it most directly meant to actively put a stop to undesirable behaviors.[88] Thus colonists would have likely interpreted this passage as "to put a stop to *and* discourage all forms of lavishness and wasteful consumption." Recovering this minor change in meaning reveals an aggressive Congress directing a forceful suppression of alleged degenerate behaviors rather than a meek one passively advising against those same practices.

Attempting to restore a sense of classical virtue and Christian community in the mainland colonies, the First Continental Congress sought to cleanse America of what it considered some of its worst vices. Hence, the Association's eighth article prohibited horse racing, cockfighting, gambling, theatergoing, extravagant funerals, and other pursuits that many felt polluted the moral purity that Congress sought to revive. These vices, as described by alarmed colonists in York, Virginia, undermined industry and frugality, underscored indolence and improvidence, and were "unbecoming [of] men" who felt the suffering of their country.[89] A strict focus on the economic elements of the Association renders Congress's assault on these social pursuits puzzling. Refraining from attending a horse race or playing cards, for instance, hardly affected the livelihoods of British manufacturers or factory laborers. And no member of Parliament aligned with king and ministry would suddenly move to repeal the Coercive Acts after learning most Americans had suspended some or all of these activities. But appreciating the Association's eighth article as a moral code designed to return simplicity to America satisfactorily connects the suspended commercial activities with those condemned cultural practices. The following paragraphs will explore the unique ways in which Congress felt these activities threatened American virtue and values.

Horse racing, by the eighteenth century, had matured in colonial America to resemble the sport's English counterpart. Enthusiasts spent much ink and many hours recounting the genealogy of their horses and seeking the best care for them, a clear indication of their social value.[90] In the middle colonies, horse racing centered around long-distance competitions. And while the Chesapeake region also hosted these longer races, the quarter-mile sprint, particularly in Virginia, remained the contest southerners enjoyed most.[91] Historian Rhys Isaac described these races in early Virginia as "combat by proxy," as gentlemen put their horses and reputations on the line during these spirited trials. Spectators enjoyed the excitement of the race, but the character of a given horse's owner also became an integral element of the unfolding drama. Beyond the bragging and betting, onlookers evaluated owners' abilities as public leaders.[92] T. H. Breen, commenting on the social dimensions of horse racing, argued these events confirmed or revised the relative social position of horse owners depending on a given contest's outcome. The touchy matter of rank tied into the equally touchy matter of honor and, as Breen explained, put on public display a gentlemen's "competitiveness, individualism, and materialism."[93] Yet during the Coercive Acts Crisis, many Americans considered those particular characteristics harmful to the resistance effort and undesirable to the proposed colonial future of simplicity. Congress prohibited this practice and instead sought to promote cooperation, communitarianism, and austerity among colonists.

Cockfighting also attracted crowds throughout British North America from all ranks of society. City dwellers, country folk, and slaves all gravitated toward this blood sport that often led to the death of one or both competing avians.[94] However, cockfighting culture, like that of horse racing, reflected values at odds with the supposed moral crisis alarmed colonists faced in 1774, as cock breeders practiced their craft in an environment rife with secrecy and potential dishonesty. Referees, feeders, even setters (men tasked with returning birds to the center of the cockpit if fighting had stalled) all came under suspicion of accepting bribes to favor one contestant over another. This favoritism came in all forms, from allowing a bird to use illegal spurs, to officials ignoring owners falsifying a combatant's weight, to setters intentionally injuring a competitor during a reset. The secrecy, distrust, and corruption that characterized cockfighting divided rather than united neighborhoods and turned men into potential enemies rather than joining them in fellowship. Even attendants, some commenters feared, became debauched by the violence that served no other purpose than to entertain.[95] Congress prohibited the practice, viewing it as an engagement that jeopardized the ethical character of Americans struggling against both Parliament and moral decay.

Horse racing and cockfighting posed yet another problem for Congress. Both pastimes created space for men to network, socialize, and, most problematically, gamble. Plenty of colonists considered gambling debasing as it allowed men to express individual dominance or fail spectacularly in their attempts. Yet it also created another debauched environment that celebrated waste and individualism, qualities many Whigs associated with English leisure and corruption.[96] The Continental Association aimed to replace individual dominance and chancy attempts at self-enrichment with public expressions of communitarian solidarity. As early as 1764, some colonists condemned gaming and gambling as wastes of time and resources that encouraged "Vice and Idleness" among American youths.[97] During the 1774 crisis, as Bostonians struggled with material shortages and Congress sought to purge the colonies of extravagance, many viewed gambling and similar vices as an affront to their efforts.

Congress also felt theatergoing threatened colonists' moral character. In England and France, subjects associated the theater with high Italian culture. In the colonies, however, many associated it with English decadence. Even before the Coercive Acts Crisis, some critics described theater culture as an assault on Christian values. The working poor, these observers lectured, ought to practice frugality and industry to support their struggling families. Frequenting stage houses, they reasoned, wasted money most could not afford to spend. And women, particularly upper-class women ostensibly sheltered from the theater's obscenity, might become debauched themselves.[98] "Is going to Plays and other theatrical Performances," one concerned colonist asked, "consistent with the Profession and Practice of Christianity?"[99] Some Americans felt theater also threatened classical virtue. Plays, they warned, turned men into women and all attendees into slaves too debauched to defend life, liberty, and property. Another commenter noted the "theater had a very considerable share in sinking the Athenians into effeminacy and indolence."[100] Delegates shared these concerns and Congress singled out theatergoing as a corruptive distraction that drained Americans of their potential virtue. Linking theatergoing to English decay also helped Congress contrast the pure and noble American with the alleged debased and effeminate Englishman.

Among the cultural practices Congress identified as morally corruptive, funerals offered the ideal environment for colonists to publicize their private political allegiance. Congress aimed to stop horse racing, cockfighting, gambling, and theatergoing altogether. It had no such intention for funerals, as these rituals had to take place. By the eighteenth century, colonial burials had developed into highly choreographed events that tied together status, wealth, and community. Those closest to the deceased purchased expensive mourning attire such as black hats, gowns, shirts, and pants to express grief and loss and highlight their closeness to the departed. The deceased's estate typically provided mourners with gifts to memorialize their life and passing, usually in the form of a ring, a scarf, or, more commonly, a pair of gloves. Mourners of a higher social station generally received better quality gifts than members of the lower ranks. This practice helped reinforce real and imagined connections within a given community while providing solace to the bereaved.[101] Yet some colonists criticized this elaborate practice as a wasteful rite that harmed local economies and proved socially divisive.[102] The Continental Association invited alarmed colonists to signal their commitment to frugality and shared suffering by eliminating lavish funerals and performing instead simple burials. Yet how exactly did Congress expect to regulate and carry out each of its directives and realize its imperial and societal goals?

Article 11 provided the blueprint for Congress's enforcement mechanism, instructing towns and counties to create and elect members to local Committees of Inspection and Observation. Congress tasked these committees with imposing the Continental Association within their respective communities. The article's final passage granted committeemen the authority to publish violators' names in local gazettes identifying them as "enemies of American liberty." It then urged inhabitants to break off all commercial and social interaction with these internal enemies.[103]

Article 12 directed local committees to inspect custom houses and publish an accurate inventory of what remained in stock. Through this directive, Congress hoped to curb price gouging and make scarce resources available in a fair and transparent fashion. In the fourteenth and final article, the Continental Association warned other colonies and provinces in British North America that they too would be declared enemies if they violated the Association. Congress described any potential violating community as "unworthy of the rights of freemen" and "inimical to the liberties of their country."[104] These powerful denunciations threatened individuals and communities alike with commercial and social death should they refuse to contribute to Congress's plans for reconciliation and moral regeneration.

This public death reimagined the Roman punishment *relegatio*, where a formal decree banished an individual from the Eternal City for a set period of time or even life. Ovid referred to his own *relegatio* as a living death, where he became an outsider among hostile strangers, precisely what Congress had in mind.[105] Puritan theology also kept its own form of exile to protect what historian David C. Brown called "communal purity." Though generally out of use by the mid-eighteenth century, the doctrine of excommunication (a holdover from Catholic and Anglican practices) provided a given community the means to maintain a pure communion by casting out a fallen member.[106] The Continental Association weaponized the threat of ostracization to cow nonsupporters into adhering to Congress's commercial and moral expectations. This potential punishment created an intellectual boundary that, once crossed, vilified and alienated violators while joining the Association's supporters in solidarity in the emerging American political community.

Congress sought to create an environment where private decisions throughout British North America found expression in public spaces and colonists calculated their actions with the community's interests (and potentially its wrath) in mind. Advocating nonimportation, nonexportation, and nonconsumption made up just part of a broader plan for imperial reconciliation and colonial moral regeneration. Urging frugality, industry, and interdependence spoke to a desire to return colonial America to the classical simplicity and vigilant Christian community many felt had slipped away. Prohibiting ostentatious expressions of leisure signaled an attempt at removing some of the moral obstacles Congress felt stood in the way of realizing this vision. And casting individuals and potentially other colonies out of this new utopia became the clearest indication that supporters of the Continental Association sought to divide the mainland colonies into Americans and their enemies. Naturally, these so-called enemies viewed the Continental Association as a form of mob rule drafted and implemented by unauthorized forces. To these imperial traditionalists, Congress, not king and Parliament, represented the greatest threat to American liberty. After Congress published its journals, traditionalists' suspicions and concerns only intensified.

On a rainy Wednesday in late October, Congress dissolved and its delegates along with some local elites attended one final evening at City Tavern to celebrate the empire's potential mending.[107] Before breaking up, however, Congress ordered 120 copies of the *Journal of the Proceedings of the Congress* printed and distributed among its delegates and their provincial congresses.[108] By late October, gazettes began advertising the sale of Congress's *Journal*.[109] Its title page displays an engraving by an unknown artist, the entirety of which is

FIGURE 1, left. Title page, *Journal of the Proceedings of the Congress* (Philadelphia: William and Thomas Bradford, 1774). FIGURE 2, right. Detail of the title page illustration depicting twelve hands, one for each colony represented in Congress. They are supporting a liberty pole crowned with a liberty cap. The pole rests on the perceived foundation of English liberty, Magna Carta. The text surrounding the engraving reads *Hanc Tuemur, Hac Nitimur*, the Latin motto, "This we defend, this we lean on." From Worthington Chauncy Ford, et al., eds., *Journals of the Continental Congress*, 34 volumes (Washington: Government Printing Office, 1904-37), vol. 1.

contained within the circular boundaries of a medallion (Figures 1 and 2). It depicts a liberty pole crowned with a liberty cap, held in place by twelve hands (six on each side), which themselves appear to be emerging out of a mist. Each hand symbolizes a colony represented in Congress, Georgia being absent. "Magna Carta" is written at the base of the pole and text within the medallion reads, "*Hanc Tuemur, Hac Nitimur*," Latin for "This we defend, this we lean on."

For many American subjects, Magna Carta represented the foundation of English liberty.[110] Indeed, throughout the crisis years, alarmed observers routinely insisted their colonial charters guaranteed them the same liberties as subjects in England, including those rights protected by Magna Carta.[111] In 1766, Virginia's Richard Bland went so far as to claim that English subjects reserved the liberties itemized in Magna Carta as part of their Anglo-Saxon birthright. Royal charters, he argued, only served to pass these liberties inviolate to American settlers.[112] Beginning in the 1760s, colonists routinely cited Magna Carta as proof that Parliament did not have authority over American affairs. From engravings produced by Paul Revere, to the cover of John Dickinson's *Letters from a Farmer in Pennsylvania*, or the title page of Congress's *Journal*, resistance actors relied on Magna Carta to illustrate a widely recognized guarantor of liberty.[113] As a young attorney, John Adams referred to that medieval charter many times to defend what he perceived to be beleaguered colonial rights.[114] Benjamin Franklin, writing under a pseudonym in London's *Public Ledger*, surveyed examples of violent social unrest in England and asked why king and Parliament did not define these riots and protests as rebellions. Why, he barbed, did English laborers, sawyers, coalheavers, and smugglers not have *their* Magna Carta stripped from them as American colonists had for doing far less?[115] And New Jersey had a borough named Runnemede, likely a nod to the site along the Thames where defensive barons imposed upon the reviled King John to seal Magna Carta in 1215.[116]

Colonial Americans appreciated Magna Carta differently than their English cousins. Even William Blackstone and Edward Coke, two jurists on whom Americans relied heavily for their understanding of British jurisprudence, did not believe Magna Carta denied Parliament the right to tax the colonies.[117] As with many Americans' understanding of the colonial past, however, the mythologized version of the charter remained a powerful influence. And in this respect, myth became reality for many Americans.

When Congress anchored American liberties to natural law, the British Constitution, and colonial charters, it considered Magna Carta as part of this bundle.[118] The inclusion of Magna Carta on the frontispiece conveyed a message that would not have been lost on contemporary readers. Congress, by including the twelve hands holding up a liberty pole resting on Magna Carta, had cast itself as a collection of benevolent American barons defending colonial liberty from a latter-day King John: Parliament.

Once Congress published its *Journal of the Proceedings of the Congress*, its work came under close scrutiny. Naturally, both delegates and outside observers expressed divergent views regarding Congress's efforts. Some of the more radical actors expressed optimism about the Continental Association's potential to convince Parliament to repeal the Coercive Acts. Virginia delegate Richard Henry Lee left Philadelphia convinced that, due to Congress's efforts, Parliament would immediately repeal the Coercive Acts.[119] Philadelphia attorney Joseph Reed expressed optimism that colonists would demonstrate "proof of public virtue and enlightened zeal" by supporting the measures of Congress.[120] No one, he warned in another letter, would dare oppose the "self-denying ordinance of the General Congress." To that end, Reed expected the Continental Association to accomplish its goals.[121]

One anonymous New Yorker sent the *Journal* to a friend in London. He claimed that thousands of copies circulated throughout the American colonies and many gentlemen had them framed and on display in their homes. They created these exhibits, the writer offered, to contrast American bravery with what he described as British effeminacy.[122] In an essay published in the *South Carolina Gazette* and reprinted in the *Pennsylvania Packet*, another writer marveled that Congress inspired and directed the united colonies to resist tyranny. "Away with the flimsy excuses driven by avarice and mistaken self-interest," this essayist lectured. "Know it ye American colonies, that true self-interest demands the exact observance of all the self-denying injunctions of the association." He confidently predicted that if colonists adhered to the Association for three months, poverty-stricken West Indian planters, as well as English and Irish manufactures, would champion the American cause "in a manner that will shake the throne of Majesty itself." Americans, this writer concluded, needed only to "wield the weapons of self-denial" Congress recommended.[123] Not all supporters, however, exuded such confidence in the delegates' work.

George Washington left Philadelphia deeply skeptical. He felt that unless colonists throughout British North America unanimously committed to a sustained nonimportation and nonexportation campaign, Parliament would not budge. Shortly after Congress dissolved,

John Adams confided to Patrick Henry his conviction that the Continental Association would cement the union of the American people. He remained convinced, however, that Congress's work would be received as "Waste Water in England," especially by the government. The fiery Virginian responded by simply stating, "We must fight." Henry, like Adams, suspected Americans would need to do more than execute a pan-colonial commercial freeze to move Parliament.[124]

If thorough radicals like Henry almost welcomed armed combat, moderates like John Dickinson recoiled at the prospect. Writing to Massachusetts agent Arthur Lee, Dickinson reflected on Congress's work and offered a few poignant predictions of his own. Now that Congress had published its recommendations, Pennsylvania's most famous farmer described Americans as unanimous in their support of the common cause. "I wish for peace," he confessed, but explained he would be surprised if the struggle for liberty ended in such fashion. The first hostile action by either the ministry or General Gage, Dickinson lamented, "will put the whole Continent in arms, from Nova Scotia to Georgia."[125] Writing to the ailing Josiah Quincy Jr., Dickinson offered an even grimmer augury. Colonists would grow more committed to resistance measures once delegates returned to their home colonies and, unless Parliament repealed the Coercive Acts quickly, he wrote, "a civil war is unavoidable." Once open conflict began, he predicted other European powers would join, deepening the misery and bloodshed. Four hundred thousand freemen, fighting for their altars and hearths, he wrote, would not easily submit to force. The moment for reconciliation was quickly passing, he cautioned, and would soon be irretrievably gone, "as the days beyond the flood."[126] Not all delegates supported Congress's efforts, however, with imperial traditionalist Joseph Galloway going so far as to denounce the Continental Association and the "Cromwellian faction" in Congress that devised it.[127] The work of the American assembly also initiated a spirited public debate outside of its Ciceronian fellowship.

Philadelphia attorney Edward Shippen remained optimistic that Congress's work would repair the empire and expected that assembly to send a copy of the "extracts from the votes &c of the Continental

Congress" directly to George III. Carrying his enthusiasm further, he hoped to "live till May to see another Congress" and anticipated this next body would also send its wisdom directly to the king.[128] Another observer defended Congress's legitimacy by reminding readers it derived its power "not from scrowls [scrolls] of parchment signed by Kings, but by the People." Those unwilling to support its directives, this writer thundered, committed treason not only against themselves and posterity, but against God. Violators, he proposed, ought to suffer corporal punishment, since they clearly had no soul or conscience. Congress instead simply wished them the infamy of being declared an enemy to the country.[129] In response to this article, the pseudonymous "Anti-Tormentor" reminded readers that American assemblymen were mortal and capable of errors in judgment. And while he disapproved of Congress's proceedings, he professed his loyalty to America. He explained that Congress, an assembly that allegedly spoke on behalf of the people, operated in total secrecy while the vilified House of Commons published its debates daily. And rather than condemning neighbors as enemies or wishing them physical harm, the writer argued (not unreasonably) a free society ought to embrace its political differences. State-sanctioned violence against domestic dissenters, he cautioned, remained more suited for imperial Rome than their Protestant kingdom.[130] More militant opponents of Congress also offered a range of responses, from predictions that most colonists would simply ignore its directives to outright fear of civil war and independence.

New York's lieutenant governor, Cadwallader Colden, expressed confidence that his constituents would ignore Congress's recommendations. Farmers would reject the Association's nonexportation directive, he predicted, and merchants already spurned nonimportation. Self-interest remained a powerful enough incentive, Colden believed, to fatally undermine the Association.[131] A British officer stationed at Boston described Congress's delegates as violent men "inflamed by sedition" and elected by a "riotous and tumultuous mob." Moderate and sensible men, he opined, had only contempt for the Association. The empire would again enjoy peace, the officer expected, once the ministry condemned Congress's resolutions.[132] Lieutenant General

Thomas Gage agreed with some of this officer's observations, assuring the Earl of Dartmouth, Britain's secretary of state for the colonies, that Congress's proceedings repulsed all good men. He voiced concern, however, that sensible colonists would likely feel too intimidated to openly defy Congress's recommendations.[133] New York Crown supporter Samuel Seabury claimed Congress's republicans aimed to radicalize colonists with the "pill of sedition." Though Congress feigned loyalty to the Crown, Seabury claimed, its actions aimed for American independence. Once the mask of loyalty came off and Congress made its intentions clear, he theorized, king and Parliament would crush America by force, bringing about "the most dreadful scenes of violence and slaughter."[134] One British merchant scoffed at the absurdity of Congress's proposals and also came away convinced American delegates sought total independence.[135] The Earl of Dartmouth agreed. From his perspective, Congress destroyed any chance for reconciliation and its scandalous work was certain to bring about "the vengeance of the mother country."[136] Yet the most perceptive and persuasive critique came from Anglican priest Thomas Bradbury Chandler, an imperial traditionalist who hoped to convince New York and other colonies to simply reject Congress outright.

Chandler carefully read Congress's *Journal*, reflected on its positions, and responded in such a clear-eyed fashion that even Congress's staunchest supporters would have struggled refuting some of his points. Americans must recognize, Chandler exclaimed, Congress now posed the greatest threat to their liberties. This treasonous body, he continued, threatened to drag America into the horrors of civil war. It demanded that Americans adhere to its Association and "become poor as dogs" and "live like savages" until Parliament repealed the Coercive Acts. Congress's nonimportation directive, he apprised, would prevent colonists from procuring medicines and other critical supplies. "[S]hould we, or our wives and children, come to struggle with sickness," at the whim of an illegitimate body, Chandler fumed? Congress sought nothing less than "a complete political revolution," which Chandler identified as the establishment of an independent American empire. He reminded readers that Britain's government protected civic and religious liberty, the glories of Englishmen. But

Congress's arrogance, the priest claimed, threatened the empire's tranquility. "For this reason," he declared, "I abhor the late Congress." For Chandler, that assembly turned out to be "a perfect monster, —a mad, blind monster."[137]

These critics offered powerful counterpoints to the deluge of print support Congress enjoyed. For a significant percentage of the colonial population, loyalty to the Crown and commitment to the empire embodied patriotism. Generations of tradition, a shared political heritage, and a deep pride in the Anglican Church and English liberty connected these colonists to their king and fellow subjects across the Atlantic.[138] Even those uneasy with Parliament's recent actions found themselves more comfortable with a minor family dispute than what they considered Congress's seeds of sedition.[139]

The king, for his part, watched the empire closely. He grew alarmed that men "who pretend to be patriots" encouraged colonists to resist Parliament's dictates. George III claimed this "motly tribe [had] boldly thrown off the mask and avowed for nothing less than a total independence of the British Legislature." Before Lords and Commons, the king committed to upholding Parliament's authority and the Crown's dignity. Both objectives, however, required subduing the American resistance movement.[140]

The Continental Association only deepened the political divisions in colonial America. For most Whigs, its directives provided a path to imperial harmony and the restoration of colonial simplicity. If successful, colonists would stimulate domestic industrial production and purge themselves of corruptive behaviors while repairing imperial infirmities. For moderates, Congress and its Association were the unfortunate outgrowths of a political environment generated by an out-of-control Parliament and American radicals. They had confidence in Congress, but remained profoundly unsettled by what might result from its directives. To some of the more confident imperial traditionalists, Congress's efforts rang hollow. They were convinced most colonists would remain committed to the Crown despite their opposition to the Coercive Acts. For alarmed traditionalists, Congress and its Association at best advocated sedition and, at worst, inched the empire closer to civil war.

Shortly after Congress published the Continental Association, towns and counties throughout British North America began electing members to local Committees of Inspection and Observation as decreed by article 11 of the Articles of Association. Once these committees started regulating their neighbors, American civil discord entered a more combustible phase. And in this moment, the most committed Whigs completed their political transformation from subjects to citizens.

Five

The Transformation of Subjects to Citizens

DURING AN EARLY DEBATE AT CARPENTERS' HALL IN SEPTEMBER 1774, South Carolina's John Rutledge cautioned his fellow assemblymen about the limits of the First Continental Congress's influence. "We have no legal authority," he asserted. Any "obedience to our determinations will only follow the reasonableness . . . of the measures we adapt."[1] And though delegates already had a grasp on what their constituents were willing to endure to secure their liberties, Rutledge's warning did not go unheeded.[2] While communities throughout British North America expressed unconditional support for Boston in the early months of the Coercive Acts Crisis, Congress recognized this enthusiasm might prove fleeting. It also remained acutely aware that not all Americans were likely to follow its directives. To preemptively combat these troubling potentialities, delegates embedded a coercive act of their own within the Continental Association.

The Association's eleventh article provided the compulsive means to carry out Congress's imperial reconciliation and colonial moral regeneration program. It directed towns and counties to elect Committees of Inspection and Observation to regulate the commercial and social practices of their constituents, effectively backing Congress's directives with the power of law.[3] It also granted committees the extraordinary authority to condemn violators as enemies of America and ostracize them from their respective communities. The Continental Association's enforcement committees did not simply monitor colonists' habits; they determined who enjoyed the basic rights of subjecthood in the mainland colonies and who counted among the political community.

This final chapter argues the Continental Association transformed cities, towns, and counties throughout British North America into hyperpoliticized zones of austerity, embroiling them in a struggle to define and defend American liberty and identity. And while many colonists observed the Association with remarkable diligence, local Committees of Inspection and Observation descended upon American seaports and streetways to enforce its directives among those who did not. In the process, resistance actors began disassociating with non-supporters, completing for many the political transformation from British subject to American citizen. Imperial traditionalists, however, reviled the Association and its committees. For these subjects, Congress's directives represented the purest form of despotism and most direct assault on liberty. Still, resistance actors' embrace of the Association received overwhelming support in the American press, crafting a narrative of virtuous compliance. This literary patriotism valorized supporters of Congress for their public efforts and villainized those unwilling to sacrifice in the name of liberty. These lived and literary forms of resistance intertwined, making compliance with the Association as prescriptive as it was descriptive for many colonists.

This chapter first surveys the election of committeemen and the methods some towns and counties used to support the Continental Association. Next it explores colonists' mixed reactions to the Association's eleventh article to draw out how Congress's directives exacerbated already pronounced political divisions among subjects. It then examines colonists' support for and enforcement of the Association as articulated in the press. The collective print narrative normalized Whig resistance and championed those suffering in the common cause. Colonists engaged this literature through reading, writing, and conversing about its charged content and connected as a literary citizenry with a shared sense of purpose.[4] Finally, these pages reveal how the shared burden of sacrifice, both real and imagined, forged a new political community.

Shortly after the First Continental Congress published the Continental Association, supportive communities began electing men to local Committees of Inspection and Observation. Signaling powerful localized support for these efforts, gazettes from New England to Georgia framed elections as necessary steps in support of American liberty.[5] The *Providence Gazette*, for example, informed readers that throughout the colonies, towns and counties were appointing members to Congress's vigilance committees to enforce the Association.[6] Other newspapers made similar claims after surveying "the public papers from the different colonies."[7] Readers learned Connecticut's New Haven County had elected committeemen for each of its towns, projecting a unified community supportive of the common cause.[8] In Maryland, inhabitants of both Anne Arundel County and Annapolis City also reported their committee elections and voiced deep support for the Association. So too did residents of Philadelphia and Boston.[9] Townsfolk of New Castle, Delaware, similarly publicized their commitment to the cause and news of their committee elections.[10] James City County, Virginia, elected its members and dedicated itself to "strictly and unviolably" observing the Association.[11] After surveying "the printed papers on this Continent," the *Massachusetts Gazette and Boston Weekly News-Letter* and Philadelphia's *Pennsylvania Gazette* declared that every town and county busied itself with electing committees "to see that the Regulations of the Congress are punctually complied with."[12] Colonists, as reflected in American newspapers, supported "the eleventh Article of the General Congress," or more generally, "the Association agreed upon by the American Congress."[13]

Even in Georgia, a colony too divided to send a delegate to Congress, many residents signaled deep support for the Association.[14] Governor Sir James Wright, venting his frustration to the Earl of Dartmouth, described his own executive authority as too weak to prevent dangerous "cabals and combinations" from supporting the resistance. He claimed that St. John's Parish, a hotbed of Whig dissent, had passed unauthorized resolutions that threated the liberty and property of the king's loyal subjects.[15] Darien, a small town in St. Andrew's Parish, joined St. John in its support for Boston and published similar resolutions in early 1775.[16] One writer, grossly oversimplifying the complicated nature of Georgia's politics, described that colony's inhabitants as awaiting to "heartily join in the Association of the General Congress."[17] Still, with few exceptions, newspapers reported communities enthusiastically supporting Congress and eager to elect their enforcement committees.[18] Since printers openly borrowed material from other gazettes, readers consumed this support as a pan-colonial movement with no real geographic center of gravity.[19]

Most accounts identified elected committeemen by name, which likely served several functions.[20] First, these lists suggest the Coercive Acts had inspired lesser-known men into enforcing the Continental Association. This expressed to readers, however imperfectly, the broad support enjoyed by Congress.[21] Newspapers also characterized committees as products of popular elections, which likely provided them a sense of political legitimacy. Finally, identifying committeemen by name allowed readers to envision the faces of enforcement. In intimate communities dependent on personal contact, an individual's face likely brought their family's history and reputation to any potential encounter, applying the flesh and sinew to Congress's skeleton of compulsion.

Every colony but New York and Georgia officially endorsed the Continental Association. Yet in the former colony, local committees still managed to stop all trade with Britain while in the latter, two parishes independently committed to Congress's directives.[22] Historian David Ammerman estimated Americans elected roughly seven thousand men to the hundreds of enforcement committees that operated in British North America during this final imperial crisis. As far as can be gleaned from surviving records, 160 committees operated in Massachusetts, 11 in both Pennsylvania and Maryland, at least 2 in each of New York, Delaware, and Georgia, 51 in Virginia and about 10 in each of the remaining colonies.[23]

The size of these committees varied greatly from as few as three members in smaller, rural communities like Maine County, Massachusetts, to as many as eighty-eight in commercial cities like Anne Arundel, Maryland.[24] Incredibly, committee membership proliferated in some spaces as the crisis deepened. For example, Prince George's County, Maryland, reported eighty-four members in November 1774, yet recorded more than double that figure by January 1775. Ammerman viewed this trend as evidence of the Association's popular appeal to all classes of colonists.[25] This remarkable infusion of new actors democratized the resistance movement at the town and county levels and provided non-elites with tremendous regulatory authority over vast political terrain.

Since Congress offered only vague guidelines as to how Committees of Inspection and Observation might regulate their respective communities, some improvised a patchwork of responsibility heavily dependent on local institutions. For instance, once Boston's assembly printed the Continental Association, it instructed committeemen to distribute copies to the "Master of a Family in each Town, who will have his Duty plainly before him."[26] Whigs naturally expected the head of each household (usually the husband) would enforce the Association among his family. This approach leaned on the institution of marriage and custom of *paterfamilias*, the traditional conception of fathers regulating familial behavioral patterns potentially out of reach (and sight) of local committees' regulatory potential.[27] Throughout the colonies, committeemen posted copies of the Continental Association in public buildings and visited each home in their respective regulatory zone to obtain signatures as proof of signers' loyalty to Congress.[28] These encounters either deepened support for the common cause or brought nonsupporters within the purview of local committees. Outside the home, some envisioned an organic hierarchy managing the resistance movement. One commenter urged

Americans to practice "virtuous self-denial," imploring each man to adhere to his local resolutions, each community to follow its provincial congress, and each province to observe the directives of the Continental Congress.[29] This organizational model theoretically integrated every level of authority and political actor into what might be described as communitarian federalism. In Virginia, George Washington sought to advertise committee elections by nailing notices on church doors.[30] Washington likely reasoned parishioners who voted in these elections would more readily support the Association.[31]

Whig leaders went to great lengths to gain support for the Continental Association. Through their efforts, towns and counties became the political front lines where Whigs clashed with traditionalists over the Association's enforcement. Family units, churches, and assemblies became nodal points connecting local resistance movements to a greater pan-colonial federation of sacrifice. During this heightened moment of partisanship, friendly gazette coverage more tightly joined these points into a single American resistance community.

Toasts, pamphlet advertisements, and poems all appeared on the pages of colonial gazettes in one form or another, usually deeply sympathetic to Congress's directives.[32] After Virginia's Provincial Congress read and approved the Continental Association, the *Virginia Gazette* reported delegates sharing a series of toasts "with much cheerfulness." These gentlemen drank in support of imperial reconciliation, Americans sacrificing for Boston, and "the true principles of our constitution." Tellingly, they offered one final sentiment of enthusiasm to the directives of Congress.[33] Readers learned an independent military society in Newburyport, New Hampshire, toasted to imperial harmony, the repeal of the Coercive Acts, the Continental Congress and all the committees throughout America.[34] Indeed, some papers early on declared, "The common toast is now, Firmness to the peoples of America, and confusion to those who would enslave them."[35]

Newspapers printed the Continental Association in full or advertised that broadside's sale, helping disseminate Congress's directives while encouraging supporters to purchase a copy as an expression of loyalty.[36] They also promoted literature that engaged with the Association. One notable example, *The Wonderful Appearance of an Angel, Devil, and Ghost,* offered readers a sobering tale of political transformation. The narrative follows a Boston traditionalist awakened by three different entities over as many nights. On the first evening, a visiting angel condemned the Bostonian for supporting Parliament's oppressive policies. Before departing, the spirit warned the man his present path led to an eternity in the "hottest place in hell." The following night, Beelzebub arrived in the traditionalist's bedchambers, confessing that even "the prince of devils" refused to support Parliament. Before returning to hell, Beelzebub declared the man an enemy to his country. On the final night, the man awoke to behold the ghost of one of his ancestors. That apparition explained he had come "to pay a friendly visit to one of his degenerate offspring." The spirit described Whigs as patriots engaged in a "righteous cause" and chastised his descendent for supporting Parliament's crushing schemes. The story concludes with the traditionalist, realizing he had become an "offender against the country" of his birth, embracing the Whig cause. The narrative defined patriotism as resistance to traditional authority and treason as submission to Parliament's current policies.[37] The parable's author hoped to convert traditionalists by appealing to the cultural authority of heaven, hell, and posterity.

"Bob Jingle," an imperial traditionalist posing as the "Poet Laureat of the Congress," produced a pamphlet satirizing colonists' resistance to Parliament's measures. Reflecting on the Continental Association's ubiquity in American newspapers, Jingle decided he would versify the "curious thing." Comically assuring readers of the quality of his verse, Jingle took aim at what he ridiculed as blind obedience to the Association:

> Then take and swallow them, and pray, About it make no fuss,
> Tis Virtue, Honor, Country's Love Commands:—They follow thus.
> Therefore we, that is you, Sirs, will go without Cloaths,
> And Victuals and Drink, tho' we're starv'd, choaked or froze;
> And when we're all dead, 'tis a Pound to a Penny,
> Of hardy Importers there'll not be found many.

And eighthly, when we are quite rid of our Trade,
And, stript of our Money, mere Shepherds are made,
We'll see no Horse-racings, nor e'en a Cock-fight,
Our only Diversion to eat, sleep, and sh-te,
And when a Son dies, we will take no more Notice,
Then, as if one should say, I know nor care who 'tis,
With a piece of black Crape, we will sit down content;
When all our old cloaths are quite tatter'd and rent,
The giving of Gloves and of Scarfs we'll decry,
Wen we've got none to give, faith, let who will die.[38]

From Jingle's perspective, the Association forced colonists into sickness and poverty. Foregoing both material culture and social engagements, he declared, reduced Americans to a more primitive state where even the death of a loved one received little notice or care. He also accused the Committees of Inspection and Observation of executing drunken, arbitrary justice. Jingle creatively tried to lodge these sentiments in his readers' minds by informing them that they could sing his lines to the melody of "What You Will," an Elizabethan-era ballad.[39]

Some printers provided space for resistance poetry too. "The Glorious Seventy-Four," published in the *Massachusetts Spy*, offered readers a heroic interpretation of Whig defiance. The author recommended singing it to "Heart of Oak," a British operatic piece glorifying the empire's military victories during the Seven Years' War.[40] The American lyrics, however, championed efforts against Parliament's measures, proclaiming, "Now unmask'd, we unite, we agree to a man/ See our stores flow to Boston, from rear to van."[41] These lines captured the spirit of unity and sacrifice prevalent throughout the mainland colonies shortly before the First Continental Congress convened. Another poem recounted the suffering that American forefathers had endured while settling the colonies. The verses claimed colonial settlers would never submit to slavery and would instead tirelessly defend their hard-earned liberties. A third poem offered a similar take but focused mainly on Boston.[42] These lines connected contemporary Whigs to a largely mythological past through the burden of shared sacrifice. One poet lamented the deception of George

III by his nefarious advisors.[43] He versified the faith many colonists kept that a patriot king would awaken and save the empire from his ministers' dark designs. Still another poet versified a fictional conversation between James II and William of Orange, in which the latter warned the Stuart king that his belief in the divine right of kings was wrong. And, according to the Dutch stadtholder, "Wrong loses the crown."[44] In this thinly veiled indictment, the tyrant James II represents George III, while the savior William embodies the righteousness of American Whig resistance. George III and Parliament behaved, from this radical perspective, as actors beyond constitutional regulation who threatened the English liberties of American subjects. James II lost his throne under similar circumstances. The reigning king, according to this poet, risked his own revolution.

By publishing celebratory toasts, pamphlet advertisements, and poems, colonial newspapers added a festive dimension to the narrative of virtuous compliance. These colorful additions to the news cycle injected a cheerful camaraderie into the Whig movement, conjuring up images of supporters drinking and singing resistance songs together. And these literary efforts reminded readers of their inclusion in a nonlocalized resistance community with a common goal. Despite the developing narrative, however, not every colonial observer championed the Continental Association and its committees.

Imperial traditionalists articulated a powerful counterpoint to American Whigs' self-described (and self-serving) narrative. Timothy Ruggles, a brigadier general in the Massachusetts militia, characterized the Committees of Inspection and Observation as "banditti, whose cruelties surpass those of savages."[45] Another writer feared the Association's eleventh article gave committeemen license to cast even respectable men as enemies of America. This terrifying form of majority rule, he warned, aimed at crushing dissent and trampling minority rights "without the shadow of a trial." For the sake of liberty and posterity, he pleaded, "Let us shun an Association designed to destroy us."[46] This observer, clearly alarmed by what he considered a power grab by unconstitutional actors, recoiled at the thought of committeemen beyond regulation. Traditionalists did not view these creatures of Congress as altruists pursuing imperial reconciliation and colonial regeneration. Rather, Crown supporters likened these new vigilance committees to mob rule or barbarians at the gates.

New Jersey Anglican priest Thomas Bradbury Chandler claimed delegates formed the Continental Association to "bind themselves and all whom they represent" to following a ruinous nonintercourse program. This statement expressed Chandler's clear understanding that the Association spoke for some, but certainly not all, of British North Americans. Instead, the Continental Association, for Bradbury, represented proof Congress wished to plunge the colonies "headlong into that abyss of misery and destruction." American subjects owed Congress nothing, he declared, and only fools and fanatics would be cowed into observing its dangerous directives. Bradbury reminded readers they were not bound to the Association since it operated outside the British Constitution. "We are at perfect liberty to judge for ourselves, and consult our own happiness," he remarked, "as if the Congress had never existed."[47]

Anglican rector Samuel Seabury also took issue with Congress's "ill-concerted association," considering it no different than a "popish Inquisition." He characterized the Committees of Inspection and Observation as mobs unlawfully policing their neighbors. Committeemen held absolute power, he howled, since the accused received no trial, sat before no jury, and could not appeal their condemnation to any impartial higher authority. Committees, Seabury warned, were not "accountable to any power on earth." And like Chandler, he declared Congress an illegitimate body. In fact, Seabury claimed Congress made up "no *body at all* [emphasis in original]."[48]

The power Congress granted local committees also deeply unnerved one New Jersey critic. In a public letter addressed to that colony's delegation, the alarmed commentator explained he would rather submit to the arbitrary whims of a king than the caprice of a mob. And like Seabury, he likened committees to the Spanish Inquisition, describing them as groups of men "clothed with power to revenge themselves upon their neighbors." And since they remained beyond regulation themselves, he predicted committees would condemn imperial traditionalists as enemies without the constitutional protections of a trial.[49] In an equally damning essay published in the *Massachusetts Gazette and Boston Weekly News-Letter*, "A Suffolk Yeoman" asked readers to look beyond Congress's disingenuous call for peace and reconciliation. According to this observer, the Association only exposed that assembly's "warlike preparations."[50] Congress and its committees, these writers feared, harbored traitors and marauders only too happy to terrorize their neighbors while destroying the empire in the process.

Critics characterized Congress and its Association as mechanisms designed to instigate civil war or an American inquisition and considered both that assembly and its enforcement committees illegal entities operating beyond constitutional regulation. Traditionalists remained utterly convinced that Whig efforts to protect colonial rights posed a greater threat to liberty than anything Parliament stood accused of. Even the sitting king, George III, took note of and became agitated by Congress and its committees. He condemned "all those Colonies who obey the mandate of Congress [the Continental Association] for non-importation, non-exportation, and non-Consumption."[51] The Hanoverian prince next condemned the dangerous "Spirit of Resistance" he saw sweeping through his mainland colonies, remarking "unlawful Combinations" threatened his kingdom's commerce.[52] For George III, Congress's committees endangered the social tranquility and economic stability of the empire and warranted his reproach.

Even Boston, universally recognized by Whigs as home to those suffering most for the common cause, experienced political backlash over the Continental Association. An obdurate General Ruggles published a loyalty association countering many of the points itemized in the Whig association. This alternative described Congress's associators as the "riotously assembled," acting without official mandate. According to this counterpact, signers joined to protect their lives, liberties, and property from unauthorized mobs and vowed to socialize and conduct business with anyone they pleased. They would not, according to this covenant, submit to the "pretended authority, of any Congress, Committee of Correspondence, or other unconstitutional Assemblies of Men."[53] In response, a critic of Ruggles's initiative scoffed that a "few asses have been terrified into compliance with this infernal scheme."[54] Virginia delegate Richard Henry Lee surmised the brigadier-general selfishly drafted his counterassociation to obtain a knighthood from the king. Lee then called for Ruggles to be beaten and dragged off to the "Tree where Traitors to their Country should all hang."[55]

Ruggles's counterassociation represented but one instance of imperial traditionalists uniting in defense of the old order. Inhabitants of Rye, New York, for example, passed articles claiming their unconditional support for the king. And in Georgia, influential men like James Habersham and Lachlan McGillivray condescendingly described Whig resolutions as being drafted by "a few persons in a tavern, with the door shut." In response to this perceived trickery, Lachlan, McGillivray, and ninety-four others signed a resolution declaring Georgia supported George III.[56] Selectmen of Ridgefield, Connecticut, also proclaimed loyalty to the Crown "against every combination in the universe," and condemned Congress's measures as "dangerous and hurtful" to their inhabitants.[57] In what likely resulted from severe social and economic pressure from their neighbors, John and Asa Pingry of Essex, Massachusetts, refused to sign resolutions supportive of Congress only to reverse their position in October 1774. "We beg for forgiveness from the gentlemen now present," they pleaded, before committing themselves to all future measures of Congress.[58] In a contrasting scenario, some New Yorkers came to regret signing articles supportive of Congress. In a letter published in *Rivington's New York Gazetteer*, they professed loyalty to the king and asked forgiveness for challenging Parliament's authority.[59] In this political environment, colonists of every political persuasion saw the middle ground of routine partisanship rapidly disintegrating. American subjects instead witnessed the very nature of political life change as they declared loyalty to dueling authorities as the sociopolitical fabric of colonial life continued to unravel.

Once towns and counties throughout British North America elected their Committees of Inspection and Observation, the Continental Association began to realign and redefine communities. And while it remains impossible to determine just how many colonists ignored or undermined the Association, surviving letters, pamphlets, and gazettes reveal a remarkable degree of compliance. The compiled narrative describes many Americans uniting through sacrifice and fiercely committing to defend their ancient liberties and customs.

The Philadelphia's Butchers' Association proclaimed its support for Congress, confident that adherence to the Continental Association would secure American liberty. It claimed members would happily "sacrifice every informant consideration of private interest" in defense of the common cause. To that end, city butchers committed themselves to limiting the slaughter of sheep as directed by the Association.[60] Butchers in Berks County, Pennsylvania, followed Philadelphia's example three weeks later.[61] The Ladies Association of Edenton, North Carolina, described moral regulations as "necessary for the publick good" and pledged themselves and their families to observe all measures with "a solemn determination."[62] New York City distillers also announced their support for the Association, warning they would not use any molasses or syrups imported from Britain or the West Indies to produce local spirits.[63]

Going beyond the Association's specific recommendations, inhabitants of Annapolis, Maryland, pledged to discontinue balls and parties "during the present time of public calamity."[64] Residents of Wilmington, North Carolina, volunteered to stop all dancing and celebrations in private homes while Boston suffered.[65] Keeping with the spirit of Congress's moral reforms, South Carolina canceled all public concerts.[66] Whigs in Baltimore encouraged townsfolk to forgo county fairs to prevent "debauching the morals of their children." They further hoped to eliminate public inebriation and other forms of "the vilest immoralities" that such frivolous exhibitions invited.[67] In yet another show of support for the Association, Wilmington, North Carolina, townsfolk offered a public condemnation of horse racing that captured the essence of the moment. Connecting self-denial with securing liberty, they declared a "patriot . . . willingly sacrifices his pleasures upon the altar of freedom."[68] These displays of voluntary compliance as represented in the press prompted one observer to remark that the "United Colonies [were] . . . all nobly exerting themselves" in observing the Continental Association.[69]

Printers also reported colonists discontinuing the corruptive engagements that Congress specifically prohibited so as to normalize adherence to the Association.

Newspapers abound with careful observations of the Continental Association's funeral regulations. When forty-one-year-old Philadelphian Jane Knox died in November 1774, the *Pennsylvania Gazette* reported her interment as proceeding with strict compliance to the Association's preferences. Conducted "in the plainest manner," Knox's burial offered neither pomp nor parade. To honor the deceased, the obituary simply asked that "every good member of society, and friend to his country," to imitate Knox's example. Mrs. Catherine Keppele's funeral followed a similar course later that month. A large crowd of mourners gathered to witness the departed wife and mother of fifteen lowered into the ground, yet "no mourning of any kind was worn, no gloves or scarfs were given." Keppele's death notice, like Knox's, simply asked all virtuous colonists to emulate her frugal procedure.[70]

In New York, Reverend John Ogilvie's funeral attracted a great crowd of mourners. The *New York Journal* reported his burial as strictly conforming to Congress's directives as the family offered attendees no gloves, scarves, or wine. In fact, the reverend's body traveled to its grave in a black casket with none of the traditional mourning decorum. And like the previous examples, Ogilvie's notice graciously asked all colonists to follow his procession's simplicity.[71] Sixty-seven-year-old Benjamin May of Roxbury, Massachusetts, revealed his own commitment to the cause less than an hour before he died. After collecting those closest to him, the ailing man lectured that delegates had designed the Continental Association to rescue America and urged those gathered to follow its moral directives. May then asked for a simple burial as outlined by Congress to contribute to revitalizing American virtue.[72] During another funeral in Providence, Rhode Island, pallbearers accepted mourning gloves "contrary to the regulations of the Continental Congress." When the men realized their infraction, however, they voluntarily returned the gloves. The merchant who had sold the items, this notice relayed, accepted the merchandise without question.[73] Outside Boston, a reverend "nobly refused" mourning gloves at a funeral. He reminded the conferrer that Congress recommended "Frugality and Oeconomy as a Means of Extricating us out of the State of Oppression we are now grievously suffering in." After this lecture, someone removed the remaining gloves from the coffin. This account lauded the reverend's commitment to liberty and asked every daughter and son of America to follow his example.[74] Newspapers reported numerous instances of colonists adhering to the restrictions of the Continental Association's eighth article.[75] And printers generally framed these gestures as virtuous efforts executed in support of colonial moral regeneration and imperial reconciliation.[76]

Communities did not expect every inhabitant to commit to the Continental Association so easily. The Committee of Inspection and Observation in Newport, Connecticut, for example, published a notice reminding inhabitants to follow the Association's funeral directives. Those who refused to support their country, the notice warned, should not expect their neighbors to attend their funerals.[77] The very public nature of funerals, from the large crowds to hired mourners, suggests how deeply colonial Americans valued this ritual.[78] A burial without visible local notice signaled the ultimate affront to the departed and their bereaved. The potential of experiencing this public insult provided another powerful incentive for indifferent colonists to observe the Association.

Certainly, the most high-profile example of compliance with the Association's funeral regulations occurred after the Second Continental Congress had convened in Philadelphia in 1775.[79] Virginia's Peyton Randolph returned as president of Congress before poor health forced him to again step down from that position. Yet he remained, according to fellow delegates, a dedicated assemblyman who worked tirelessly for the common cause.[80] On October 22, Randolph accepted an invitation to dine with Philadelphia merchant Harry Hill.[81] Yet shortly before dinner that evening, Randolph suffered an "Apoplectic Fit." Several hours later, the Virginian died. John Adams wrote that every delegate planned to attend Randolph's funeral "in as much Mourning as our Laws will permit."[82] The day after Randolph's death, Congress passed a resolution reminding members to adhere to the Continental Association and wear nothing but crepe around their left arms. It also permitted delegates to mourn for one month and asked that Jacob Duché prepare a fitting sermon for the funeral.[83]

Visiting medical student Solomon Drowne paid his respects to President Randolph, recording that a great collection of mourners had gathered to honor "that friend of America." He described the procession as a somber scene accompanied by muffled drums and tolling bells. Reverend Duché preached "a most excellent Sermon," according to Drowne, before pallbearers placed Randolph's remains into a vault at Christ Church.[84] Upon learning of Randolph's death, the Williamsburg Masonic Lodge asked members to remain in a state of mourning "until the corps shall arrive" back in Virginia.[85] After disinterment the following fall, Randolph's coffin finally made its way to Williamsburg in late November 1776. Mourners reinterred his remains in Wren Chapel at William and Mary College at the behest of his "afflicted and inconsolable widow."[86]

Colonial funerals were solemn, public performances that whole communities experienced on some level. During the Coercive Acts Crisis, these rites became layered with political theater, allowing Whig actors to publicly perform their commitment to moral purification through self-denial. Newspaper reports of compliance reminded geographically distant individuals of their inclusion in a broader intellectual community joined by sacrifice.[87]

American theater also found itself in the crosshairs of the Continental Association. Throughout the 1760s, bookstores and public auctions advertised their literary inventories that typically included collections of "Books in Divinity, history, and plays."[88] If colonists were not privately reading plays, they were experiencing them live, as playhouses enjoyed strong attendance in the colonies into the 1770s.[89] Once the Coercive Acts Crisis began, however, theatergoers risked public censure for ostensibly contributing to the moral corruption of colonial America.[90] The Articles of Association signaled the end to a vibrant theater culture for the immediate future; even the most successful traveling troupe, David Douglass's American Company of Comedians, left the mainland colonies for Jamaica to survive.[91] As long as Boston suffered, resistance-minded Americans refrained from ostentatious displays of leisure and enjoyment. Advocates of the cause hoped to regenerate American morality by promoting individual restraint, frugality, and industry, the inverse of values typically associated with the theater. Despite the disgrace associated with *attending* a theatrical performance, however, Whigs viewed *reading* plays as an engagement through which colonists might receive political and moral instruction.

Dating back to the classical world, theater served as an important medium that offered audiences more than entertainment. Many playwrights intended their works to educate viewers in history, ethics, and contemporary politics.[92] This practice continued in Tudor, Stuart, and Hanoverian England with Shakespeare's historical plays and, by 1713, Joseph Addison's *Cato: A Tragedy*.[93] Beginning around 1765 and continuing throughout the American Revolution, Whig writers supplied colonists with a steady supply of propagandistic plays designed to inspire resistance to Parliament's perceived constitutional infringements. Mercy Otis Warren, Hugh Henry Breckenridge, Philip Freneau, and others helped create what scholar Jason Shaffer dubbed "theatrical republicanism," in which playwrights advocated subordinating life, liberty, and private desire in defense of American liberty.[94] Yet despite the many available American plays written for private consumption and instruction, it was Addison's *Cato: A Tragedy* that most captivated American readers.[95]

The widespread availability of pamphlets, plays, and newspapers helped create, connect, and coordinate a reading political community in Revolutionary America. Each literary form identified perceived public problems and proposed potential solutions.[96] However, few pieces of literature circulated more widely than did *Cato* in the leadup to the Coercive Acts Crisis. This play, at first glance, appears to offer little political guidance for American Whigs. Over the course of its five acts, the protagonist commits suicide and Caesar conquers Rome. Yet as historian Forrest McDonald pointed out, Addison's central message is not Cato's failure to rescue Rome, but rather classical virtue's triumph over avarice. Americans idolized Addison's Cato because he conducted himself as a disinterested statesman acting on behalf of the commonwealth without private consideration.[97] Cato's willingness to sacrifice for Rome resonated deeply with a developing political community that was itself weaponizing self-denial in defense of its country. Resistance leaders believed that if enough colonists modeled themselves after this character, they might succeed where that senator had failed. Simply put, Addison's *Cato* captured the American imagination. The idealized Roman stoic inspired George Washington to the extent that some of his private correspondence and even his style of politics reveals an Addisonian influence.[98] Not every American, however, expressed support for or acted within the scope of the Continental Association. In these instances, the Committees of Inspection and Observation coerced their defiant neighbors into supporting the Association and publicly condemned those who refused. These moments of enforcement received glowing press coverage throughout much of British North America.

Committees of Inspection and Observation in port cities spent much of their time culling the cargoes of incoming vessels to make certain that captains and merchants operated within the bounds of the Association.[99] Gazette coverage mostly framed encounters between committees and violators as gentlemanly engagements. Printers typically depicted committeemen as benevolent arbiters and nonsupporters as misguided but ultimately repentant men. In Portsmouth, Connecticut, for example, committeemen caught a man smuggling sixty pounds of tea. By his own admission, he had intended to sell that condemned commodity for a handsome profit. Once confronted, however, he acknowledged his poor judgment and personally set the tea ablaze before an elated crowd.[100] When committeemen of Newburyport, Massachusetts, discovered a ship captain had sold several chests of tea, regulators confronted the mariner. He immediately turned over his profits "for the benefit of the Poor in this once flourishing, but now unhappy Town."[101] Once New York committeemen learned of the arrival of a vessel from Scotland loaded with prohibited cargo, they quickly seized the ship. After provisioning it with water, they instructed the captain to return to his port of origin, "agreeable to the tenth article of the continental association." The captain, according to this account, complied without an utterance of resistance.[102] A similar scene unfolded in Philadelphia, when a vessel laden with pipes of wine arrived at port. Once the recipient of the illicit spirits learned of their arrival, he personally alerted his local committee. Before both the committeemen and a gathering crowd, he refused the cargo, sending the ship away "agreeable to the direction of the Congress."[103]

By reporting so many of these instances as moments of brotherly interference, American newspapers portrayed vigilance committees as regulating their mistaken neighbors in an orderly and amicable fashion. Newspapers also gave violators the benefit of the doubt, portraying them as men who recognized their error and remained part of the community afterward. And while violators may or may not have actually repented, editors likely framed these encounters as redemptive tales to discredit traditionalists' claims that committees acted in a lawless and mob-like fashion.

Contemporary press coverage and private correspondence also reveals Committees of Inspection and Observation preventing violators from smuggling resources out of the colonies. For instance, inhabitants of New York discovered sheep had been spirited onto a ship set for the West Indies. They alerted local committeemen who, upon their arrival, explained to the vessel's captain that exporting sheep ran "Contrary to a Resolution of the Continental Congress." When the mariner pledged not to depart with the animals, the committee, still not satisfied, called for the owner of the livestock. Bowing to the pressure of committeemen and onlookers, the summoned man asked the captain to remove the sheep. Once relieved of the chattel, the committee allowed the vessel to depart.[104] New Hampshire governor John Wentworth complained that his subjects submitted to the Continental Association as a matter of delusion rather than judgment. He reported a local committee forced a captain to unload fifty sheep before allowing him to depart for the West Indies.[105] Readers learned, as well, that committees for the "Seaport towns of Connecticut" prevented illicit sheep exports, "agreeable to the 7th article of the Association of Congress."[106] The committee in Newport, Rhode Island, complained that some inhabitants sought to violate the Continental Association with alarming frequency. Despite violators' efforts, however, the committee boasted it had prevented dozens of sheep from being unlawfully shipped to Africa. It praised merchants for their conviction and remained convinced most colonists would carry on with "a punctual regard to the Association."[107] Gazette coverage portrayed committees as tireless groups patrolling their regulatory zones preventing smugglers from evading the Association.[108] These same reports also presented committeemen as exercising their authority courteously when possible and sternly when necessary.

In South Carolina, the Georgetown committee intercepted a suspicious vessel on the Santee River in December 1775. The ship's captain sought to purchase rice to sell in the West Indies, "contrary to the Resolves of the Continental Congress." The St. James Santee committee, not Georgetown, had the responsibility of monitoring the area in question. Georgetown apologized to the St. James River committee for regulating beyond its borders but insisted the action "was intended for publick utility."[109] St. James Santee informed Georgetown they had indeed captured a schooner loaded with rice, "ready for Sea." The captain, however, refused to divulge his destination to the committee. To prevent him from circumventing the Continental Association, committeemen removed the vessel's sails, stranding captain, crew, and cargo.[110]

Some colonists had already placed orders they could not reasonably cancel before the continental boycott began on December 1, 1774. When this prohibited merchandise arrived at colonial ports, recipients had three options by which to lawfully dispose of their goods: send orders back to Britain, allow local committees to store the goods until the present crisis resolved, or sell the merchandise at public vendue. This final option allowed purchasers to recoup costs and send any profits to those struggling in Boston. American newspapers regularly published accounts of these auctions, inviting potential buyers to obtain supplies while supporting the common cause. Committees advertised these auctions as "agreeable to the American Congress Association," and colonists could expect to find raisins, glass, cheese, beer, Irish linens, coal, and even maritime materials.[111] An irritated Henry Laurens privately noted in early 1775 that plenty of goods had found their way into American markets that should not have been permitted to land.[112] Yet according to the *South Carolina Gazette*, every owner of prohibited merchandise happily complied with the Association, most opting to sell at auction.[113] Print media's narrative once again characterized compliance with the Association as voluntary and committees as helpful and organized.

Resistance leaders George Washington and Thomas Jefferson also nearly found themselves operating outside of Congress's directives. After an order of merchandise failed to arrive at Mount Vernon before nonimportation began, Washington promptly wrote his agent and canceled it in recognition of the Association.[114] Jefferson had purchased windows from London in June 1774. Yet when he learned his shipment would not likely arrive until early January, he worried lest observers might think he had simply ignored the Association. Writing his committee, Jefferson defended his purchase, noting not even "the spirit of prophecy" could have predicted the current commercial freeze when he had placed his order. He agreed to "submit [to] the disposal of them" to avoid running afoul of the Association.[115] These two notable examples did not become part of the carefully crafted compliance narrative framed by local gazettes. Yet Washington and Jefferson protected that narrative from the perception that resistance leaders flaunted the directives of Congress. In this respect, both recognized any damage to their personal reputations might also weaken support for the Association and ultimately threaten Congress's attempt at imperial reconciliation and moral regeneration.

Committees regulated the commercial and cultural behaviors of their neighbors beyond just ports and custom houses. When Portsmouth, Connecticut, locals learned some colonists continued to play cards and billiards contrary to the Association, they immediately alerted their committee. Right away it published a warning, demanding violators "discontinue their unjustifiable proceedings" during this moment of "deep distress and danger" to the United Colonies. The committee threatened to brand anyone caught violating the Association as an enemy of America and ostracize them.[116] Boston's committee learned of an individual "attempting to divert the Public" by planning a show of horsemanship. It quickly shut down the event.

The *Boston Evening Post* praised the committee's prompt action as "A worthy Example" before urging it to stop the daily parade that also diverted attention from the present crisis.[117] This consistent focus on restraint reminded Americans to remain vigilant and supportive of Congress's objectives.

Those unwilling to support the Association risked Committees of Inspection and Observation declaring them enemies of America. For example, when Andrew Miller, a merchant from Halifax County, North Carolina, refused to sign the Association, committeemen visited his home and once more sought his support. Miller again declined, explaining, not unreasonably, that he felt it unjust that the Association denied colonists the freedom to use their property as they saw fit. Unpersuaded by Miller's position, the committee asked inhabitants to refrain from purchasing goods from the obstinate merchant and anyone consorting with him. It also directed them to avoid socializing with the unapologetic Miller, lest they too be tainted with the stigma of violation.[118]

Inhabitants of Caroline County, Virginia, accused nine merchants of raising their prices contrary to articles 9 and 13 of the Association and reported them to their committee. Committeemen asked to compare the merchants' current rates to their prices in previous years. Three complied, clearing them of any suspicion. Yet the rest refused, and committeemen deduced they had raised prices contrary to the Association. To that end, it asked townsfolk to break off all social and commercial dealings with these "enemies of *American* Liberty."[119] In a similar situation, Maryland merchant Thomas Charles Williams enjoyed profiting from selling tea before coming to the attention of Anne Arundel's committee. This blatant disregard for the Association prompted the committee to condemn Williams as a man who "supported the assumed power of Parliament to tax America." Cowed into compliance, the once-brazen Williams apologized and signed the Association on January 2, 1775, to avoid ostracism.[120] Likewise, when a vessel carrying tea arrived in Charleston, South Carolina, it did not escape notice of local committeemen. They summoned the tea's owners, forced them onto the vessel, and demanded they personally toss the reviled merchandise overboard. According to the report, the men obliged the committee and expressed relief they had escaped bodily harm from the "Thousands of Spectators."[121]

The committee in Epsom, New Hampshire, mixed some local bigotry and xenophobia with its enforcement of the Continental Association when it described the "Scotch" as a self-interested people who were "no friends to our country." As such, the committee banned Scottish merchants from conducting business in Epsom. Should persistent sellers refuse to comply, the committee warned it would confiscate their goods and dress them in "a new suit, agreeable to the modern mode."[122] This sartorial comment alluded to the torturous practice of tarring and feathering.[123] In Georgia, two individuals experienced this barbarous ritual firsthand. On July 24, 1775, shipmaster John Hopkins toasted "Damnation to America" at a tavern in Savannah. In response, an angry crowd surrounded Hopkins's home. The mob dragged Hopkins outside and tarred and feathered him before parading its victim through town as a reviled outsider. Crowd leaders threatened to hang the defiant captain if he refused to recant his previous sentiment and drink instead to "Damnation to all Tories and Success to American Liberty." Fearing for his life, Hopkins promptly complied. In Augusta, two Englishmen faced a similarly threatening crowd. After expressing disdain for the Association, angry men alerted the local Sons of Liberty and the visitors quickly found themselves fleeing a bloodthirsty gang. One managed to escape, but self-styled "Liberty Boys" caught the other. They tarred and feathered him before dragging him around in a cart for all to see.[124] Some inhabitants deepened the alienation of this unfortunate man by hurling insults, threats, and debris during his degradation. Reading about these instances of draconian violence likely coerced some on the political fence to simply follow Congress's directives.

Some Whigs viewed any criticism of Congress and its Association as a threat to liberty and colonial unity. Committeemen of Middlesex, New Jersey, decried all "insidious scribblers" who disseminated lies "behind prostituted presses" to weaken colonial harmony.[125] In Ulster, New York, committee members publicly read a pamphlet supportive of the crown and claimed its author intended to "destroy the union." They condemned that broadside and any similar writings to public burning. Going further still, they directed inhabitants to treat any author, printer, or peddler of such poisonous literature as "ene-mies of their country."[126] The committee chairman in Elizabethtown, New Jersey, described all critical literature as designed to "sow the seeds of discord" among Americans. He then directed the committee to collect any dangerous writings and have them "publickly burnt, in detestation."[127]

In Philadelphia, subjects penned a letter to their committee ex-pressing concern over what they considered the divisive nature of similar pamphlets. They demanded the committee discover the au-thors' identities and asked that every newspaper on the continent de-nounce them as enemies of America.[128] The Loyalist-leaning New York publisher James Rivington came under fire for printing pam-phlets that committees in Morris County and Woodbridge, New Jer-sey, felt defamed Congress and threatened American unity. These committees asked supporters of the common cause to stop purchas-ing Rivington's paper, end all commercial and social dealings with him, and consider the printer "a person inimical to the liberties of this country."[129] Rivington suddenly found himself a political outcast among American Whigs.

Traditionalists felt quite differently about James Rivington and other critics of Congress. One observer from Annapolis, Maryland, praised Rivington for boldly publishing patriotic literature that de-fended king and Parliament. He went on to declare the First Conti-nental Congress and "their satellites, the Committee-men" as the purest examples of tyranny.[130] Another commenter described Amer-ica as "chained down with the Shackles of Anarchy." Governing by congresses, committees, and associations, the critic proclaimed, went against the laws of God and man. Most men who spoke of unanim-ity, expressed the writer, felt "obliged to put on the mask of Union" out of fear. This alarming state of intolerance, instigated by the Con-tinental Association and intensified by its enforcement committees, created an atmosphere where thoughts provoked violence and dis-senters risked ostracization or worse.

Two Connecticut men endured perhaps the most elaborate display of exile while passing through a neighboring town. At Wethersfield, they stopped at a tavern and found themselves engaged in a heated political debate with some locals. When they revealed their contempt for Congress, patrons petitioned to have the transients expelled from Wethersfield. For these strangers, their odyssey of abuse had just begun. A collection of men forcibly removed them and marched them, like prisoners, to a neighboring town and notified this new community of the travelers' politics. After learning the men supported the Crown, their new hosts likewise drummed them out of town. This next settlement also notified the new host community of the two travelers' views. This choreographed ostracization continued until Whigs had forced the two unfortunate traditionalists, against their will, back to their hometown. Wethersfield committeemen cited a law regulating "strolling ideots, lunaticks, &c" as the legal basis for the unfortunate pair's sudden eviction. Whigs forcibly escorted the dissenters from town to town while onlookers hissed and groaned at them. One observer noted that Wethersfield's inhabitants no longer tolerated individuals unsupportive of Congress to live among them.[131] This unforgiving attitude toward political opponents transformed dissenters into either unwelcome outsiders or internal enemies.

One of the most extreme and unfortunate examples of majoritarian abuse unfolded in Virginia. In June 1774, David Wardrobe, a schoolteacher in Westmoreland County, wrote a letter to a friend in Glasgow, Scotland, offering his assessment of the unfolding political crisis that summer. Without Wardrobe's consent, the *Glasgow Journal* obtained and published the letter in August 1774, and someone sent a copy back to Westmoreland County.[132] The letter outraged local Whigs and brought the unfortunate Wardrobe to the attention of Westmoreland's committee.

In the letter, Wardrobe claimed Whigs did not enjoy universal support throughout Virginia despite what most newspapers reported. During a moment of political activism, he recorded, local Whigs hanged Lord North in effigy. As this street theater unfolded, Wardrobe remained "particularly attentive to the countenances of the spectators." And despite local elites voicing their delight at the mock hanging, the educator noted nearly all others in attendance expressed little enthusiasm for the spectacle. Wardrobe surmised that even the outspoken elites hardly supported nonimportation and nonexportation, predicting they would abandon all pretenses of indignation and fall back in line at the slightest inconvenience. Any imposition on their lifestyles, Wardrobe remarked, would convince most planters the true threat rested not in Parliament's poison, but America's antidote.[133] At a moment when resistance leaders felt the Whig cause required universal support, Wardrobe's letter naturally provoked outrage among Congress's supporters.

When the letter came to the attention of Westmoreland's Committee of Inspection and Observation, members accused the teacher of spreading falsehoods that threatened American liberty. The committee asked that Cople Parish deny Wardrobe classroom space in its vestry house and directed all parents to immediately withdraw their children from his tutelage. Local leaders then demanded Wardrobe appear before the committee and asked inhabitants to treat him as "a wicked enemy to America." They then ordered their judgment published in the press.

Wardrobe, likely terrified of potential physical reprisals, refused to appear before the committee. The shaken educator instead wrote a letter to the committee and community begging "on my knees" for forgiveness for his offense. He simply asked to "subsist among the people I greatly esteem."[134] The record is silent on what became of David Wardrobe. What is clear, however, is that Whig leaders felt the veneer of unity so important that they proved willing to ruthlessly crush dissenters, deny them a livelihood, ban them from their communities, and brand them as enemies.

In another extreme case, Georgia found itself temporarily ostracized from the American political community. The divided politics of that colony strained its relationship with Whig leaders throughout the colonies. South Carolina, in the spirit of the Association's fourteenth article, eventually cut off all social and commercial contact with Georgia over its refusal to support the resistance. Georgia's temporary estrangement reveals the challenges Whigs faced trying to maintain the narrative of colonial unity against the much thornier political reality on the ground.

The enforcement of the Continental Association only deepened Georgia's complicated politics. While the Coercive Acts alarmed many Georgians, most appreciated that their colony relied heavily on Parliament's annual stipend to fund their government and the British Army to secure their borders against the Creeks. Without Parliament, these observers reasonably assumed, Georgia could not survive.[135] South Carolina, meanwhile, pressured Georgia to embrace the Continental Association to no avail.[136] Yet radical St. John's Parish, followed by St. Andrew (as mentioned above), embraced the Association. These two outliers supported Boston because so many of their inhabitants were themselves transplanted Massachusetts Congregationalists. Leaders from St. John and St. Andrew broke with Christ Church Parish, the seat of Georgia's leadership, over the latter's failure to join the Association and support the common cause.[137] According to leaders from St. John, though Georgia adopted a form of the Association, the compromise relaxed so many of Congress's directives that it evaded what delegates had hoped to achieve.[138] Disgusted by this failure to support the Association, St. John incredibly sent delegates to Charleston in an attempt to secede from Georgia and become annexed by South Carolina.[139] Greater Georgia's flagrant disregard for the Association, as might be imagined, did not go unnoticed by her northern neighbor.

The Charleston committee lauded St. John's commitment to the common cause but refused to welcome that parish into the arms of South Carolina.[140] Instead, South Carolina ultimately broke off all dealings with its southern neighbor over what its Council of Safety described as the "Apostasy of Georgia."[141] As a result, the Charleston committee characterized Georgians as "unworthy of the rights of freemen" and "inimical to the liberties of their country."[142] South Carolina delegate Christopher Gadsden put it more bluntly, writing "we have determin'd to have nothing farther to do with them, as they have not agreed to the American Association."[143] Even after Georgia's Provincial Congress formally adopted the Association on July 4, 1775, illicit trade continued to plague Whig leadership. Charleston's committee wryly noted how Georgia continued to go out of her way to help America's enemies by shipping them supplies. At this moment of high crisis, the committee lectured, "every true lover of Liberty and his Country should have determined to forego his own interest." And since Georgia insisted on continuing its dishonorable practices, it concluded, "She must be held to be an Enemy."[144]

Why South Carolina refused to recognize St. John remains unclear. That parish had gone out of its way to support Boston and Congress and even elected Lester Hall as delegate to the First Continental Congress (Hall joined the Second Continental Congress in May 1775). The most likely answer is that the First Continental Congress determined American liberty flowed directly from natural law, the British Constitution, and colonial charters.[145] Colonists from all political backgrounds expressed alarm over Parliament altering Massachusetts's charter after the Boston Tea Party. Subjects from Maine to Georgia feared Parliament might arbitrarily abolish or rewrite any charter at its pleasure. If resistance leaders found it acceptable to alter colonial charters, what separated them from Parliament?

Whig leaders worked tirelessly to normalize resistance to Parliament and secure pan-colonial unity. Friendly printers reported most colonists as cheerfully adhering to the Association and Committees of Inspection and Observation offering occasional brotherly intervention. But Whigs were also pragmatic. Local organizers understood the resistance could not succeed if its demands were unreasonable or if Whigs were a decided minority within the mainland colonies. Resistance leaders sensed they held both the moral high ground and numerical superiority, which provided many committees license to ostracize obstinate outliers and declare them enemies. In the case of Georgia, it was the poorest, least populated, most vulnerable colony. It was also the southernmost colony, so it did not disrupt the contiguous union among the mainland majority. Resistance actors likely would have reacted quite differently had the outlier been say Virginia or Pennsylvania. Still, unity and sacrifice, for Whig leaders, remained the fundamental components for imperial reconciliation and moral regeneration.

Surveying the colonies after committees began enforcing the Continental Association, Samuel Adams continued to support self-denial as the surest way to secure American liberty. He also felt it was helping colonists restore "the ancient purity of principles and manners in our country."[146] In another letter, Adams claimed Americans must mimic the Roman Republic's commitment to sacrifice, lest they suffer the fate of "the degenerate Romans, who upon the fall of Julius set up Augustus."[147] Adams linked simplicity and classical virtue as a panacea for America's ills. Congress's plan for imperial reconciliation and moral regeneration, he hoped, might yet solve the current political crisis and cure Americans of their alleged corruptive behaviors. One enthusiastic commenter, in an essay published in the *Massachusetts Spy*, described communities throughout the mainland colonies as vigorously supporting the common cause. History offered no comparable example, according to this writer, of "human laws that were more strictly and religiously observed" than the Continental Association.[148] The United Colonies had come together to execute the First Continental Congress's measures and only "disappointed, factious Tories" ignored the Association, reported another observer.[149] In a deeply revealing letter, Abigail Adams captured the struggle shared by so many when she addressed the difficulty in taming the "fire and pride of private ambition" to meet the needs of the "publick weal." She praised those joined in self-denial for committing to "so noble an undertaking."[150] This commitment to sacrifice, for many colonists, carved a new community out of an old one. For alarmed Whigs, supporting the Continental Association united them as Americans. Throughout the mainland colonies, press coverage portrayed most colonists as engaged in a voluntary, pan-colonial movement of sacrifice. Many private letters likewise reveal colonists witnessing and participating in this literary and lived solidarity. While most American newspapers contributed to the narrative of virtuous compliance, however, many printers also memorialized imperial traditionalists' anxiety over Congress's perceived goals.

From this vantage point, Congress and its Association threatened the harmony of the empire. One traditionalist condemned the radical nature of Congress, claiming its "proceedings, the resolves, [and] association" clearly revealed a scheme for independence. Delegates, he claimed, were working against reconciliation.[151] Another writer wondered, in April 1776, "In what shape we shall hereafter exist as a people?" Resistance leaders, according to this observer, were exploring the "dark and untrodden way of Independence and Republicanism."[152] A Connecticut town publicly disapproved of Congress, describing its measures "as unconstitutional, as subversive of our real liberties, and as countenancing licentiousness."[153] New Jersey governor William Franklin described colonists adhering to the Association as delusional and looked forward to the king reducing all "rebellious Subjects to obedience."[154] Imperial traditionalists did not envision Congress as a benign assembly seeking salvation for the empire, but as a collection of American radicals seeking to usurp constitutional authority.

Even conservative men deeply unsettled by the Coercive Acts like Joseph Galloway, New York's Isaac Low, and Anglican reverend Jacob Duché could not, in the end, bring themselves to turn their proverbial backs on the old empire.[155] For imperial traditionalists, supporting Crown and homeland remained a single, inseparable concept. Indeed, many traditionalists feared radical Americans aimed to turn a family quarrel into a civil war. During the Coercive Acts Crisis, traditionalists viewed themselves as true Englishmen and their opponents as treasonous and deplorable opportunists.

American Whigs also considered themselves equally committed to Crown and country. Mercy Otis Warren declared that sensible men raised under monarchy hoped to remain governed by the king "under certain limitations."[156] This qualification, however, recognized the awakening of a new community, men and women unwilling to remain part of the empire should king and Parliament not meet what they considered their reasonable demands. Once formerly unasked and ultimately unanswerable constitutional questions seized Britain's public discourse, some colonists considered their continued inclusion within the imperial structure as conditional. Even when the Second Continental Congress offered one final petition to George III proclaiming American loyalty, it still denied Parliament's right to tax Americans. It also only offered the king conditional loyalty, self-preservation again taking precedence above even allegiance to the Crown.[157] Tellingly, while moderate delegates wrote this final olive branch, radicals simultaneously composed the militant Declaration for the Cause and Necessity for Taking Up Arms, which laid out a colonial justification for armed conflict.[158] As the crisis deepened, reconciliation within the empire seemed, from all perspectives, the least likely outcome.

Even faith in the supposed patriot king disintegrated once Whigs learned George III had declared the colonies in open rebellion in August 1775.[159] The Hanoverian prince issued another fiery condemnation of resistance efforts two months later, blaming traitorous leaders for dragging his colonies into a "rebellious War." This time, the king threatened to crush his American enemies "by the most decisive Exertions."[160] For many alarmed colonists, George III had finally revealed himself as firmly supportive of enslaving America.

News of the second speech reached the colonies in November 1775, prompting Thomas Jefferson to declare George III both a tyrant and an enemy of America. Jefferson and other Whigs concluded they belonged to a political community separate from that of the reigning king. The Virginia congressman noted that the colonies had "drawn the sword," and lamented open war remained the next, only, and final move. He claimed Americans required neither "inducement nor power to declare and assert separation." The American community, he observed, needed only the determination to do so. "[B]y the God that made me," Jefferson threatened, "I will cease to exist before I yield to a connection" to England under king and Parliament's oppressive terms.[161] The spirit of Jefferson's prose resonated with plenty of Americans who shared his grim assessment of the rapidly deteriorating political situation.

In sum, imperial traditionalists felt horrified by the emerging resistance community. Even George III recognized his American detractors as a separate, dangerous faction threatening his empire. And Jefferson (among others) recognized no connection to the king whatsoever. He felt the emerging American community represented the colonial majority and could leave the empire whenever it chose. It is this last point that separated self-identifying Americans from imperial traditionalists.

Whigs identified one another by homespun clothing, cultural behaviors and consumption practices, qualities itemized by Congress and carefully regulated by the Committees of Inspection and Observation. As James Madison explicitly noted, the Continental Association became "the method used among us to distinguish friends from foes."[162] A willingness to sacrifice for American liberty provided the building blocks of community that birthed a separate political identity for resistance actors. Colonists' temporary commitment to material simplicity and moral purification ultimately transformed many British subjects into republican citizens. Once the likelihood of imperial reconciliation all but dried up, Whigs proved able to separate loyalty to homeland from loyalty to king. Most chose the former, opting to protect local identities and liberties from an empire they feared threatened both. For supporters of the Continental Association, communities divided themselves into Americans and their internal enemies. These newly awakened Americans experienced this transformation as a process, however, and it came more quickly for some than others.

As early as May 26, 1774, the *Massachusetts Spy* published lyrics attributed to Joseph Warren set to the tune of "The British Grenadiers." Warren's "A Song on Liberty" became quite popular and its lyrics celebrated belonging to a distinct American community:

> We led fair Freedom hither, and lo the desert smil'd,
> A paradise of pleasure now open'd in the wild;
> Your harvest, bold Americans, no pow'r shall snatch away
> Preserve, preserve, preserve your rights in free America
> Torn from a world of Tyrants beneath this western sky
> We form'd a new dominion, a land of liberty;
> The world shall own we're freemen here, and such will ever be,
> Huzza! huzza! huzza! huzza for love and liberty . . .
> Lift up your hearts, my heroes, and swear with proud disdain,
> The wretch that would ensnare you shall spread his net in vain;
> Should Europe empty all her force we'd meet them in array,
> And shout huzza! huzza! huzza for brave America.[163]

The lyrics reminded colonists of their American heritage of liberty at the moment communities throughout the mainland were passing resolutions expressing solidarity with Boston and calling for union through suffering. In another letter published in the *New England Chronicle* in November 1775, "A Freeman" described those serving in the Continental Army as "Guardians of America." This writer claimed he had "the honour to be an American, and one among the

Free Millions." The "American people," he claimed, were prepared to "form into a Grand Republic of the American United Colonies," since they no longer felt connected to Britain.[164]

In September 1774, Patrick Henry declared before his fellow delegates in Congress, "The distinctions between Virginians, Pennsylvanians, New Yorkers and New Englanders, are no more. I am not a Virginian, but an American."[165] The Coercive Acts Crisis, for Henry, became the crucible by which he transformed his identity. The grassroots resistance that summer, according to the bombastic Virginian, shaped colonists into Americans as they joined in solidarity with Boston to defend liberty. Silas Deane, writing to Henry after Congress had dissolved, considered the First Continental Congress the mechanism by which colonies had formed a union. He expected a second congress to "effect a complete and perfect American Constitution," regardless of whether the colonies remained within the empire.[166] According to Deane, Americans had already united as a political community to defend their rights and would remain as one with or without a British king. They needed only to memorialize their fundamental law to delineate and protect their liberties. Philadelphia's Joseph Reed offered one of the more nuanced appreciations of the emerging yet fragile political community in February 1775. He recognized there remained profound political differences among those supportive of Congress's measures, but identified the basic principle that unified the resistance as a people. Americans, he claimed, universally denied Parliament's right to interfere in their local affairs.[167] This basic belief, coupled with the willingness to sacrifice in defense of local rule, united Americans during the Coercive Acts Crisis. Those who supported Parliament's authority over colonial affairs or refused to adhere to the Continental Association, by this logic, were not Americans.

John Adams described colonists' struggle as "a compleat Revolution," and cautioned America's future depended on its inhabitants' continued willingness to "sacrifice their private Pleasures, Passions, and Interests . . . when they Stand in Competition with the Rights of society."[168] Adams recognized the political transformation taking place but agonized over whether Americans would remain virtuous or succumb to self-interest. Thomas Jefferson, gauging the general sentiments of delegates before they signed the Declaration of Independence, recorded how many of his colleagues felt that that document's language revealed little new about the American community. As the Virginian remembered it, some claimed the document simply declared "a fact which already exists."[169] For many colonists, a new American identity had emerged as a result of their shared struggle during the Coercive Acts Crisis.

More than two decades after signing the Declaration of Independence, President John Adams penned a statement to the federal senate remarking on the death of George Washington. After commending the late president's virtue, the second chief executive reflected on the spirit of union and the shared identity he felt had formed around those suffering in Boston in 1774. Washington once belonged to "that memorable league of the continent in 1774," eulogized Adams, that "first expressed the sovereign will of a free nation in America."[170] For President Adams, those who joined in sacrifice during the Coercive Acts Crisis transformed into a new community and offered the earliest expressions of political sovereignty. They became, from the president's perspective, the first American citizens. The Continental Association, for Whig actors, breathed life into a new citizenry. But that citizenry did not sustain itself without assistance.

During the uncertainty of the first Washington administration, historian David Ramsey also meditated on the formation of an American political community. Ramsey theorized, "The pen and the press had merit equal to that of the sword." Awakening and uniting Americans, the historian claimed, required the "tongues and pens of the well-informed citizens."[171] For Ramsey, print culture was every bit as vital to the founding of the American Republic as was the Continental Army. The army fought and won the war; the press connected Americans and convinced enough of them to support the cause. And a significant element of that support involved voluntary self-denial. Reading about unity and sacrifice in public papers, according to Ramsey, ultimately educated supporters on their public responsibilities to the common cause.

The Continental Association offered colonists a plan to realize imperial reconciliation and colonial moral regeneration. Cities, towns, and counties throughout colonial America expressed their enthusiasm for Congress's directives by immediately holding elections for Committees of Inspection and Observation and voluntarily complying with the Association. Whether forgoing horse races and theatrical performances, refraining from gaming and gambling, or committing to frugality in other ways, public simplicity signaled support for the resistance. American printers memorialized these moments of self-denial, at once describing and prescribing the shared burden of sacrifice. Toasts, pamphlet advertisements, and poetry contributed to the narrative of virtuous compliance and American papers typically framed the hard work of enforcement as teachable moments of brotherly guidance. The reading public also learned of committees casting obstinate violators as enemies of America. These accounts of ostracism and violence served as clear warnings to those still reluctant to support the Continental Association. Colonists read about compliance, support, and enforcement from all over British North America, connecting them to an extralocal community of Americans suffering in the common cause.

The political community that separated from the British Empire identified as American. Yet it is critical to note this new community was not as much a well-defined national identity with set civic notions of citizenship as it was a loosely described federation of united communities that feared their liberties were under assault. The American political community was, fundamentally, a resistance movement joined through shared fears and anxieties. American Whigs did not set out to establish a federal government. They sought to restore the local liberty and autonomy they felt had come under fire from Parliament. Liberty and autonomy varied by colony, county, and town, making it virtually impossible to create anything resembling a modern national identity. The fundamental national qualities that these first political Americans shared were a jealous vigilance over local identities and a willingness to join in sacrifice to protect them. This vigilance and union through self-denial connected the many communities of suffering into a pan-colonial resistance movement committed to protecting their various identities. Ultimately, union through suffering metamorphized many American subjects into republican citi-zens. Once colonial Whigs determined monarchy posed the greatest threat to their cherished liberties and local identities, this political transformation became the necessary and logical conclusion of their imperial struggle.

CONCLUSION

"No Longer Subjects of the British King"

H ISTORIANS HAVE PRODUCED CONFLICTING RESEARCH ON THE First Continental Congress and the Articles of Association. Congress, depending on the scholar, represented either a cautious body unwilling to aggressively defend American liberties, an innovative assembly that coordinated many local resistance movements, a failed institution, or something in between.[1] Regarding the Continental Association, historians most commonly focus their attention on its economic aspects. Fitting within the tenets of the neo-progressive school, this model traces the commercial coercion American Whigs hoped to apply to Britain's manufacturing sector. If properly executed, colonists expected merchants to apply political pressure on members of the House of Commons to repeal the Coercive Acts. T. H. Breen argued this position most persuasively, claiming colonists weaponized their economic potency to address a political crisis they could not otherwise constitutionally resolve.[2]

While considering the neo-Whig interpretation, scholars such as David Ammerman and Hermann Wellenreuther examined the underappreciated democratizing effects of the Continental Association.

Ammerman claimed the Association invited thousands of new activists, men dedicated to the Whig cause, into the resistance movement, a development he described as "a psychological victory of the first magnitude."[3] Wellenreuther argued that the Association's Committees of Inspection and Observation pulled Americans out of a state of nature, reclaimed sovereignty from king and Parliament and their colonial subsidiaries, and served as de facto governments.[4] Scholar Anne Fairfax Withington offered a rare exploration exclusively into the cultural regulations proposed by Congress.[5] She claimed that assembly designed the Association's moral regulations to encourage Americans to sustain the boycott effort through acts of public virtue. In the process, she contended, widespread sacrifice pushed colonists toward republican government.[6] *No Longer Subjects of the British King* offers a bridge between these interpretive models while addressing political identity formation during the Coercive Acts Crisis in the process.

The American political community forged in an environment of suffering and voluntary sacrifice. After disguised agitators in Boston destroyed roughly ninety-two thousand pounds of the East India Company's tea, Parliament responded by closing that port, protecting British officials from trial by local juries, opening unused buildings for billeting the king's soldiers, and altering Massachusetts's charter. American Whigs began viewing themselves as distinct from the broader imperial community following the implementation of the Coercive Acts and the crisis at Boston impelled them to join in solidarity with that seaport town. Many cities, towns, and counties memorialized this solidarity through local resolutions that condemned Parliament, championed colonial union, and called forth the First Continental Congress.[7] This sudden, unexpected and remarkable spirit of unity laid the foundation of a pan-colonial political identity in Britain's mainland colonies. The core tenets of this identity were a desire to retain local liberties and identities and a willingness to join in sacrifice in their defense. Americans joined in resistance, then, to defend the right of local rule for each American community. And the Whig embrace of and support for provincial differences characterized the American political community.

When the First Continental Congress convened in September 1774, delegates from twelve colonies arrived in Philadelphia as an assembly of strangers. During the next two months, however, many became well-acquainted with each other and formed a fellowship based on Ciceronian principles.[8] At social engagements outside Carpenters' Hall, this elite fraternity pronounced its support for the common cause and American liberties through performative politics. Engaging in a series of toasts and boasts, delegates revealed their abilities, character, and commitment to safeguarding what they considered colonial America's besieged rights.[9] Joined in the public's cause, this fellowship emerged as an elite leadership class of the pan-colonial resistance and a symbol of American union.

During congressional sessions, the better-organized radicals outmaneuvered both moderates and imperial traditionalists to seize the political initiative. These machinations led to Congress's selection of Carpenters' Hall (itself a symbol of local radicalism) as its meeting place and the election of radical Charles Thomson as secretary.[10] Once Thomson assumed his office, he recorded many of Congress's policies as passing *nemine contradicente* despite the actual internal divisions that persisted among the delegates.[11] These carefully choreographed and publicized early moves signaled Congress's radical nature to the public and communicated a politically-manipulated veneer of artificial unity among the delegates.

Looking beyond Thomson's sanitized minutes and into delegates' letters, the substance of congressional debates reveals an assembly aggressively defending the rights of American subjects. Congress officially rooted the origins of American liberty in natural rights, which implied, theoretically, that colonists enjoyed their privileges with or without king and empire.[12] This raised concerns among traditionalists in Congress, most notably Joseph Galloway and James Duane, who recognized at once the implications of such a radical declaration. Galloway felt radicals aimed to break off any connection to Britain and declare the American colonies an independent nation.[13] When Paul Revere delivered the Suffolk Resolves, radicals scored another victory. Against imperial traditionalists' protests, Congress read the Resolves into the record. Galloway described the Suffolk Resolves as nothing less than a declaration of war against Britain. Congress next voted to support Suffolk's positions and had the Resolves, Congress's official endorsement, and a scathing rebuke of Parliament published in the American press. Galloway and Duane both voted against this position and vehemently protested when Thomson recorded this motion as passing *nemine contradicente.* By supporting the Suffolk Resolves, Congress further embraced a radical approach to protecting white Americans' liberty from the perceived encroachments of Parliament. Among other bold claims, the Resolves stated (and Congress publicly validated) that self-preservation, the reflexive human desire to survive, remained any political entity's chief objective, above even loyalty to the British Crown.[14]

Congress employed the doctrine of self-preservation in its letter to Lieutenant General Thomas Gage, Address to the People of Great Britain, Memorial to the Inhabitants of North America, and Petition to the King.[15] In each of these missives, Congress claimed the continued survival of American liberty and community took precedence over any connection to the Crown or inclusion in the empire. Despite declaring fealty to king and empire, Congress warned of potential violence should Parliament fail to meet American demands. Delegates hoped for imperial reconciliation but on American terms. This aggressive and uncompromising position exposes that Congress's attachment to the empire did not outweigh its firm commitment to retaining local American identities and liberties.

A combination of classical virtue and Protestant resistance informed Congress's work. The Articles of Association's nonimportation and nonexportation directives, to be sure, aimed to achieve imperial reconciliation through economic coercion.[16] Still many activists also hoped to purge American culture of the corruptive forces they felt had already debauched and demoralized England. Resistance leaders used the Association and its Committees of Inspection and Observation to regenerate virtue and foster republican simplicity. In unmistakable language, numerous Americans embraced this attempt at moral redemption.[17] The new American political community found commonality in sacrifice, with members voluntarily stopping commercial engagement with the greater empire and discontinuing certain social behaviors so long as Boston suffered in the common cause.[18] Colonial printers publicized the performative nature of sacrifice and in the process helped develop and strengthen a narrative of virtuous compliance.[19] Congress's directives and this heroic narrative intertwined and self-denial and political identity became, for many Americans, synonymous. Yet it is important to remember that those subjects unwilling to follow Congress's directives, in many instances, faced the regulatory wrath of the Committees of Inspection and Observation.

The resistance movement denied imperial traditionalists freedom of the press, freedom of expression, the right to freely dispose of their private property, the security of trial by jury, even the liberty to participate openly in certain pastimes or practice certain behaviors.[20] Simply put, self-described patriots saw no contradiction in denying liberty to some, to ostensibly secure those liberties they believed to be under threat by Parliament. Traditionalists endured tremendous social and economic pressure and endured their own form of suffering and sacrifice. So-called patriots socially and economically ostracized nonsupporters, declared them enemies of America, and tarred and feathered them to enforce Congress's directives and assert local dominance. Local committees decided which members of their communities deserved the basic rights many Whigs felt Parliament threatened. This moment in the colonial past offers a startling starting point to an American tradition of crushing dissent and suppressing liberties in times of high crisis.

As the political crisis deepened, Congress began modifying some of its commercial directives. For example, by July 1775 it started regulating privateering and allowing merchants to import war materials and export domestic goods to pay for these wares. The moral proscriptions, however, remained.[21] Yet even with these necessary adjustments, that assembly ultimately failed to achieve its immediate political and cultural objectives. Writing to John Jay in 1775, John Adams claimed the Continental Association worked better in theory than in practice. Preventing merchants from importing goods and producers from exporting resources, he reasoned, burdened Americans with a likely unsustainable commitment to self-denial.[22] And after Lexington and Concord, the commercial aspects of the Association mattered little in terms of altering British policy. Following the success of the Franco-American alliance in the War for Independence, the desire for moral purification also waned among Americans. By the middle of the 1780s, for example, horse racing enjoyed a resurgence throughout the new nation. Americans also again began indulging themselves with theatrical performances, while cockfighting, gambling, and elaborate funeral practices all became normalized before the denouement of the eighteenth century.[23] Congress did not succeed in negotiating imperial reconciliation or realizing moral regeneration. It did, however, succeed in securing something every bit as important—the American liberties and identities it felt under threat at the beginning of the Coercive Acts Crisis. Securing these liberties and identities required, according to the American political community, colonial independence and the repudiation of monarchy as a system of governance.

Once the United Colonies officially declared independence from Britain, Samuel Adams marveled that Americans were "no longer the Subjects of the British King."[24] They now regulated themselves with governments they constructed, he claimed, and "Monarchy seems to be generally exploded."[25] Not every American wrote or uttered these words explicitly, but plenty of former subjects must have reflected on this powerful socioemotional transformation. For a generation of Britons only familiar with constitutional monarchy, severing the connection to the British Crown likely left them in a state between fear and exhilaration. Thomas Jefferson likened this moment to American Whigs simply discarding the robes of monarchy for those of republicanism.[26]

Jefferson's claim that colonists changed governments as easily as changing into new clothes remains an apt description of the process Americans experienced while transforming from subjects to citizens. But Jefferson never did reveal why the proverbial "new suit" fit so well for so many colonists.[27] Remarkably, the key to understanding this is deceptively simple: Governments, like clothing, serve a function. The functionality of clothing is quite basic—without considering aesthetics or fashion, clothes offer protection from the environment. If new clothes failed to meet this basic requirement, most would not bother donning them in the first place. Colonists in eighteenth-century British North America felt the function of the British government was to protect English liberties and facilitate commercial exchange. Yet when Parliament determined to punish Boston for hurling East India tea into the harbor in December 1773 by closing its port, altering its charter, and discontinuing trial by jury, many colonists expressed a profound fear (expectation, even) that Parliament would extend its drastic measures well beyond Boston. Indeed, many anticipated Parliament's subjugation of the rest of the mainland colonies as part of an insidious design to enslave America.

This overwhelming sense of fear awakened an American political community committed to sacrificing for the common cause, which helped grow and sustain it. The British system had, for many colonists, lost its functionality. Yet while colonists did, in the end, change their form of government, its function proved quite similar to the old order in some critical ways. Local people continued to elect local leaders to solve local problems. And those locally elected officials exercised the exclusive right to govern the affairs of their constituents, whether through taxation or legislation. John Adams noted in January 1775 that Congress had "drawn a line by the banks of the ocean," and he identified that assembly's proceedings as "the temper and principles of America." Among the principles that defined the American people, Congress believed the "exclusive jurisdiction in all interior concerns, and in all cases of taxation" ranked chief among them.[28] The clothes might have been new, but for Americans, they served the same familiar function in an immediate sense. Local identities, liberties, and traditions remained intact, and the American political community embraced republicanism as the form of government best able to secure and guarantee them.

NOTES

INTRODUCTION

1. Thomas Jefferson to Benjamin Franklin, August 3, 1777, in *The Papers of Thomas Jefferson*, eds. Julian P. Boyd et al., 43 vols. (Princeton, NJ: Princeton University Press, 1950–2018), 2:26. For Benjamin Franklin as ambassador to France, see Morris Bishop, "Franklin in France," *Daedalus* 86, no. 3 (1957):214–30.

2. The Articles of Association's opening statement advanced this characterization. See Worthington C. Ford et al., eds., *Journals of the Continental Congress, 1774–1789*, 34 vols. (Washington, DC, 1904–1937), 1:75.

3. Some works exploring the development of early national identity include Peter S. Onuf, *Jefferson's Empire: The Language of American Nationhood* (Charlottesville: University Press of Virginia, 2009); Simon P. Newman, *Parades and the Politics of the Street: Festive Culture in the Early American Republic* (Philadelphia: University of Pennsylvania Press, 1997); David Waldstreicher, *In the Midst of Perpetual Fetes: The Making of American Nationalism* (Chapel Hill: University of North Carolina Press, 1997); David Armitage, *The Declaration of Independence: A Global History* (Cambridge, MA: Harvard University Press, 2007).

4. Joseph J. Ellis, *The Quartet: Orchestrating the Second American Revolution, 1783-1789* (New York: Vintage Books, 2015), xi–xx. John M. Murrin made a similar point in "A Roof Without Walls: The Dilemma of American National Identity," in *Beyond Confederation: Origins of the Constitution and National Identity*, eds. Richard Beeman, Stephen Botein, and Edward C. Carter (Chapel Hill: University of North Carolina Press, 1987), 333–48. Murrin, however, did not advocate the "top-down" model Ellis not unreasonably embraced in his work. Instead, Murrin argued Americans' deification of the federal constitution connected widely dispersed and culturally diverse people once British institutions collapsed.

5. For works on southern nationalism, see Paul D. Escott, *After Secession: Jefferson Davis and the Failure of Confederate Nationalism* (Baton Rouge: Louisiana State University Press, 1978); Drew Gilpin Faust, *The Creation of Confederate Nationalism: Ideology and Identity in the Civil War South* (Baton Rouge: Louisiana State University Press, 1988); Drew Gilpin Faust, "Altars of Sacrifice: Confederate Women and the Narratives of War," *Journal of American History* 76, no. 4 (1990):20–128; John McCardell, *The Idea of a Southern Nation: Southern Nationalists and Southern Nationalism, 1830–1860* (New York: W.W. Norton & Company, 1981). For northern nationalism, see Melinda Law-

son, *Patriot Fires: Forging a New American Nationalism in the Civil War North* (Lawrence: University Press of Kansas, 2002); Susan-Mary Grant, *North over South: Northern Nationalism and American Identity in the Antebellum Era* (Lawrence: University Press of Kansas, 2000); Gary W. Gallagher, *The Union War* (Cambridge, MA: Harvard University Press, 2011). For the reconciliation of both northern and southern white American identity at the expense of African Americans, see David Blight, *Race and Reunion: The Civil War in American Memory* (Cambridge, MA: Belknap Press of Harvard University Press, 2001).
6. For some general surveys, see Edmund S. Morgan and Helen M. Morgan, *The Stamp Act Crisis: Prologue to Revolution* (Chapel Hill: University of North Carolina Press, 1962); Bernard Bailyn, *The Ideological Origins of the American Revolution* (Cambridge, MA: Harvard University Press, 1967), 99–102; Robert Middlekauff, *The Glorious Cause: The American Revolution, 1763–1789* (New York: Oxford University Press: 1982), 74–97, 142–58; John Ferling, *A Leap in the Dark: The Struggle to Create the American Republic* (New York: Oxford University Press, 2003), 32–40, 57–79; Pauline Maier, *From Resistance to Revolution: Colonial Radicals and the Development of American Opposition to Britain, 1765–1776* (New York: W.W. Norton & Company, 1972); Benjamin Carp, *Defiance of the Patriots: The Boston Tea Party and the Making of America* (New Haven, CT: Yale University Press, 2011).
7. David Ammerman, *In the Common Cause: American Response to the Coercive Acts of 1774* (New York: W.W. Norton and Company, 1974), 5–10.
8. Some examples include Edmund Pendleton to Joseph Chew, June 20, 1774, in *The Letters and Papers of Edmund Pendleton*, ed. David John Mays, 2 vols. (Charlottesville: University Press of Virginia, 1967), 1:92–93; "Proceedings and Resolves of the Gentlemen Chosen by the Several Towns in Cumberland County, Massachusetts Bay," *Rivington's New York Gazetteer*, October 13, 1774; "Committee of Correspondence at Westerly (Rhode Island) to the Committee of Boston," in *American Archives: Consisting of a Collection of Authentic Records, State Papers, Debates, And Letters And Other Notices of Publick Affairs, the Whole Forming a Documentary History of the Origins and Progress of the North American Colonies; of the Causes and Accomplishments of the American Revolution; and of the Constitution of Government for the United States, to the Final Ratification Thereof: Fourth Series*, ed. Peter Force, 6 vols. (Washington, DC, 1837–1853), 1:315–16, 336–37. For secondary examinations, see T.H. Breen, *The Marketplace of Revolution: How Consumer Politics Shaped American Independence* (New York: Oxford University Press, 2004), 2–4; Ammerman, *Common Cause*, 15.
9. Ann Fairfax Withington, *Toward a More Perfect Union: Virtue and the Formation of American Republics* (New York: Oxford University Press, 1991); Patrick Griffin, *America's Revolution* (New York: Oxford University Press, 2013), 109–10; Jack P. Greene, *The Constitutional Origins of the American Revolution* (New York: Cambridge University Press, 2011), 153–54; Ammerman, *Common Cause*, 14.
10. T. H. Breen, "The Baubles of Britain: The American and Consumer Revolu-

tions of the Eighteenth Century," *Past & Present*, no. 119 (1988):73–104; Neil L. York, "Imperial Impotence: Treason in 1774 Massachusetts," *Law and History Review* 29, no. 3 (2011):657–701.

11. Henry Laurens to John Knight, March 17, 1774, in *The Papers of Henry Laurens*, eds. David R. Chestnut et al., 16 vols. (Columbia: University of South Carolina Press, 1981–2003), 10:359–60.

12. Henry Laurens to John Laurens, March 22, 1774, in Chestnut, *The Papers*, 10:363–64.

13. Samuel Adams to Richard Randolph, February 1, 1775, in *The Papers of Samuel Adams*, ed. Harry Alonzo Cushing, 4 vols. (New York: Knickerbocker Press, 1904–1907), *Writings of Adams*, 4:175–76.

14. Donation for the Boston Poor from Chesterfield County, Virginia, December 17, 1774, in *Papers of John Adams*, Robert J. Taylor et al., 17 vols. (Cambridge, MA: Harvard university Press, 1977), 2:203.

15. Thomas Gage to Lord William Barrington, November 2, 1774, in *The Correspondence of General Thomas Gage with Secretaries of State, and with the War Office and the Treasury, 1763-1775*, ed. Clarence Edwin Carter, 2 vols. (New Haven, CT: Yale University Press, 1931–1933), 2:658–59.

16. George Washington to William Fairfax, June 10, 1774, in *The Papers of George Washington, Colonial Series*, eds. W. W. Abbot and Dorothy Twohig, 10 vols. (Charlottesville: University Press of Virginia, 1983–1995), 10:94–101.

17. George Washington to Bryan Fairfax, July 20, 1774, in *The Papers of George Washington*, eds. Abbot and Twohig, 10:128–31.

18. George Washington to Bryan Fairfax, August 24, 1774, in *The Papers of George Washington*, eds. Abbot and Twohig, 10:154–56.

19. Samuel Adams to Charles Thomson, May 30, 1774, in Cushing, *Writings of Adams*, 3:122–23.

20. Morgan and Morgan, *Stamp Act Crisis*, 84–91, 297; Green, *Constitutional Origins*, 114–16; Middlekauff, *Glorious Cause*, 241.

21. Ammerman, *Common Cause*, 147.

22. As chapter 1 explores in more detail, resistance leaders on the town and county levels passed a multitude of grassroots resolutions advocating material sacrifice in support of Boston. Some examples include "Queen Anne, Maryland Resolutions, 13 May 1774" and "Baltimore County, Maryland Resolutions, 31 May 1774" in Force, *American Archives*, 1:366–67.

23. See for example "Prince George County, Virginia Resolutions, June 1774" and "Fauquier County, Virginia Resolutions, 9 July 1774" in Force, *American Archives* , 1:493–95, 528–29.

24. "Letter from a Private Individual to Peyton Randolph," October 20, 1774, in Force, *American Archives*, 1:944.

25. Ford et al., *Journals of Congress*.

26. For the Continental Association as a call to action, see Maier, *Resistance to Revolution*, 278; Ammerman, *Common Cause*, 91; Ferling, *Leap in the Dark*, 121.

27. Withington, *More Perfect Union*, 218–20.

28. Middlekauff, *Glorious Cause*, 252–54; Ammerman, *Common Cause*, 84–85.
29. Maier, *Resistance to Revolution*, 251–53; *Pennsylvania Packet*, November 28, 1774.
30. Withington, *More Perfect Union*, 13–14.
31. Ford et al., *Journals of Congress*, 1:76.
32. Steven C. Bullock and Sheila McIntyre, "The Handsome Tokens of a Funeral: Glove-Giving and the Large Funeral in Eighteenth-Century New England," *William and Mary Quarterly* 69, no. 2 (2012):305–46.
33. Ford et al., *Journals of Congress*, 1:77.
34. Benjamin Lincoln, "In Provincial Congress," *Massachusetts and Boston Weekly*, November 3, 1774.

CHAPTER ONE

1. Observers used this phrase early and often during the Coercive Acts Crisis to describe Bostonians enduring hardship. Samuel Adams likely coined this phrase. See Samuel Adams to Arthur Lee, May 18, 1774," in Cushing, *The Writings of Samuel Adams*, 3:117–19.
2. James Warren to John Adams, January 3, 1774, in *The Papers of John Adams*, eds. Robert J. Taylor, et al., 18 vols. (Cambridge, MA: Harvard University Press, 1977), 2:6–7. For a thorough account of the Boston Tea Party, see Benjamin L. Carp, *Defiance of the Patriots: The Boston Tea Party and the Making of America* (New Haven, CT: Yale University Press, 2010).
3. Samuel Adams to Arthur Lee, January 25, 1774, in Cushing, *Writings of Samuel Adams*, 3:78–79.
4. David Ammerman, *In the Common Cause: American Response to the Coercive Acts of 1774* (New York: W. W. Norton & Company, 1974), 12–13.
5. "The King's Message, 7 March 1774," in *American Archives: Consisting of a Collection of Authentic Records, State Papers, Debates, And Letters And Other Notices of Publick Affairs, the Whole Forming a Documentary History of the Origins and Progress of the North American Colonies; of the Causes and Accomplishments of the American Revolution; and of the Constitution of Government for the United States, to the Final Ratification Thereof: Fourth Series*, ed. Peter Force, 6 vols. (Washington, DC, 1837–1853), 1:5.
6. For Parliament formulating a response to the Boston Tea Party, see Robert Middlekauff, *The Glorious Cause: The American Revolution, 1763–1789* (New York: Oxford University Press, 1982), 233–37; Ammerman, *Common Cause*, 13–15.
7. "House of Commons, 14 March 1774," in Force, *American Archives*, 1:38.
8. T. H. Breen, *The Marketplace of Revolution: How Consumer Politics Shaped American Independence* (New York: Oxford University Press, 2004), 302–4.
9. For a survey of the Coercive Acts, see Ammerman, *Common Cause*, 5–12; Edmund Cody Burnett, *The Continental Congress* (New York: MacMillan Company, 1941), 18–19; Middlekauff, *Glorious Cause*, 235–37.
10. See, for example, "Proceedings in the Fields, New York, 6 July 1774" and "Committee of Correspondence at Westerly, Rhode Island to the Committee of

Boston, 19 May 1774," in Force, *American Archives:* 1:312, 336–37. For colonial fears that the Coercive Acts endangered every mainland colony see Breen, *Marketplace of Revolution*, 2–4.

11. Henry Laurens to John Laurens, March 22, 1774, in *The Papers of Henry Laurens*, eds. David R. Chestnut et al, 16 vols. (Columbia: University of South Carolina Press, 1981–2003), 9:363.

12. Edmund Pendleton to Joseph Chew, June 20, 1774, in *The Letters and Papers of Edmund Pendleton*, ed. David John Mays, 2 vols. (Charlottesville: University Press of Virginia, 1967), 1:92–93.

13. Colonists used the phrase "enemies of American liberties," or some variation ("inimical to this country") to describe those unwilling to sacrifice for Boston. See, for example, the "Virginia Resolutions," *Pennsylvania Gazette*, August 24, 1774; *Massachusetts Spy*, September 8, 1774; "Chestertown, Maryland, 18 May 1774," in Force, *American Archives*, 1:334–35.

14. As pointed out by Jeffery Pasley, resistance leaders weaponized the press during the crisis years. While printers sympathetic to the crown continued to publish newspapers supportive of Parliament, the clear majority of papers found their financial support from resistance actors. As such, the print coverage most colonists engaged with presented a decidedly pro-Whig narrative. See Pasley, *The Tyranny of Printers: Newspaper Politics in the Early Republic* (Charlottesville: University of Virginia Press, 2001), 33–40.

15. For examples of "Grand American Congress," see *New-Hampshire Gazette*, August 12, 1774; *Newport Mercury*, August 15, 1774; for "general Congress," see "Resolutions of Baltimore County, Maryland," *Essex Journal*, June 22, 1774; "New-London, Connecticut Committee of Correspondence," *Connecticut Gazette*, July 15, 1774.

16. Jerrilyn Greene Marston, *King and Congress: The Transfer of Political Legitimacy, 1774–1776* (Princeton, NJ: Princeton University Press, 1987), 43–44; Ammerman, *Common Cause*, 20–21; Burnett, *Continental Congress*, 19–20.

17. "A Gentleman in London to One in New York, 27 April 1774," in Force, *American Archives*, 1:248.

18. George Washington to George William Fairfax, June 10, 1774, in *The Papers of George Washington: Colonial Series*, eds. W. W. Abbot, and Dorothy Twohig, 10 vols. (Charlottesville and London: University Press of Virginia, 1995), 10:94–101.

19. George Washington to Bryan Fairfax, July 4, 1774, in *The Papers of George Washington* , eds. Abbot and Twohig, 10:109–10.

20. "Extracts from Letters from London, 7 April 1774, to Persons in New York and Philadelphia," in Force, *American Archives*, 1:289–92.

21. Henry Laurens to Thomas Savage, April 9, 1774, in Chestnut et al., *Papers of Laurens*, 9:386–88.

22. "To the Freeman of America, 18 May 1774," in Force, *American Archives*, 1:335–36.

23. Breen, *Marketplace of Revolution*, 302–3; Ammerman, *Common Cause*, 15; Ferling, *A Leap in the Dark: The Struggle to Create the American Republic* (New York: Oxford university Press, 2003), 108–10.

24. For a comprehensive exploration into this theme, see Forrest McDonald, *Novus Ordo Seclorum: The Intellectual Origins of the Constitution* (Lawrence: University of Kansas, 1985).

25. The standard for this interpretation of colonial history is Thomas Jefferson's "A Summary View of the Rights of British America," in *The Papers of Thomas Jefferson*, eds. Julian P. Boyd et al., 43 vols. (Princeton: Princeton University Press, 1950–2018), 1:121–25; see also Bernard Bailyn, *The Ideological Origins of the American Revolution*, enlarged ed. (Cambridge, MA: Belknap Press of Harvard University Press, 1992), 80–83; Caroline Robbins, "Rights and Grievances at Carpenters' Hall, September 5–October 26, 1774," *Pennsylvania History: A Journal of Mid-Atlantic Studies* 43, no. 2 (1976):100–18.

26. Herman Wellenreuther, "Introduction," in *The Revolution of the People: Thoughts and Documents on the Revolutionary Process in North America, 1774-1776*, ed. Hermann Wellenreuther (Göttingen: University of Göttingen, 2006), 16.

27. "Governor Franklin to the Earl of Dartmouth, 18 June 1774" in Force, *American Archives*, 1:428–29. This letter reveals Franklin's accurate understanding of colonial politics. Franklin identified the resistance movement's principal objective as securing American liberties on constitutional grounds to prevent future imperial disruptions.

28. "Sir James Wright to Governor Gage, 27 June 1775," in Force, *American Archives*, 2:1110.

29. Some examples include "Proceedings and Resolves of the Gentlemen Chosen by the Several Towns in Cumberland County, Massachusetts Bay," *Rivington's New York Gazetteer*, October 13, 1774; "Connecticut Resolutions, 12 May 1774" in Force, *American Archives*, 1:355–57.

30. "A Zealous Friend of Both Countries," *Pennsylvania Gazette*, August 24, 1774.

31. "Proceedings and Resolves of the Gentlemen Chosen by the Several Towns in Cumberland County, Massachusetts Bay," *Rivington's New York Gazetteer*, October 13, 1774.

32. "Rhode-Island Resolves, 13 June 1774" in Force, *American Archives*, 1:416–17.

33. "Connecticut Resolutions, 12 May 1774" in Force, *American Archives*, 1:355–57.

34. For more examples, see "Connecticut Resolutions, 12 May 1774," "Essex County, New Jersey Resolutions, 11 June 1774," "City and County of Philadelphia, Pennsylvania Resolutions, 18 June 1774," and "Northampton County, Pennsylvania Resolutions, 21 June 1774," in Force, *American Archives*, 1:355–57, 403–4, 426–27, 435–36.

35. "South-Haven, New York Resolutions, 13 June 1774," in Force, *American Archives*, 1:407–8.

36. "Morris County, New Jersey Resolutions, 27 June 1774," in Force, *American Archives*, 1:452.

37. "Freehold, New Jersey Resolutions, 6 June 1774," in Force, *American Archives*, 1:390.

38. "Annapolis, Maryland, 26 May 1774," in Force, *American Archives*, 1:352–53.

39. "Queen Anne, Maryland Resolutions, 13 May 1774," in Force, *American Archives*, 1:366.

40. "Westmoreland County, Virginia Resolutions, 22 June 1774," in Force, *American Archives*, 1:437–38.

41. "Prince George County, Virginia Resolutions, 30 June 1774," and "Fauquier County, Virginia Resolutions, 9 July 1774," in Force, *American Archives*, 1:493–95, 528–29.

42. Georgia was the most vulnerable and least populated colony in British North America. See Kenneth Coleman, *The American Revolution in Georgia, 1763–1789* (Athens: University of Georgia Press 1958); W. W. Abbot, *The Royal Governors of Georgia, 1754–1775* (Chapel Hill: University of North Carolina Press, 1959); Ronald G. Killion and Charles T. Waller, *Georgia and the Revolution* (Atlanta, GA: Cherokee Publishing Company, 1975).

43. "Georgia Resolutions, 10 August 1774," in Force, *American Archives*, 1:700–1.

44. "Letter from Philadelphia," *Massachusetts Spy*, October 20, 1774.

45. *Georgia Gazette*, September 7, 1774; Leslie Hall, *Land and Allegiance in Revolutionary Georgia* (Athens: University of Georgia Press, 2001), 20.

46. Edmund Pendleton to Joseph Chew, June 20, 1774, in Mays, *Papers of Pendleton*, 1:92–93.

47. "Notice to Call for the First Virginia Revolutionary Convention, 31 May 1774," in Mays, *Papers of Pendleton*, 1:89–90.

48. James Bowdoin to Benjamin Franklin, September 6, 1774, in *The Papers of Benjamin Franklin*, eds. Leonard W. Labaree et al., 42 vols. (New Haven, CT: Yale University Press, 1959–present), 21:281–84.

49. *Providence Gazette*, June 11, 1774.

50. *Providence Gazette*, June 18, 1774.

51. *Pennsylvania Gazette*, June 1, 1774; *Providence Gazette*, June 11, 1774.

52. *Providence Gazette*, June 18, 1774.

53. *Pennsylvania Gazette*, June 8, 1774.

54. *Providence Gazette*, July 30, 1774.

55. *Virginia Gazette* (Dixon and Hunter ed.), November 24, 1774.

56. "Morris County, New Jersey Resolutions, 27 June 1774," "Hunterdon County, New Jersey Resolutions, 8 July 1774," "Monmouth County, New Jersey Resolutions, 19 July 1774," and "Middlesex County, New Jersey Resolutions, 15 July 1774," in Force, *American Archives*, 1:452, 524, 610–11, 553.

57. "City and County of Philadelphia, Pennsylvania Resolutions, 18 June 1774" in Ibid., 1:426-27.

58. "Northampton County, Pennsylvania Resolutions, 21 June 1774," in Force, *American Archives*, 1:435–36.

59. "Norfolk Borough, Virginia Resolutions, 6 July 1774," and "James County, Virginia Resolutions, 1 July 1774," in Force, *American Archives*, 1:518, 499.

60. "Boston, Massachusetts Resolutions, 17 June 1774," in Force, *American Archives*, 1:423–24.
61. *Massachusetts Gazette*, August 18, 1774, May 19, 1774.
62. *Pennsylvania Packet*, November 28, 1774.
63. *Pennsylvania Gazette*, August 17, 1774; *Essex Journal and Merrimack Packet*, October 19, 1774.
64. *Essex Journal and Merrimack Packet*, October 19, 1774; *Pennsylvania Gazette*, October 5, 1774.
65. *Pennsylvania Packet*, December 19, 1774.
66. *Essex Journal and Merrimack Packet*, October 29, 1774; *Massachusetts Spy*, October 20, 1774, September 29, 1774.
67. *Massachusetts Spy*, September 1, 1774.
68. *Rivington's New York Gazetteer*, September 2, 1774.
69. *Pennsylvania Gazette*, August 17, 1774.
70. *Providence Gazette*, July 16, 1774, August 13, 1774, August 20, 1774; *Massachusetts Gazette*, August 25, 1774, September 1, 1774, October 20, 1774, December 8, 1774, December 16, 1774, December 22, 1774, December 29, 1774.
71. *Massachusetts Gazette*, September 8, 1774.
72. "Extract from a Letter from a Gentleman at Norwich-Landing," in *Massachusetts Gazette*, September 8, 1774.
73. *Providence Gazette*, May 28, 1774.
74. *Rivington's New York Gazetteer*, October 27, 1774; *Massachusetts Spy*, September 29, 1774.
75. *Pennsylvania Packet*, November 28, 1774.
76. *Massachusetts Spy*, September 1, 1774.
77. *Pennsylvania Packet*, December 19, 1774.
78. *Rivington's New York Gazetteer*, September 29, 1774.
79. *Essex Journal and Merrimack Packet*, October 5, 1774.
80. *Massachusetts Spy*, September 29, 1774; *Georgia Gazette*, October 12, 1774.
81. *Massachusetts Spy*, September 29, 1774.
82. See, for example, *Norwich Packet*, September 22, 1774; *Pennsylvania Packet*, November 11, 1774; *Boston Evening-Post*, November 14, 1774; *Essex Gazette*, November 15, 1774; *Massachusetts Spy*, November 17, 1774; *Dunlap's Pennsylvania Packet*, November 28, 1774.
83. *Massachusetts Spy*, September 15, 1774.
84. *Essex Journal and Merrimack Packet*, September 7, 1774.
85. Joseph Greenleaf to Robert Treat Paine, September 27, 1774, in *The Papers of Robert Treat Paine*, eds. Stephen T. Riley and Edward W. Hanson, 5 vols. (Charlottesville: University of Virginia Press, 2012-2020), 3:7.
86. *Essex Journal and Merrimack Packet*, September 7, 1774.
87. *Pennsylvania Packet*, October 17, 1774.
88. *Massachusetts Spy*, September 22, 1774.
89. *Massachusetts Spy*, October 6, 1774.
90. *Georgia Gazette*, October 12, 1774.

91. *Massachusetts Spy*, September 22, 1774, October 13, 1774, October 20, 1774, October 27, 1774.

92. Philip Freeman's advertisement ran roughly every week in the *Massachusetts Spy*, beginning June 2, 1774, through December of the same year. It ran at least once in the *Boston News-Letter*, December 22, 1774.

93. "Farmington, Connecticut, 19 May 1774," in Force, *American Archives*, 1:336.

94. Colonists occasionally referred to Congress as the "Grand Continental Congress." See "Salem, August 9," *Newport Mercury*, August 15, 1774; *New-Hampshire Gazette*, August 12, 1774. This title came with variations, such as the hardly distinctive "General Congress." See *Pennsylvania Packet*, September 19, 1774.

95. "A Gentlemen in London to a Friend in Annapolis, 31 March 1774," Force, *American Archives*, 1:230–31.

96. "Arthur Lee to Francis Lee, 18 March 1774," in Force, *American Archives*, 1:229–30.

97. Samuel Adams to Arthur Lee, April 4, 1774, in Cushing, *Writings of Adams*, 3:100.

98. "From a Gentlemen in London to One in New York, 5 April 1774," in Force, *American Archives*, 1:240–41.

99. Burnett, *The Continental Congress*, 18–22; "Town Meeting in Boston, 13 May 1774" in Force, *American Archives*, 1:331–32; Samuel Adams to Arthur Lee, May 18, 1774, in Cushing, *Writings of Adams*, 3:117–19.

100. "Philadelphia Committee of Philadelphia to the Committee of Boston, Sent by Mr. Paul Revere, 21 May 1774," and "New-York, 23 May 1774," in Force, *American Archives*, 1:341–42, 29699.

101. For some background to these resolutions, see Middlekauff, *Glorious Cause*, 237–39; Burnett, *Continental Congress*, 19. For the actual text, see "Resolutions of the House of Burgesses Designating a Day of Fasting and Prayer, 24 May 1774," in Boyd et al., *Papers of Jefferson*, 1:105–7.

102. For Governor Dunmore dissolving the House of Burgesses, see Burnett, *Continental Congress*, 19–20.

103. "An Association, By the Members of the Late House of Burgesses, May 1774" in Force, *American Archives*, 1:350–51; *Virginia Gazette* (Dixon and Hunter ed.), May 27, 1774.

104. For a summary of delegate selection, see Burnett, *Continental Congress*, 19–22; Middlekauff, *Glorious Cause*, 239–40.

105. Hall, *Land and Allegiance*, 20; Coleman, *Revolution in Georgia*, 40–42.

106. Coleman, *Revolution in Georgia*, 40–42.

107. For Georgia's internal conflict, see Harvey H. Jackson, "Factional Politics in Revolutionary Georgia, 1774–1777," *Georgia Historical Quarterly* 59, no. 4 (Winter, 1975):388–401; Coleman, *Revolution in Georgia*, 40, 50.

108. "Extract from a Letter from Philadelphia, 3 September 1774," *Georgia Gazette*, September 14, 1774; Coleman, *Revolution in Georgia*, 43.

109. *Newport Mercury*, September 12, 1774.

110. See Jackson, "Factional Politics," 388–401; Coleman, *Revolution in Georgia*, 50.

111. "Charleston, South Carolina, 4 June 1774," in Force, *American Archives*, 1:382–84.

112. "Extract from a Letter from London, 27 July 1774," *Massachusetts Spy*, September 29, 1774.

113. "Extract from a Letter from London, 16 July 1774," *Pennsylvania Gazette*, September 14, 1774.

114. "Junius Americanus," *Essex Journal and Merrimack Packet*, September 7, 1774.

115. For a study on cultural and political identity and community expression, see Adrian Oldfield, "Citizenship and Community: Civic Republicanism and the Modern World," in *The Citizenship Debates*, ed. Gershon Shafir (Minneapolis: University of Minnesota Press, 1998), 75–89.

116. "Charleston, South Carolina, 4 June 1774," in Force, *American Archives*, 1:382–84.

117. Nicholas Cresswell, *The Journal of Nicholas Cresswell* (New York: Dial Press, 1924), 42–46.

118. Henry Laurens to James Laurens, February 5, 1774, in Chestnut et al., *Papers of Laurens*, 9:264–70.

119. Henry Laurens to James Laurens, May 7, 1774, in Chestnut, *Papers of Laurens*, 9:431–38.

120. George Washington to Bryan Fairfax, July 20, 1774, in Abbot and Twohig, *Papers of Washington*, 10:128–31.

121. "House of Commons, 5 December 1774," in Force, *American Archives*, 1:1474.

CHAPTER TWO

1. John Ferling, *A Leap in the Dark: The Struggle to Create the American Republic* (New York: Oxford University Press, 2003), 108–10; Robert Middlekauff, *The Glorious Cause: The American Revolution, 1763–1789* (New York: Oxford University Press, 2005), 240–41; Jack Rakove, *The Beginnings of National Politics: An Interpretive History of the Continental Congress* (Baltimore, MD: Johns Hopkins University Press, 1979), 23; David Ammerman, *In the Common Cause: American Response to the Coercive Acts of 1774* (New York: W. W. Norton & Company, 1974), 22–34.

2. This aspect of the chapter relies on the groundbreaking work of Jürgen Habermas, *The Structural Transformation of the Public Sphere* (Cambridge, MA: MIT Press, 1991); Benedict Anderson, *Imagined Communities: Reflections on the Origin and Spread of Nationalism* (London: Verso, 1983); Michael Warner, *The Letters of the Republic: Publication and the Public Sphere in Eighteenth-Century America* (Cambridge, MA: Harvard University Press, 1990). Habermas argued the emergence of print culture in the West during the seventeenth and eighteenth centuries created a negotiated space between traditional power structures and civil society. Since print media operated outside of both, it acted as a regulatory medium that criticized the state and the people, ultimately influencing and shap-

ing both in the process. For Anderson, print culture invited people to imagine themselves connected to a wider community that had no definable geographic centrality. Readers ostensibly shared common concerns, goals, and cultural practices and found identity with others consulting the same literature. For Warner, print media transformed political discourse in the critical eighteenth century by codifying a language of republicanism that informed and engaged colonists, helping them imagine a wider, extralocal community that could act as a people separate from the state. This development activated and encouraged, so far as this argument goes, political divisions and partisan identity formation.

3. See James Warren to John Adams, January 3, 1774, in *The Papers of John Adams*, eds. Robert J. Taylor et al., 18 vols. (Cambridge, MA: Harvard University Press, 1977–) 2:6–7; Samuel Adams to Arthur Lee, January 25, 1774, in *The Writings of Samuel Adams*, ed. Harry Alonzo Cushing, , 4 vols. (New York: G. P. Putnam's Sons, 1904-08), 3:78–79; Arthur Lee to Richard Henry Lee, March 18, 1774, in *American Archives: Consisting of a Collection of Authentic Records, State Papers, Debates, And Letters And Other Notices of Publick Affairs, the Whole Forming a Documentary History of the Origins and Progress of the North American Colonies; of the Causes and Accomplishments of the American Revolution; and of the Constitution of Government for the United States, to the Final Ratification Thereof: Fourth Series*, ed. Peter Force, 6 vols. (Washington, DC, 1837–1853), 1:228–29.

4. *Pennsylvania Gazette*, June 29, 1774.

5. "From a Gentleman in London to One in New York, 5 April 1774," in Force, *American Archives*, 1:241.

6. *Providence Gazette*, May 14, 1774.

7. *Pennsylvania Gazette*, June 29, 1774.

8. *Massachusetts Gazette and Boston Weekly News-Letter*, June 2, 1774.

9. *Massachusetts Gazette and Boston Weekly News-Letter*, June 2, 1774.

10. Eran Shalev, *Rome Reborn on Western Shores: Historical Imagination and the Creation of the American Republic* (Charlottesville: University of Virginia Press, 2009); Carl J. Richard, *The Founders and the Classics: Greece, Rome, and the American Enlightenment* (Cambridge, MA: Harvard University Press, 1994); Gordon S. Wood, "The Legacy of Rome in the American Revolution," in *The Idea of America: Reflections on the Birth of the United States*, ed. Gordon S. Wood (New York: Penguin, 2011), 57–79.

11. "To the Inhabitants of the British Colonies in America," *Providence Gazette*, July 30, 1774.

12. Rakove, *National Politics,* 16, 29–30; Caroline Robbins, "Rights and Grievances at Carpenters' Hall, September 5 to October 26, 1774," *Pennsylvania History: A Journal of Mid-Atlantic Studies* 43, no. 2 (1976), 111.

13. "To the Free and Brave Americans," *Massachusetts Spy*, June 9, 1774.

14. "A Letter from the Committee of Correspondence in the Province of Pennsylvania, to the Committee in the Province of Massachusetts-Bay," *Massachusetts Gazette and Boston Weekly News-Letter*, July 28, 1774.

15. "Proceedings of the Committee of Correspondence New-York," *Massachusetts Gazette and Boston Weekly News*, August 4, 1774.

16. "Anglo Americanus," *Providence Gazette*, August 6, 1774.

17. "Extract of a Letter from a Gentleman of Distinction, in Philadelphia, to his Friend in the Town," *Massachusetts Spy*, September 29, 1774.

18. "Extract of a Letter Received in London from Maryland, 28 September 1774," in Force, *American Archives*, 1:809.

19. James Madison to William Bradford, August 23, 1774, in *The Papers of James Madison: Congressional Series*, eds. William T. Hutchinson et al., , 17 vols. (Chicago: University of Chicago Press, 1962–1991), 1:120–22.

20. Abigail Greenleaf to Robert Treat Paine, October 8, 1774, in *The Papers of Robert Treat Paine*, eds. Stephen T. Riley and Edward W. Hanson, 5 vols. (Charlottesville: University of Virginia Press, 2012–2020), 3:8–10.

21. Caesar Rodney to Thomas Rodney, September 9, 1774, in *Letters to and from Caesar Rodney: Member of the Stamp Act Congress and the First and Second Continental Congresses; Speaker of the Delaware Colonial Assembly*, ed. George Herbert Ryden (Philadelphia: University of Pennsylvania Press, 2017), 46–47.

22. John Adams, Diary, August 15, 1774, in *Diary and Autobiography of John Adams*, ed. L. H. Butterfield, 4 vols. (Cambridge, MA: Harvard University Press, 1961), 2:98.

23. James Bowdoin to Benjamin Franklin, September 6, 1774, in *The Papers of Benjamin Franklin*, eds. Leonard W. Labaree et al., 42 vols. (New Haven, CT: Yale University Press, 1959–present), 21:28.

24. *Pennsylvania Gazette*, June 8, 1774.

25. "A Letter from the Committee of Correspondence in the Province of Pennsylvania, to the Committee in the Province of Massachusetts-Bay," *Massachusetts Gazette and Boston Weekly News-Letter*, July 28, 1774.

26. Abigail Adams to John Adams, August 19, 1774, in *Adams Family Correspondence*, eds. L. H. Butterfield et al., 13 vols. (Cambridge, MA: Harvard University Press, 1963–), 1:142–43.

27. "Letters from Men in Philadelphia," *Massachusetts Spy*, September 22, 1774.

28. "Solomon Drowne, Jr., to Solomon Drowne, Sr., 5 October 1774," in *Pennsylvania Magazine History and Biography* 48, no. 3 (1924), 231–33.

29. "Solomon Drowne to Sally Drowne, 5 October 1774," in *Pennsylvania Magazine History and Biography* 48, no. 3 (1924), 233–34.

30. Joseph Reed to [Charles Pettit?], September 4, 1774, in New York Historical Society, American Manuscripts, *Joseph Reed Papers, 1757–1874, Part I, 1757–1776*, accessed November 15, 2020, https://cdm16694.contentdm.oclc.org/digital/collection/p16124coll1/id/47504/rec/38.

31. "A Westchester Farmer," [Samuel Seabury], *The Congress Canvassed: Or, An Examination into the Conduct of the Delegates at their Grand Convention, Held in Philadelphia, September 1, 1774. Addressed to the Merchants of New-York* (New York: 1775), 12.

32. Herbert Friedenwald, "The Journals and Papers of the Continental Congress," *Pennsylvania Magazine of History and Biography* 21, no. 2 (1897):161–84.

33. *Rivington's New York Gazetteer*, September 2, 1774.

34. *Rivington's New York Gazetteer*, September 2, 1774.

35. "Chaubullagungamuggensis," in *Rivington's New York Gazetteer*, September 22, 1774.

36. Joseph Reed to [Charles Pettit?], September 4, 1774, in New York Historical Society, American Manuscripts, *Reed Papers*, accessed November 15, 2020, https://cdm16694.contentdm.oclc.org/digital/collection/p16124coll1/id/47504/re c/38.

37. *Massachusetts Spy*, September 20, 1774.

38. *Pennsylvania Gazette*, August 17, 1774.

39. *Georgia Gazette*, September 21, 1774.

40. *New York Gazette and Weekly Mercury*, September 5, 1774; *Pennsylvania Gazette*, September 15, 1774.

41. John Adams, Diary, August 10, 1774, in Butterfield, *Adams Diary*, 2:97.

42. *Massachusetts Gazette and Boston Weekly News-Letter*, September 8, 1774.

43. *Connecticut Gazette*, August 19, 1774; *Connecticut Journal*, August 19, 1774.

44. For more on community-building through print capitalism and readership, see Habermas, *Structural Transformation*; Anderson, *Imagined Communities*; Warner, *Letters of the Republic*.

45. *Massachusetts Gazette and Boston Weekly News-Letter*, August 25, 1774.

46. John Adams, Diary, August 16,1774, in Butterfield, *Adams Diary*, 2:99–100.

47. *Connecticut Journal*, August 19, 1774.

48. Anderson, *Imagined Communities*.

49. For population figures, see Benson Bobrick, *Angel in the Whirlwind: The Triumph of the American Revolution* (New York: Simon and Schuster, 1997), 41. For the influence of German newspaper editors supportive and apathetic about the American Revolution, see John Joseph Stoudt, "The German Press in Pennsylvania and the American Revolution," *Pennsylvania Magazine of History and Biography* 59, no. 1 (1935):74–90. For German support in colonies outside of Pennsylvania, see Joseph George Rosengarten, *Frederick the Great and the American Revolution* (Cambridge, MA: Harvard University Press, 1906).

50. John Adams, Diary, August 31, 1774, in Butterfield, *Adams Diary*, 2:117–18.

51. *Pennsylvania Packet*, August 3, 1774.

52. John Adams to Abigail Adams, September 25, 1774, in Butterfield et al., *Adams Family Correspondence*, 1:162–63.

53. John Adams to William Tudor, September 29, 1774, in. Taylor et al., *Adams Papers*, 2:117–18.

54. John Adams, Diary, October 10, 1774, in Butterfield, *Adams Diary*, 2:150.

55. William Bradford to James Madison, October 17, 1774, in Hutchinson, et al., *Madison Papers: Congressional Series*, 1:125–28.

56. "Extract from a Letter from Philadelphia," *Georgia Gazette*, September 21, 1774.

57. "To the Inhabitants of Pennsylvania, August 1774," in Force, *American Archives*, 1:753–54.

58. Silas Deane to Mrs. Deane, September 1, 1774, and Joseph Galloway to the governor of New Jersey, September 3, 1774, in *Letters of the Members of the Continental Congress*, eds. Edmund C. Burnett et al., 24 vols. (Washington, DC: Carnegie Institution of Washington, 1921–1936), 1:4–6.

59. Connecticut delegates to the governor of Connecticut, October 10, 1774, in Burnett, *Letters of the Members*, 1:69–70.

60. Gordon S. Wood, *The Radicalism of the American Revolution* (New York: Vintage Books, 1991), 101–2; Judith Nisse Shklar, "Politics and Friendship," *Proceedings of the American Philosophical Society* 137, no. 2 (1993):207–12; Adrian Oldfield, "Citizenship and Community: Civic Republicanism and the Modern World," in *The Citizenship Debates*, ed. Gershon Shafir (Minneapolis: University of Minnesota Press, 1998), 75–89.

61. See, for example, Stephen Botein, "Cicero as Role Model for Early American Lawyers: A Case Study in Classical 'Influence,'" *Classical Journal* 73, no. 4 (1978):313–21; Paul A. Rahe, "Cicero and the Classical Legacy in America," in *Thomas Jefferson, the Classical World, and Early America*, eds. Peter S. Onuf and Nicholas Cole (Charlottesville: University of Virginia Press, 2011), 248.

62. Botein, "Cicero as Role Model," 314.

63. John Adams to William Tudor, August 4, 1774, in Taylor et al., *Adams Papers*, 2:125–27.

64. Silas Deane to Mrs. Deane, September 10, 1774, in Burnett et al., *Letters of the Members*, 1:28–29.

65. Cicero, *De Amicitia*, trans. Andrew P. Peabody (Boston, MA: Little, Brown and Company, 1887).

66. Shklar, "Politics and Friendship," 207–12.

67. For work on the functions and sociopolitical purposes of colonial American taverns, see Peter Thompson, *Rum Punch and Revolution: Taverngoing and Public Life in Eighteenth-Century Philadelphia* (Philadelphia: University of Pennsylvania Press, 1999); David W. Conroy, *In Public Houses: Drink and the Revolution of Authority in Colonial Massachusetts* (Chapel Hill: University of North Carolina Press, 1995); Kym S. Rice, *Early American Taverns: For the Entertainment of Friends and Strangers* (New York: Regnery Gateway, 1983); Robert Earle Graham, "The Taverns of Colonial Philadelphia," *Transactions of the American Philosophical Society* 43, no. 1 (1953):318–25.

68. Thompson, *Rum Punch and Revolution*, 147, 161.

69. George Washington, Diary, September 1–4, 1774, in Jackson and Twohig, eds., *Diaries of Washington*, 3:274–75,

70. John Adams, Diary, August 23, 1774, in Butterfield, *Adams Diary*, 2:108–9.

71. John Adams, Diary, August 29, 1774, in Butterfield, *Adams Diary*, 2:114–15.

72. John Adams to Abigail Adams, September 8, 1774, in Butterfield et al., *Adams Family Correspondence*, 1:150–51.

73. John Adams to Abigail Adams, September 29, 1774, in Butterfield et al., *Adams Family Correspondence*, 1:163–64.

74. Silas Deane to Mrs. Deane, September 12–16, 1774, in Burnett et al., *Letters of Members*, 1:32.

75. Silas Deane to Mrs. Deane, September 17, 1774, in Burnett et al., *Letters of Members*, 1:34.

76. John Adams, Diary, September 2, 1774, in Butterfield, *Adams Diary*, 2:119–20.

77. John Adams, Diary, September 3, 1774, in Butterfield, *Adams Diary*, 2:120–22.

78. John Adams, Diary, October 20, 1774, in Butterfield, *Adams Diary*, 2:155.

79. Peter Thompson, "The Friendly Glass: Drink and Gentility in Colonial Philadelphia," *The Pennsylvania Magazine of History and Biography*, 113, no. 4 (1989):564.

80. Richard J. Hooker, "The American Revolution Seen Through a Wine Glass," *William and Mary Quarterly* 11, no. 1 (1954):52–77.

81. Washington recorded few details in his diary during this period, usually his location, company, and sometimes the weather. Still, a look through those pages for both September and October 1774 reveals a quite vibrant social life with an impressive cast of characters. See Jackson and Twohig, *Diaries of Washington*, 3:273–88.

82. Robert Mackenzie to George Washington, September 13, 1774, in W. W. Abbot and Dorothy Twohig, *The Papers of George Washington: Colonial Series*, 10 vols. (Charlottesville: University of Virginia Press, 1983–1995), 10:161–62.

83. George Washington to Robert McKenzie, October 9, 1774, in *The Papers of George Washington*, Abbot and Twohig, 10:171–72.

84. "A Westchester Farmer," *The Congress Canvassed*, 12.

85. *Rivington's New York Gazetteer*, September 15, 1774.

86. *Essex Journal and Merrimack Packet*, October 5, 1774.

87. *Rivington's New York Gazetteer*, October 6, 1774.

88. "Extract from a Philadelphia Letter," *Essex Journal and Merrimack Packet*, October 5, 1774.

89. Worthington Chauncy Ford et al., eds., *Journals of the Continental Congress*, 34 vols. (Washington, DC: Government Printing Office, 1904–1937), 1:26.

90. Rick K. Wilson and Calvin Jillson, "Leadership Patterns in the Continental Congress: 1774–1789," *Legislative Studies Quarterly* 14, no. 1 (1989):5–37.

91. Thomas Cushing to Mrs. Cushing, October 4, 1774, in Burnett et al., *Letters of the Members*, 1:62.

92. John Adams to Abigail Adams, September 18, 1774, in Butterfield et al., *Adams Family Correspondence*, 1:35.

93. William Bradford to James Madison, October 17, 1774, in Hutchinson et al., *Madison Papers: Congressional Series*, 1:126.

94. John Adams to Abigail Adams, October 9, 1774, in Butterfield et al., *Adams Family Correspondence.*, 1:166–67.

95. John Adams, Diary, August 31, 1774, in Butterfield, *Adams Diary*, 2:117–18.

96. John Adams, Diary, September 12, 1774, in *Adams Diary*, 2:132–33.

97. Samuel Adams to Joseph Warren, September 25, 1774, in Cushing, *Writings of Adams*, 3:157–58.

98. Silas Deane to Mrs. Deane, September 1–3, 1774, in Burnett et al., *Letters of the Members*, 1:4.

99. Silas Deane to Mrs. Deane, September 10, 1774, in Burnett et al., *Letters of the Members*, 1:28.

100. Silas Deane to Mrs. Deane, September 6, 1774, in Burnett et al., *Letters of the Members*, 1:11.

101. Caesar Rodney to Thomas Rodney, September 9, 1774, in Ryden, *Rodney Letters*, 46–47.

102. *Pennsylvania Packet*, September 19, 1774; *Pennsylvania Gazette*, September 21, 1774; *Rivington's New York Gazetteer*, September 22, 1774, September 29, 1774; *Essex Journal and Merrimack Packet*, September 28, 1774; *Massachusetts Spy*, September 29, 1774.

103. Silas Deane to Mrs. Deane, September 12–16, 1774, in Burnett et al., *Letters of Members*, 1:32.

104. George Washington, Diary, September 16, 1774, in Jackson and Twohig, *Diaries of Washington*, 3:278.

105. *Pennsylvania Packet*, September 19, 1774.

106. *Pennsylvania Packet*, September 19, 1774.

107. Jonathan Williams Jr., to Benjamin Franklin, October 28, 1774, in Labaree et al., *Franklin Papers*, 21:342–44.

108. *Massachusetts Gazette*, November 10, 1774; *Rivington's New York Gazetteer*, November 17, 1774.

109. "Nathaniel Appleton to Josiah Quincy, November 15, 1774," in Force, *American Archives*, 1:980.

110. *Massachusetts Gazette*, December 16, 1774.

111. *Massachusetts Gazette*, December 22, 1774.

112. *Rivington's New York Gazetteer*, November 24, 1774; "Address from the Committee of Mechanicks of New York, Presented to the Delegates Who Represented this City at the General Congress," in Force, *American Archives*, 1:987.

113. *Virginia Gazette* (Dixon and Hunter ed.), November 10, 1774.

114. *Pennsylvania Packet*, November 14, 1774.

115. "To the Honourable Peyton Randolph, Esquire, Late President of the American Continental Congress," October 1774, in Force, *American Archives*, 1:939–45.

116. Robert Treat Paine to Stephen Collins, February 25, 1775, in Riley and Hanson, *Paine Papers*, 3:34–36.

117. Richard Henry Lee to Samuel Adams, February 4, 1775, in Curtis James Ballagh, *The Letters of Richard Henry Lee*, 2 vols. (New York: MacMillan Company, 1911–1914), 1:127–30.

118. Silas Deane to Patrick Henry, January 25, 1775, in Burnett, *Letters to Delegates*, 1:291.

119. Peyton Randolph to Charles Thomson, November 18, 1774, in Ford et al., *Journals of the Continental Congress*, 1:115.

120. "Joseph Reed to Josiah Quincy, 25 October 1774," in *Life and Correspondence of Joseph Reed: Military Secretary of Washington, at Cambridge; Adjutant General of the Continental Army; Member of the Congress of the United States; and President of the Executive Council of the State of* Pennsylvania, ed. William B. Reed, 2 vols. (Philadelphia: Lindsay and Blakiston, 1847), 1:85

121. Joseph Reed to Lord Dartmouth, October 15, 1774, in Reed, *Life and Correspondence of Joseph Reed: Military Secretary of Washington, at Cambridge; Adjutant General of the Continental Army; Member of the Congress of the United States; and President of the Executive Council of the State of Pennsylvania*, 82.

122. John Adams, Autobiography, in Butterfield, *Adams Diary*, 4:41–43.

123. "Letters from a Distinguished American, 6 February 1782" in Taylor et al., *Adams Papers*, 9:568–70.

CHAPTER THREE

1. There are several studies of the Continental Congress, though more often than not they combine both the First and Second Congress in the same work and typically have far more to say about the latter. For work on just the First Continental Congress, see David Ammerman, *In the Common Cause: American Response to the Coercive Acts of 1774* (New York: W. W. Norton and Company, 1974); H. James Henderson, *Party Politics in the First Continental Congress* (New York: McGraw-Hill Book Company, 1974); Jerrilyn Greene Marston, *King and Congress: The First Continental Congress Assumes Authority* (Princeton, NJ: Princeton University Press, 1987); Henry Wellenreuther, ed., *The Revolution of the People: Thoughts and Documents on the Revolutionary Process in North America, 1774–1776* (Gottingen: University of Gottingen, 2006). For studies that combine both the First and Second Congress, see Edmund Cody Burnett, *The Continental Congress* (New York: Macmillan Company, 1941); Jack P. Rakove, *The Beginnings of National Politics: An Interpretive History of the Continental Congress* (Baltimore, MD: Johns Hopkins University, 1979); Calvin Jillson and Rick K. Wilson, *Congressional Dynamics: Structure, Coordination, and Choice in the First American Congress, 1774–1789* (Stanford, CA: Stanford University Press, 1994).

2. Gregory J. W. Urwin, "'Abandoned to the Arts & Arms of the Enemy': Placing the 1781 Virginia Campaign in Its Racial and Political Context," in *The Harmon Memorial Lectures in Military History, 1988*-2017, ed. Mark Grotelueschen, (Montgomery, AL: Air University Press, 2020), 49–74.

3. Herbert Friedenwald, "The Continental Congress," *Pennsylvania Magazine of History and Biography* 19, no. 2 (1895):197–207.

4. See Worthington Chauncey Ford's prefatory note in Ford et al., eds., *Journals of the Continental Congress*, 34 vols. (Washington, DC: Government Printing Office, 1904–1937), 1:5–6.

5. Edmund Cody Burnett, "The 'More Perfect Union': The Continental Congress Seeks a Formula," *Catholic Historical Review* 24, no. 1 (1938):1–29.

6. Burnett, *Continental Congress*, vii, ix.

7. Rakove, *National Politics*, 27.

8. Rick K. Wilson and Calvin Jillson, "Leadership Patterns in the Continental Congress: 1774–1789," *Legislative Studies Quarterly* 14, no. 1 (1989):5–37.

9. See Richard R. Beeman, "The Democratic Faith of Patrick Henry," *Virginia Magazine of History and Biography* 95, no. 3 (1987):301–16. For an early biography that contains the little Henry actually wrote down, see Henry Wirt, *Patrick Henry, Life, Correspondence and Speeches*, 3 vols. (New York: Charles Scribner's Sons, 1891). For a modern biography, see Richard R. Beeman, *Patrick Henry: A Biography* (New York: McGraw-Hill, 1974).

10. See Middlekauff, *Glorious Cause*; Ferling, *Leap in the Dark*; John Ferling, *Setting the World Ablaze: Washington, Adams, Jefferson, and the American Revolution* (New York: Oxford University Press, 2000).

11. Silas Deane to Mrs. Deane, September 1–3, 1774, in *Letters of the Members of the Continental Congress*, eds. Edmund C. Burnett et al., 23 vols. (Washington, DC: Carnegie Institution of Washington, 1921–1936), 1:4–5.

12. Charles E. Peterson, "Carpenters' Hall," *Transactions of the American Philosophical Society* 43, no. 1 (1953):96–128.

13. John Adams, Diary, September 5, 1774, in *Diary and Autobiography of John Adams*, ed. L. H. Butterfield, 4 vols. (Cambridge, MA: Harvard University Press, 1961), 2:122.

14. Edward M. Riley, "The Independence Hall Group," *Transactions of the American Philosophical Society* 43, no. 1 (1953):7–42.

15. "Solomon Drowne to William Drowne, 9 November 1774," in *Pennsylvania Magazine of History and Biography* 48, no. 3 (1924), 237–38.

16. Peterson, "Carpenters' Hall," 96–97, 100.

17. John Adams, Diary, September 5, 1774, in Butterfield, *Adams Diary*, 2:122–24.

18. Cyril M. White, "Charles Thomson: The Irish-Born Secretary of the Continental Congress, 1774–1789," *Studies: An Irish Quarterly Review* 68, no. 268 (1979):33–45; Peterson, "Carpenters' Hall," 100–1.

19. Silas Deane to Mrs. Deane, September 5, 1774, in Burnett et al., *Letters to Members*, 1:11; James E. Hutson, "An Investigation of the Inarticulate: Philadelphia's White Oaks," *William and Mary Quarterly* 28, no. 1 (1971):3–25.

20. Peterson, "Carpenters' Hall," 100–1.

21. Caroline Robbins, "Rights and Grievances at Carpenters' Hall, September 5–October 26, 1774," *Pennsylvania History: A Journal of Mid-Atlantic Studies* 43, no. 2 (1976):100–18.

22. James Duane, "Notes on Proceedings," September 5, 1774, in Burnett et al., *Letters to Members*, 1:8.

23. John Adams, Diary, August 30, 1774, in Butterfield, *Adams Diary*, 2:122.

24. Silas Deane to Mrs. Deane, September 5, 1774, in Burnett et al., *Letters to Members*, 1:11.

25. James Duane, "Notes of Proceeding," September 5, 1774, in Burnett et al., *Letters to Members*, 1:8.

26. John Adams, Diary, September 5, 1774, in Butterfield, *Adams Diary*, 2:121–22.

27. James Duane, "Notes on the Proceedings," September 5, 1774 in Burnett et al., *Letters to Members*, 1:8.

28. "Joseph Galloway to William Franklin, 5 September 1774," in *Archives of the State of New Jersey: First Series, Documents Relating to the Colonial History of the State of New Jersey*, eds. Frederick W. Ricord and William Nelson, 10 vols. (Newark, NJ: Daily Advertiser Printing House, 1880–1886), 10:475–76.

29. Joseph Galloway to the Governor of New Jersey, September 5, 1774, in Burnett et al., *Letters to Members*, 1:9.

30. This quote, and more on Charles Thomson's participation in the radical politics of the American Revolution, can be found in the dated but still useful survey by Lewis R. Harley, *The Life of Charles Thomson: Secretary of the Continental Congress and Translator of the Bible from the Greek* (Philadelphia: George W. Jacobs & Company, 1900), 61–124.

31. John Sanderson, "Biography of the Signers of the Declaration of Independence," *American Quarterly Review* 1 (1827):30–31.

32. Sanderson, "Biography," 30–31.

33. John Adams, Diary, February 17, 1776, in *The Works of John Adams: Second President of the United States with A Life of the Author*, ed. Charles Francis Adams, 10 vols. (Boston: Charles C. Little and James Brown, 1851–1856), 3:29. Though Adams recorded this entry long after the First Continental Congress dissolved, this particular passage reveals the brewing frustration Adams had with Charles Thomson's method of recording Congress's minutes.

34. Galloway makes note of the journal's silence on debate and dissent several times, the most expansive account being Joseph Galloway, "Statement to a Committee of the House of Commons," October 14, 1774, in Burnett et al., *Letters to Members*, 1:76.

35. Thomas Bradbury Chandler, *What Think Ye of the Congress Now? or, An Inquiry, How Far Americans are Bound to Abide by and Execute the Decisions of, the Late Congress* (New York: James Rivington, 1775), 12–20.

36. Ford et al., *Journals of Congress*, 1:15–24, 30.

37. James Duane, "Notes of Proceedings," September 5, 1774, in Burnett et al., *Letters to Members*, 1:8–9.

38. Ford et al., *Journals of Congress*, 1:25.

39. John Adams, Diary, September 5, 1774, in Butterfield, *Adams Diary*, 2:122–24.

40. James Duane, "Notes of Proceedings," September 6, 1774, in Burnett et al., *Letters of Members*, 1:12–13.

41. John Adams, Diary, September 6, 1774, in, 2:124–26.

42. John Adams, Diary, September 6, 1774, in Butterfield, *Adams Diary*, 2:124.

43. Silas Deane to Mrs. Deane, September 5–6, 1774, in Burnett et al., *Letters to Members*, 1:11.

44. James Duane, "Notes of Proceedings," September 6, 1774, in Burnett et al., *Letters to Members*, 1:13.

45. John Adams, Diary, September 6, 1774, in Butterfield, *Adams Diary*, 2:124.

46. John Adams, Diary, September 8, 1774, in Butterfield, *Adams Diary*, 2:128.

For a survey of William Livingston's poetic endeavors, see Frank Shuffelton, "'Philosophic Solitude' and the Pastoral Politics of William Livingston," *Early American Literature* 17, no. 1 (1982):43–53. For a useful study of Livingston's legal mind, see Milton M. Klein, "The Rise of the New York Bar: The Legal Career of William Livingston," *William and Mary Quarterly* 15, no. 3 (1958):334–58.

47. For two articles on Galloway's commitment to and vision for the British Empire, see John Ferling, "Joseph Galloway: A Reassessment of the Motivations of a Pennsylvania Loyalist," *Pennsylvania History: A Journal of Mid-Atlantic Studies* 39, no. 2 (1972):163–86; John Ferling, "Compromise or Conflict: The Rejection of the Galloway Alternative to Rebellion," *Pennsylvania History: A Journal of Mid-Atlantic Studies* 43, no. 1 (1976):4–20.

48. Diary of Samuel Ward, September 9, 1774, in Burnett et al., *Letters of Members*, 1:27.

49. For more on this theme, see Forrest McDonald, *Novus Ordo Seclorum: The Intellectual Origins of the Constitution* (Lawrence: University of Kansas, 1985).

50. Joseph Galloway, *The Historical and Political Reflections on the Rise and Progress of the American Rebellion* . . . (London: G. Wilkie, 1780), 66.

51. Samuel Adams to Arthur Lee, January 29, 1775, in *The Writings of Samuel Adams*, ed. Harry Alonzo Cushing, 4 vols. (New York: Knickerbocker Press, 1904-7), 3:169–72.

52. Samuel Adams to Thomas Young, October 17, 1774, in Cushing, *The Writings of Samuel Adams* 3:162–63.

53. "John Dickinson to Arthur Lee, 27 October 1774" in Peter Force, ed., *American Archives: Consisting of a Collection of Authentic Records, State Papers, Debates, And Letters And Other Notices of Publick Affairs, the Whole Forming a Documentary History of the Origins and Progress of the North American Colonies; of the Causes and Accomplishments of the American Revolution; and of the Constitution of Government for the United States, to the Final Ratification Thereof: Fourth Series*, 6 vols. (Washington, DC, 1837–1853), 1:947.

54. See, among other publications, *Providence Gazette*, September 24, 1774; *Massachusetts Gazette and Boston Post-Boy*, September 26, 1774; *Massachusetts Spy*, September 29, 1774. For a good secondary survey see David Hackett Fischer, *Paul Revere's Ride* (New York: Oxford University Press, 1994), 26–27.

55. Galloway, *American Rebellion*, 66.

56. Joseph Galloway, "Statement," September 28, 1774, in Burnett et al., *Letters to Members*, 1:55.

57. Fischer, *Revere's Ride*, 26; Ford et al., *Journals of Congress*, 1:31–37.

58. Ford et al., *Journals of Congress*, 1:31–37.

59. Joseph Galloway, "Statement," September 28, 1774, in Burnett et al., *Letters to Members*, 1:55.

60. Joseph Galloway, "Statement," September 28, 1774, in Burnett et al., *Letters to Members*, 1:54; Galloway, *American Rebellion*, 69; Henderson, *Party Politics*, 38.

61. Joseph Galloway, "Statement," September 28, 1774, in Burnett et al., *Letters of Members*, 1:56.

62. John Adams, Diary, September 17, 1774, in Butterfield, *Adams Diary*, 2:134–35.

63. Ford et al., *Journals of Congress*, 1:39.

64. Samuel Adams to Charles Chauncy, September 19, 1774, in Cushing, *Writings of Adams*, 3:155–56.

65. Ford et al., *Journals of Congress*, 1:39–40.

66. Marston, *King and Congress*, 44.

67. *Rivington's New York Gazetteer*, September 29, 1774.

68. "Letter from Rye, New York, 24 September 1774" in *Rivington's New York Gazetteer*, November 10, 1774.

69. Thomas Bradbury Chandler, *A Friendly Address to All Reasonable Americans, on the Subject of Our Political Confusions: In Which the Necessary Consequences of Violently Opposing the King's Troops, and of a General Non-Importation Are Fairly Stated* (New York: James Rivington, 1774).

70. Ford et al., *Journals of Congress*, 1:41.

71. Ford et al., *Journals of Congress*, 1:43.

72. Ford et al., *Journals of Congress*, 1:51–52.

73. John Adams, Diary, September 28, 1774, in Butterfield, *Adams Diary*, 2:140.

74. John Adams, Diary, September 28, 1774, in Butterfield, *Adams Diary*, 2:141–44.

75. Joseph Galloway, "Statement Relative to his Plan of Union," September 28, 1774, in Burnett et al., *Letters to Members*, 1:56–57.

76. Ferling, "Compromise or Conflict," 5.

77. Ferling, "Joseph Galloway," 177; Ferling, *A Leap in the Dark*, 118.

78. Joseph Galloway to Richard Jackson, August 10, 1774, in *Colonies to Nation: A Documentary History of the American Revolution*, ed. Jack P. Greene, (New York: W. W. Norton and Company, 1967), 238–39.

79. Joseph Galloway, "Statement Relative to his Plan of Union," September 28, 1774, in Burnett et al., *Letters to Members*, 1:57.

80. Galloway, *American Rebellion*, 77, 78, 80.

81. Congress did not include the actual plan as presented to Congress in its journals. Galloway provided an outline in his *American Rebellion*, 70. A more expansive discussion can be found in his 1775 pamphlet, *A Candid Examination of the Mutual Claims of Great-Britain, and the Colonies: With a Plan of Accommodation, on Constitutional Principles*, in *The American Revolution: Writings from the Pamphlet Debate, 1764-1776*, ed. Gordon S. Wood, 2 vols. (New York: Library of America, 2015), 2:411–57.

82. Joseph Galloway, "Statement Relative to his Plan of Union," September 28, 1774, in Burnett et al., *Letters of Members*, 1:56–59.

83. Robert Calhoun, "'I Have Deduced Your Rights': Joseph Galloway's Concept of His Role, 1774–1775," *Pennsylvania History: A Journal of Mid-Atlantic Studies* 35, no. 4 (1968):356–78; Julian P. Boyd, *Anglo-American Union: Joseph Galloway's Plans to Preserve the British Empire, 1774–1788* (Philadelphia: University of Pennsylvania Press,1941), 5–6, 16–17.

84. "Joseph Galloway to William Franklin, 3 September 1774," in Ricord and Nelson, *Archives of New Jersey*, 10:476; Henderson, *Party Politics*, 40–41.

85. Samuel Adams to Arthur Lee, May 18, 1774, in Cushing, *Writings of Adams*, 3:117–19.

86. "To the Freemen of America," in *Pennsylvania Gazette*, May 18, 1774; "To the Freemen of America," in *Connecticut Journal*, May 27, 1774; "To the Freemen of America," in *Massachusetts Spy*, June 2, 1774.

87. *New-York Gazette*, September 29, 1774; *Massachusetts Spy*, October 13, 1774.

88. "Connecticut Resolutions, 12 May 1774," in Force, *American Archives*, 1:356–57.

89. "Westmoreland Resolutions, 22 June 1774," in Force, *American Archives*, 1:437–38.

90. "South Carolina Resolutions, 8 July 1774," in Force, *American Archives*, 1:525–26.

91. "Essex County Resolutions, 9 July 1774," in Force, *American Archives*, 1:527–28.

92. Ford et al., *Journals of Congress*, 1:31–37.

93. Ford et al., *Journals of Congress*, 1:55–56.

94. Samuel Ward, Diary, October 6, 1774, in Burnett et al., *Letters to Members*, 1:64; Ford et al., *Journals of Congress*, 1:57.

95. Ford et al., *Journals of Congress*, 1:59–60.

96. "The Continental Congress to General Gage," October 10, 1774, in Cushing, *Writings of Adams*, 3:159–62.

97. Ford et al., *Journals of Congress*, 1:59–61.

98. Ford et al., *Journals of Congress*, 1:81–90.

99. Ford et al., *Journals of Congress*, 1:89–90.

100. Ford et al., *Journals of Congress*, 1:62. There is some controversy over who exactly sat on the committee to draft the "Memorial to the People of British America." Curators found a complete manuscript draft of the memorial in John Dickinson's papers in his own hand, though the records of Congress do not list Dickinson, who had only taken his seat as delegate for Pennsylvania on October 17, 1774, as a member of the committee.

101. Ford et al., *Journals of Congress*, 1:101.

102. Ford et al., *Journals of Congress*, 1:101.

103. "American Biography," *American Quarterly Review* 1:414.

104. John Adams to Thomas Jefferson, November 12, 1813, in *The Papers of Thomas Jefferson: Retirement Series*, ed. J. Jefferson Looney, 14 vols. (Princeton, NJ: Princeton University Press, 2004–2017), 6:612–14

105. Like the "Memorial to the People of British America," there is some controversy surrounding the exact authorship of Congress's "Petition to the King." For an outstanding examination, see Edwin Wolf, "The Authorship of the 1774 Address to the King Restudied," *William and Mary Quarterly* 22, no. 2 (1965):189–224.

106. Ford et al., *Journals of Congress*, 1:115–21.

CHAPTER FOUR

1. James Duane, "Notes of Proceedings," September 6, 1774, in *Letters of the Members of the Continental Congress*, eds. Edmund C. Burnett et al., 24 vols. (Washington, DC: Carnegie Institution of Washington, 1921–1936), 1:12–13.
2. John Adams to Abigail Adams, September 16, 1774, in *Adams Family Correspondence*, eds. L. H. Butterfield et al., 13 vols. (Cambridge, MA: Harvard University Press, 1963–), 1:156–57.
3. Worthington Chauncy Ford et al., eds., *Journals of the Proceedings of Congress*, 34 vols. (Washington, DC: Government Printing Office, 1904–1937), 1:26; James Duane, "Notes of Proceedings," September 6, 1774, in *Letters to Members*, eds. Burnett et al., 1:13. For an early but useful examination of Duché's role in Congress, see Edward Neill and John Hancock, "Jacob Duché, the First Chaplain of Congress," *Pennsylvania Magazine of History and Biography* 2, no. 1 (1878):58–73.
4. James Duane, "Notes on Proceedings," September 7, 1774, in *Letters to Members*, eds. Burnett et al., 1:13.
5. Ps.35: 1–4, 13, 14, 17, 27 (NRSV).
6. Silas Deane to Mrs. Deane, September 7, 1774, in *Letters to Members*, eds. Burnett et al., 1:18.
7. "Samuel Ward Diary, 7 September 1774," in *Magazine of American History with Notes and Queries* 1, no. 1 (1877):440.
8. James Duane, "Notes on Proceedings," September 7, 1774, in *Letters to Members*, eds. Burnett et al., 1:15.
9. John Adams to Abigail Adams, September 16, 1774, in *Adams Family Correspondence*, eds. Butterfield et al., 1:156–57.
10. Martin J. Medhurst, "From Duché to Provoost: The Birth of Inaugural Prayer," *Journal of Church and State* 24, no. 3 (1982):573–88.
11. *Boston Gazette*, September 26, 1774.
12. John Adams, Diary, September 10, 1774, in *Diary and Autobiography of John Adams*, ed. L. H. Butterfield 4 vols. (Cambridge, MA: Harvard University Press, 1961), 2:157.
13. For more on this, see J. P. Sommerville, *Royalists and Patriots: Politics and Ideology in England, 1603–1640* (New York: Longman, 1986); Michael Braddick, *God's Fury, England's Fire: A New History of the English Civil Wars* (New York: Penguin, 2009).
14. For the most recent study that reveals the popular nature of the Glorious Revolution, see Steve Pincus, *1688: The First Modern Revolution* (New Haven, CT: Yale University Press, 2009). For the Glorious Revolution and its effects in the colonies, see Owen Stanwood, *The Empire Reformed: English America and the Glorious Revolution* (Philadelphia: University of Pennsylvania Press, 2011); Richard Johnson, "The Revolution of 1688–89 in the American Colonies" in *The Anglo-Dutch Moment: Essays on the Glorious Revolution and its World Impact*, ed. Jonathan Israel (Cambridge: Cambridge University Press, 1991), 215–40. For a valuable exploration of high court politics that led to the Glorious Revolution, see W. A. Speck, *Reluctant Revolutionaries: Englishmen and the Revolution of 1688* (Oxford: Oxford University Press, 1988).

15. Pauline Maier, *From Resistance to Revolution: Colonial Radicals and the Development of American Opposition to Britain, 1765–1776* (New York: W. W. Norton & Company, 1972), 4–12.

16. John Ferling, *A Leap in the Dark: The Struggle to Create the American Republic* (New York: Oxford University Press, 2003), 66.

17. Robert Middlekauff, *The Glorious Cause: The American Revolution, 1763–1789* (New York: Oxford University Press, 1982), 92–93. See also Dirk Hoeder, *Crowd Action in Revolutionary Massachusetts, 1765–1780* (New York: Academic Press, 1977); Arthur Meier Schlesinger, "Political Mobs and the American Revolution, 1765–1776," *Proceedings of the American Philosophical Society* 99, no. 4 (1955):244–50; Maier, *Resistance to Revolution*, 86–87.

18. T. H. Breen, *The Marketplace of Revolution: How Consumer Politics Shaped American Independence* (New York: Oxford, 2004), 19–20.

19. For a survey of colonial efforts to repeal the Stamp Act, see C. A. Weslager, *The Stamp Act Congress* (Newark: University of Delaware Press, 1976); Edmund S. Morgan and Helen M. Morgan, *The Stamp Act Crisis: Prologue to Revolution* (Chapel Hill: University of North Carolina Press, 1965).

20. For an exploration into the repeal of the Stamp Act, see Middlekauff, *Glorious Cause*, 111–14; Morgan and Morgan, *Stamp Act Crisis*, 49–50. For Samuel Adams on the Townshend Acts, see Adams to Arthur Lee, October 31, 1771, in *Writings of Samuel Adams*, ed. Harry Alonzo Cushing, 4 vols. (New York: G. P. Putnam's Sons, 1904–1908), 2:267; Breen, *Marketplace*, 19.

21. For a close study of the friendship between George Washington and George Mason, see Peter R. Henriques, "An Uneven Friendship: The Relationship Between George Washington and George Mason," *Virginia Magazine of History and Biography* 97, no. 2 (1989):185–204. See also Peter R. Henriques, *Realistic Visionary: A Portrait of George Washington* (Charlottesville: University of Virginia Press, 2006), 33–34.

22. George Washington to George Mason, April 5, 1769, in *The Papers of George Washington: Colonial Series*, eds. W. W. Abbot and Dorothy Twohig, 10 vols. (Charlottesville: University Press of Virginia, 1983-95), 8:177–81.

23. Breen, *Marketplace*, 20.

24. Samuel Adams to Stephen Sayre, November 16, 1770, in Cushing, *Writings of Adams*, 2:56–60.

25. Ferling, *A Leap in the Dark*, 89.

26. For a detailed account of this event, see Benjamin L. Carp, *Defiance of the Patriots: The Boston Tea Party and the Making of America* (New Haven, CT: Yale University Press, 2011), 227–33. See also Ferling, *Leap in the Dark*, 103–7.

27. Henry Laurens to John Laurens, January 21, 1774, in *The Papers of Henry Laurens*, eds. David R. Chestnut et al., 16 vols. (Columbia: University of South Carolina Press, 1981–2003), 9:245.

28. *New York Mercury*, December 11, 1752; *Independent Reflector*, May 3, 1753; *Boston Evening Post*, April 4, 1763.

29. *New York Gazette*, November 7, 1754.

30. *Independent Reflector*, May 3, 1753.

31. A standard study connecting virtue and avarice to happiness and decay is J. G. A. Pocock, *The Machiavellian Moment: Florentine Thought and the Atlantic Republican Tradition* (Princeton, NJ: Princeton University Press, 1975). See also Drew McCoy, *The Elusive Republic: Political Economy in Jeffersonian America* (New York: W. W. Norton and Company, 1980).

32. Morgan and Morgan, *Stamp Act Crisis*, 21–26; Ferling, *Leap in the Dark*, 30–31; Middlekauff, *Glorious Cause*, 65.

33. Frederick Bernays Wiener, "The Rhode Island Merchants and the Sugar Act," *New England Quarterly* 3, no. 3 (1930):464–500.

34. "Instructions of the Town of Boston to its Representatives in the General Court," May 24, 1764, in Cushing, *Writings of Adams*, 3:1–7.

35. Morgan and Morgan, *Stamp Act Crisis*, 21–26; Ferling, *Leap in the Dark*, 30–31, 34; Middlekauff, *Glorious Cause*, 65.

36. *Newport Mercury*, August 20, 1764; *Boston Newsletter*, September 13, 1764.

37. Morgan and Morgan, *Stamp Act Crisis*, 54–74.

38. Larry Gerlach, *Prologue to Independence: New Jersey and the Coming of the Revolution* (New Brunswick, NJ: Rutgers University Press, 1976), 117–19.

39. Anton-Hermann Chroust, "The Lawyers of New Jersey and the Stamp Act," *American Journal of Legal History* 6, no. 3 (1962):286–97; Gerlach, *Prologue to Independence*, 117–19.

40. *Pennsylvania Gazette*, October 10, 1765; Gerlach, *Prologue to Independence*, 117.

41. "Reflections of Patriotism," *Connecticut Courant*, April 24, 1769.

42. "Thoughts on Patriotism by the Celebrated Rousseau," *Boston Chronicle*, February 6, 1768.

43. "Publican Patriotism," *Boston Evening Post*, January 20, 1768.

44. *Boston Evening Post*, January 20, 1768.

45. George Mason to George Washington, April 5, 1769, in *Papers of Washington: Colonial Series*, eds. Abbot and Twohig, 8:182–84.

46. "Portius," *New York Gazette*, August 13, 1770.

47. "A Citizen," *Pennsylvania Gazette*, October 11, 1770.

48. "A Husbandman," *New Hampshire Gazette*, June 12, 1772.

49. *Newport Mercury*, February 7, 1774.

50. "For the Pennsylvania Packet: On Patriotism," *Pennsylvania Packet*, October 11, 1773; *Boston Evening Post*, November 8, 1773.

51. "On Declensions of Government" in *American Magazine or General Repository*, March 1769, at David Library of the American Revolution. Film 381. APS I. Reel 2.

52. "John Hancock's Address of March 5, 1774 to Commemorate the Bloody Tragedy," in *Royal American Magazine*, March 1774, at David Library of the American Revolution. Film 381. APS I. Reel 26.

53. H. James Henderson, *Party Politics in the First Continental Congress* (New York: McGraw-Hill Book Company, 1974), 81–85.

54. For a brief survey of this thinking see Paul A. Rahe, *Republics Ancient and Modern: New Modes and Orders in Early Modern Political Thought*, 3 vols. (Chapel Hill: University of North Carolina Press, 1994), 3:21-23.

55. Patrick Mullins, *Father of Liberty: Jonathan Mayhew and the Principles of the American Revolution* (Lawrence: University Press of Kansas, 2017), 45–49; Mark A. Knoll, "The American Revolution and Protestant Evangelicalism," *Journal of Interdisciplinary History* 23, no. 3 (1993):615–38; Middlekauff, *Glorious Cause*, 59.

56. Carl J. Richard, *The Founders and the Classics: Greece, Rome, and the American Enlightenment* (Cambridge, MA: Harvard University Press, 1994); Gordon S. Wood, "The Legacy of Rome in the American Revolution," in *The Idea of America: Reflections on the Birth of the United States*, ed. Gordon S. Wood (New York: Penguin, 2011), 57–79.

57. Wyger R. E. Velema, "Conversations with the Classics: Ancient Political Virtue and Two Modern Revolutions," *Early American Studies* 10, no. 2 (2012):415–38; Eran Shalev, *Rome Reborn on Western Shores: Historical Imagination and the Creation of the American Republic* (Charlottesville: University of Virginia Press, 2009); Richard, *The Founders and the Classics*; Wood, "The Legacy of Rome in the American Revolution," in *The Idea of America*, ed. Wood, 57–79.

58. McCoy, *The Elusive Republic*, 48–75.

59. "Gracchus," *Pennsylvania Packet*, October 17, 1774.

60. "Lucius Publicola," *Pennsylvania Packet*, October 24, 1774.

61. Velema, "Conversations with the Classics," 438.

62. See Margalit Finkelberg, "Virtue and Circumstances: On the City-State Concept of Arete," *American Journal of Philology* 123, no. 1 (2002):35–49; Paul Rahe, *Republics Ancient and Modern*, 3 vols. (Chapel Hill: University of North Carolina Press, 1994), 1:33.

63. Catalina Balmaceda, *Virtus Romana: The Concept of Virtus* (Chapel Hill: University of North Carolina Press, 2017), 16–41.

64. "Self-Denial Not the Essence of Virtue," in *Pennsylvania Gazette*, February 18, 1774. This essay explores the nature of virtue and concludes that self-denial for its own sake, like refraining from eating or drinking too much, is not exactly a virtue. Sacrificing for the public good and supporting the community, according to Franklin's essay, demonstrated political virtue.

65. Balmaceda, *Virtus Romana*, 16–41.

66. For an excellent survey on Puritanism and its influence on the revolutionary mind, see Edmund S. Morgan, "The Puritan Ethic and the American Revolution," in *William and Mary Quarterly* 24, no. 1 (1967):3–43; Carolyn Robbins, "Rights and Grievances at Carpenters' Hall, September 5–October 26, 1774," *Pennsylvania History: A Journal of Mid-Atlantic Studies* 43, no. 2 (1976):100–18; Henderson, *Party Politics*, 84.

67. For a survey of American dissent and the marginalization of its intellectual basis, see Andrew Shankman, "Liberty and Dignity in America," *The Remnant Review* 1, no. 1, 2005:67–112. See also Mullins, *Father of Liberty*, 47–49; Pincus, *1688*.

68. Mullins, *Father of Liberty*.

69. John Adams to Hezekiah Niles, February 13, 1818, in *The Works of John Adams*, ed. Charles Francis Adams, 10 vols. (Boston, MA: Little, Brown and Company, 1856), 10:271–72.
70. Mullins, *Father of Liberty*, 53–54; Jonathan Mayhew, *A Discourse Concerning Unlimited Submission and Non-Resistance to the Higher Powers* (Boston, MA: Daniel Fowle, 1750); Jonathan Mayhew, *The Snare Broken, a Thanksgiving-Discourse, Preached at the Desire of the West Church, in Boston* (Boston, MA: Richard and Samuel Draper, Edes and Gill, 1766).
71. Mullins, *Father of Liberty*, 51–52.
72. Samuel Adams to Thomas Young, October 17, 1774, in Cushing, *Adams Writings*, 3:162–63.
73. John Adams to Abigail Adams, September 20, 1774, in Butterfield et al., *Adams Family Correspondence*, 1:156–57.
74. Abigail Adams to John Adams, October 16, 1774, in Butterfield et al., *Adams Family Correspondence*, 1:172–74.
75. William Tudor to John Adams, September 26, 1774, in *The Papers of John Adams*, eds. Robert J. Taylor et al. 18 vols. (Cambridge, MA: Harvard University Press, 1977–2016), 2:174-76.
76. William Tudor to John Adams, September 26, 1774, in *The Papers of John Adams*, 2:174–76.
77. See, for example, "Prince George County (Virginia) Resolutions, 30 June 1774," and "Fauquier County (Virginia) Resolutions, 9 July 1774," in *American Archives: Consisting of a Collection of Authentic Records, State Papers, Debates, And Letters And Other Notices of Publick Affairs, the Whole Forming a Documentary History of the Origins and Progress of the North American Colonies; of the Causes and Accomplishments of the American Revolution; and of the Constitution of Government for the United States, to the Final Ratification Thereof: Fourth Series*, ed. Peter Force, 6 vols. (Washington, DC: 1837–1853), 1:493–95, 528–29
78. Ford et al., *Journals of Congress*, 1:75–76.
79. Ford et al., *Journals of Congress*, 1:76.
80. Vernon P. Creviston, "'No King Unless it be a Constitutional King': Rethinking the Place of the Quebec Act in the Coming of the American Revolution," *Historian* 73, no. 3 (2011):463–79; Paul Langston, "'Tyrant and Oppressor!': Colonial Press Response to the Quebec Act," *Historical Journal of Massachusetts* 34, no. 1 (2006):1–17. For a study that contextualizes the Quebec Act with American lawlessness on the frontier, see Matthew L. Rhoades, "Blood and Boundaries: Virginia Backcountry Violence and the Origins of the Quebec Act, 1758–1775," *West Virginia History* 3, no. 2 (2009):1–22.
81. For some standard examples, see Ferling, *Leap in the Dark*, 121; Middlekauff, *Glorious Cause*, 251–52; Maier, *Resistance to Revolution*, 251–52.
82. Ford et al., *Journals of Congress*, 1:75–76.
83. Ford et al., *Journals of Congress*, 1:77–79.
84. David Ammerman, *In the Common Cause: American Response to the Coercive Acts of 1774* (New York: W.W. Norton & Company, 1974), 114–15.

85. Hermann Wellenreuther, ed., *The Revolution of the People: Thoughts and Documents on the Revolutionary Process in North America, 1774–1776* (Göttingen: University of Göttingen, 2006) and Ammerman, *Common Cause*, are exceptions.
86. Ford et al., *Journals of Congress*, 1:78; McCoy, *Elusive Republic*, 69–75; Breen, *Marketplace*, 263–65; Eric Nelson, *The Greek Tradition in Republican Thought* (Cambridge: Cambridge University Press, 2004), 196–201, 245–46.
87. Ford et al., *Journals of Congress*, 1:78.
88. *Dictionarium Brittanicum: Or a More Compleat Universal Etymological English Dictionary* (London: Lamb, 1730), s.v. "Countenance."
89. "York County, Virginia Resolves, 18 July 1774," in Force, *American Archives*, 1:595–97.
90. *Pennsylvania Chronicle*, March 30, 1767; Rhys Isaac, *The Transformation of Virginia, 1740–1790* (Chapel Hill: University of North Carolina Press, 1982), 99–101.
91. Peter Clark, "Games and Sports in the Long Eighteenth Century: Failures in Transmission," in *Leisure Cultures in Urban Europe, 1700-1870: A Transitional Perspective*, eds. Peter Borsay and Jan Hein Furnée (Manchester: Manchester University Press, 2015), 72–89; N. L. Struna, *People of Prowess: Leisure and Labor in Early Anglo-America* (Urbana: University of Illinois Press, 1996), 76, 96.
92. Isaac, *The Transformation of Virginia*, 99–101.
93. T. H. Breen, "Horses and Gentlemen: The Cultural Significance of Gambling Among the Gentry of Virginia," *William and Mary Quarterly* 34, no. 2 (1977):239–57.
94. Isaac, *Transformation of Virginia*, 103; Struna, *People of Prowess*, 12.
95. Anne Fairfax Withington, *Toward a More Perfect Union: Virtue and the Formation of the American Republics* (New York: Oxford University Press, 1991), 186–91.
96. Kenneth Cohen, "'The Entreaties and Perswasions of our Acquaintance': Gambling and Networks in Early America," *Journal of the Early Republic* 31, no. 4 (2011):599–638.
97. *Pennsylvania Gazette*, November 1, 1764.
98. Withington, *More Perfect Union*, 20–24.
99. *Boston News Letter*, October 30, 1760.
100. "Philander," "Votaries of the Theater," *New-York Journal*, February 4, 1768.
101. For some insightful work on colonial funeral practices, see Steven C. Bullock and Sheila McIntyre, "The Handsome Tokens of a Funeral: Glove-Giving and the Large Funeral in Eighteenth-Century New England," *William and Mary Quarterly* 69, no. 2 (2012):305–46; Withington, *More Perfect Union*, 92–143; Isaac, *Transformation of Virginia*, 326–32.
102. See Withington, *More Perfect Union*, 92–143.
103. Ford et al., *Journals of Congress*, 1:79.
104. Ford et al., *Journals of Congress*, 1:79.
105. Gordon P. Kelly, *A History of Exile in the Roman Republic* (Cambridge: Cambridge University Press, 2009). For an exploration into Ovid's experience

in exile, see Sabine Grebe, "Why Did Ovid Associate His Exile with a Living Death," *Classical World* 103, no. 4 (2009):491–509.

106. For a study of excommunication, from its Roman roots to the shores of New England, see David C. Brown, "The Keys to the Kingdom: Excommunication in Colonial Massachusetts," *New England Quarterly* 67, no. 4 (1994); 531–66.

107. George Washington, Diary, October 26, 1774, in *Diaries of George Washington*, eds. Donald Jackson and Dorothy Twohig, 6 vols. (Charlottesville: University of Virginia, 1976–1979), 3:289; John Adams, Diary, October 26, 1774, in Butterfield, *Adams Diary*, 2:157.

108. Ford et al., *Journals of Congress*, 1:81.

109. Some examples include *New York Gazette and the Weekly Mercury*, October 31, 1774; *New York Journal*, November 3, 1774; *Boston Post-Boy*, November 7, 1774; *Massachusetts Spy*, November 10, 1774; *Connecticut Journal*, November 11, 1774; *Providence Gazette*, November 12, 1774; *Rivington's New York Gazetteer*, November 17, 1774.

110. Robert Aitken and Marilyn Aitken, "Magna Carta," *Litigation* 35, no. 3 (2009):59–62; Nicholas Vincent, "Magna Carta: From King John to Western Liberty," in *Magna Carta: History, Context, and Influence*, ed. Lawrence Goldman (London: University of London Press, 2018), 25–40.

111. A. E. Dick Howard, *The Road from Runnymede: Magna Carta and Constitutionalism in America* (Charlottesville: University of Virginia Press, 1968), 25.

112. Richard Bland, *An Inquiry into the Rights of the British Colonies* (Williamsburg, 1766), in *The American Revolution: Writings from the Pamphlet Debate*, ed. Gordon S. Wood, 2 vols. (New York: Library of America, 2015), 1:305–30.

113. Harry T. Dickinson, "Magna Carta in the American Revolution," in Goldman, *Magna Carta*, 70–100.

114. For example, John Adams condemned the Stamp Act as an unlawful tax that illegally forced violators to be tried in an admiralty court. See "Instructions Adopted by the Braintree Town Meeting, 24 September 1765," in *The Adams Papers: The Papers of John Adams*, eds. Robert J. Taylor, 18 vols. (1977–2016), 1:137–40. Adams defended John Hancock against a fine for smuggling wine by questioning the legality of the admiralty courts. He argued that the court's jurisdiction in that matter overturned Magna Carta. See L. Kinvin Wroth and Hiller B. Zobel, eds., *The Adams Papers: The Legal Papers of John Adams*, 3 vols. (Cambridge, MA: Harvard University Press, 1965), 2:194–210.

115. "A Londoner," March 9 (?), 1774, in *The Papers of Benjamin Franklin*, eds. Leonard W. Labaree et al., 42 vols. (New Haven, CT: Yale University Press, 1959-present), 21:134–38.

116. William W. Leap, *The History of Runnymede, New Jersey, 1626–1976* (New Jersey: Borough of Runnymede, 1981).

117. Dickinson, "Magna Carta and the American Revolution," 70–100.

118. Vincent, "Magna Carta," 36.

119. John Adams to William Wirt, January 23, 1818, in *The Works of John Adams: Second President of the United States*, ed. Charles Francis Adams, 10 vols. (Boston, MA: Little, Brown and Company, 1850–1856), 10:277–79.

120. Joseph Reed to Josiah Quincy, October 25, 1774, in *Life and Correspondence of Joseph Reed*, ed. William R. Reed, 2 vols. (Philadelphia, PA: Lindsay and Blakiston, 1847), 1:85.
121. Joseph Reed to William Legge, 2nd Earl of Dartmouth, December 10, 1774, in Reed, *Life and Correspondence* 1:88
122. "Extract from a Letter from a Gentleman in New York to His Correspondent in London, November 7, 1774," Force, *American Archives*, 1:969.
123. *Pennsylvania Packet*, November 28, 1774.
124. John Adams to William Wirt, January 23, 1818, in Adams, *Works of Adams*, 10:277–79.
125. "John Dickinson to Arthur Lee, 27 October 1774," in Force, *American Archives*, 1:947.
126. "John Dickinson to Josiah Quincy, Jr.," October 28, 1774, in Force, *American Archives*, 1:947–48.
127. Joseph Galloway, *Historical and Political Reflections on the Progress of the American Rebellion* (London: G. Wilkie, 1780), 91.
128. Edward Shippen Sr. to Joseph Shippen, Jr., November 25, 1774. New Jersey Historical Society. Manuscript Group 375. Shippen Family Papers, 1750–1775.
129. "Political Observations, Without Order: Addressed to the People of America," *Pennsylvania Packet*, November 14, 1774.
130. "Anti-Tormentor," *Pennsylvania Packet*, November 21, 1774.
131. "Lieutenant Governor Cadwallader Colden to William Legge, 2nd Earl of Dartmouth, November 2, 1774," in Force, *American Archives*, 1:957.
132. "Extract of a Letter from an Officer at Boston Camp to his Friend in Edinburgh, 3 November 1774," in Force, *American Archives*, 1:957–58.
133. "Extract of a Letter from the Honourable Governor Gage to William Legge, 2nd Earl of Dartmouth, 15 November 1774," in Force, *American Archives*, 1:981.
134. Samuel Seabury, *The Congress Canvassed: Or, An Examination into the Conduct of the Delegates at their Grand Convention, Held in Philadelphia, September 1, 1774. Addressed to the Merchants of New-York* (New York: James Rivington, 1775), 7, 15, 26, 27.
135. "Extract from a Letter received in New York, from a Mercantile House in Yorkshire, 31 December 1774," in Force, *American Archives*, 1:1080.
136. "John Legge, 2nd Earl of Dartmouth to Lieutenant Governor Cadwallader Colden, 7 January 1775," in Force, *American Archives*, 1:1101.
137. Thomas Bradbury Chandler, *What Think Ye of the Congress Now? or, An Inquiry, How Far Americans are Bound to Abide by and Execute the Decisions of, the Late Congress* (New York: James Rivington, 1775).
138. Edmund S. Morgan, *Inventing the People: The Rise of Popular Sovereignty in England and America* (New York: W. W. Norton and Company, 1988), 17–37. For an exploration into Loyalist clergymen and their support of the old order, see Gregg L. Frazer, *God against the Revolution: The Loyalist Clergy's Case against the American Revolution* (Lawrence: University Press of Kansas, 2018).
139. Leonard Woods Labaree, *Conservatism in Early America* (Ithaca, NY: Cornell University Press, 1948), 164–65.

140. "George III, Address to the House of Lords, 30 November 1774," in Force, *American Archives*, 1:1465.

CHAPTER FIVE

1. John Adams, Diary, September 6, 1774, in *Diary and Autobiography of John Adams*, ed. L. H. Butterfield, 4 vols. (Cambridge, MA: Harvard University Press, 1961), 2:124–26.
2. Jerrilynn Marston Greene, *King and Congress: The Transfer of Political Legitimacy* (Princeton, NJ: Princeton University Press, 1987), 67–99.
3. Worthington Chauncy Ford et al., eds., *Journals of the Proceedings of Congress*, 34 vols. (Washington, DC: Government Printing Office, 1904–1937), 1:79; David Ammerman, *In Common Cause: American Response to the Coercive Acts of 1774* (New York: W. W. Norton and Company, 1974), 84–85; Hermann Wellenreuther, "Associations, the People, Committee of Observation and Inspection and the Culture of Rights, 1774–1776," in *The Revolution of the People: Thoughts and Documents on the Revolutionary Process in North America, 1774-1776*, ed. Hermann Wellenreuther (Göttingen: University of Göttingen Press, 2006), 26.
4. This aspect of this chapter relies on the work of Jürgen Habermas, *The Structural Transformation of the Public Sphere* (Cambridge, MA: MIT Press, 1991); Benedict Anderson, *Imagined Communities: Reflections on the Origin and Spread of Nationalism* (London: Verso, 1983); Michael Warner, *The Letters of the Republic: Publication and the Public Sphere in Eighteenth-Century America* (Cambridge, MA: Harvard University Press, 1990).
5. As pointed out by Jeffery Pasley, resistance leaders weaponized the press during the crisis years. And while printers sympathetic to the Crown continued to publish gazettes critical of Congress and supportive of Parliament, the majority of papers found their financial support from resistance actors. The print coverage most colonists engaged with presented a decidedly pro-Whig narrative. See Pasley, *The Tyranny of Printers: Newspaper Politics in the Early Republic* (Charlottesville: University of Virginia Press, 2001), 33–40.
6. *Providence Gazette*, December 3, 1774.
7. *Essex Journal*, December 12, 1774.
8. *Connecticut Journal*, November 18, 1774.
9. For support in Maryland, see *Pennsylvania Gazette*, December 12, 1774. For support from Philadelphia, see *Boston Gazette*, November 28, 1774, *Massachusetts Gazette and Boston Weekly News-Letter*, December 22, 1774. For support at Boston see *Massachusetts Gazette and Boston Weekly News-Letter*, December 1, 1774, December 16, 1774.
10. *Essex Journal*, November 28, 1774; *Pennsylvania Gazette*, November 28, 1774, December 12, 1774.
11. *Virginia Gazette* (eds. Purdie and Dixon), December 1, 1774.
12. *Massachusetts Gazette and Boston Weekly News-Letter*, December 16, 1774, December 22, 1774; *Pennsylvania Gazette*, November 28, 1774, December 12, 1774.
13. *Connecticut Journal*, November 18, 1774; *Boston Gazette*, November 28, 1774; *Massachusetts Gazette and Boston Weekly News-Letter*, November 17,

1774; *Rivington's New York Gazetteer*, November 10, 1774, November 24, 1774; *Pennsylvania Packet*, November 7, 1774, November 21, 1774, December 12, 1774; *Pennsylvania Gazette*, November 2, 1774.

14. Harvey H. Jackson, "Factional Politics in Revolutionary Georgia, 1774–1777," *Georgia Historical Quarterly*, 59 no. 4 (1975):388–401; Ronald G. Killion and Charles T. Waller, *Georgia and the Revolution* (Atlanta, GA: Cherokee Publishing Company, 1975); Kenneth Coleman, *The American Revolution in Georgia, 1763–1789* (Athens: University of Georgia Press 1958); Leslie Hall, *Land and Allegiance in Revolutionary Georgia* (Athens: University of Georgia Press, 2001).

15. "Governor Sir James Wright to John Legge, 2nd Earl of Dartmouth, 24 August, 1774," in *American Archives, Consisting of a Collection of Authentic Records, State Papers, Debates, And Letters And Other Notices of Publick Affairs, the Whole Forming a Documentary History of the Origins and Progress of the North American Colonies; of the Causes and Accomplishments of the American Revolution; and of the Constitution of Government for the United States, to the Final Ratification Thereof: Fourth Series*, Peter Force, ed., 6 vols. (Washington, DC: 1837–1853) 1:731.

16. "Darien, Georgia Resolutions, 12 January 1775," in Force, *American Archives*, 1:1135–36.

17. "Extract from a Letter from Philadelphia, December 10, 1774," in *Essex Journal*, December 28, 1774.

18. For more examples, committees in New York City and Providence, Rhode Island, embraced Congress and dedicated themselves to supporting its measures, see *Massachusetts Gazette and Boston Weekly News-Letter*, December 16, 1774.

19. For open borrowing in the early years of the press, see Pasley, *Tyranny of Printers*, 8. For print media connecting geographically separated spaces, see Anderson, *Imagined Communities*; Warner, *Republic of Letters*.

20. For example, Woodbridge, New Jersey, named twenty-one committeemen to enforce the Continental Association. See "Woodbridge, New Jersey Endorses the Articles of Association, 7 January 1775," in Force, *American Archives*, 1:1102–03. Gloucester, New Jersey, identified seventy-seven men to make certain locals "punctually observed" the Association. See *Essex Journal*, December 12, 1774. Cumberland County, New Jersey, listed thirty-five men. See *Pennsylvania Packet*, January 9, 1775. James City, Virginia, named twenty-nine men. See "General Meeting at James County, Virginia," *Virginia Gazette* (eds. Purdie and Dixon), December 1, 1774. Anne Arundel County and Annapolis City each elected and publicized forty-four men to their committees, while Philadelphia listed sixty-one. See *Boston Gazette*, November 28, 1774; Boston identified sixty-three men. See *Massachusetts Gazette and Boston Weekly News-Letter*, December 16, 1774.

21. John Adams to Edward Biddle, December 12, 1774, in *The Papers of John Adams*, eds. Robert J. Taylor et al, 17 vols. (Cambridge, MA: Harvard University Press, 1977–2016), 2:199; Ammerman, *Common Cause*, 107–9.

22. Ammerman, *Common Cause*, 103.

23. Ammerman, *Common Cause*, 106–7.

24. Ammerman, *Common Cause*, 106–10. For the Continental Association in Georgia, see Coleman, *Revolution in Georgia*, 60–65; Hall, *Land and Allegiance*, 20–25.

25. Ammerman, *Common Cause*, 107–8.

26. *Boston Gazette*, December 12, 1774.

27. Gordon S. Wood, *The Radicalism of the American Revolution* (New York: Vintage Books, 1991), 43–47; Robert A. Gross, *The Minutemen and Their World* (New York: Hill and Wang, 1976), 78–80. For a useful study that fleshes out the origins of these trends, see Philip J. Greven Jr., "Family Structure in Seventeenth-Century Andover, Massachusetts," in *Colonial America: Essays in Politics and Social Development*, eds. Stanley N. Katz, John M. Murrin, and Douglas Greenburg (New York: McGraw Hill, 1983), 137–44.

28. Wellenreuther, "Associations," in Wellenreuther, *Revolution of the People*, 23–26.

29. "A Zealous Friend of Both Countries," *Pennsylvania Packet*, December 26, 1774.

30. For church and sociability in colonial Virginia, see Rhys Isaacs, *The Transformation of Virginia, 1740–1790* (Chapel Hill: University of North Carolina Press, 1982), 60.

31. George Washington to Townshend Dade Jr., November 19, 1774, in *The Papers of George Washington: Colonial Series*, eds. W. W. Abbot and Dorothy Twohig, 10 vols. (Charlottesville: University Press of Virginia, 1983–1995), 10:187.

32. For an example of literature critical of Congress and the Continental Association, see "Free Thoughts on the Proceedings of the Grand Continental Congress" advertised in *Rivington's New York Gazetteer*, November 24, 1774.

33. *Virginia Gazette* (Purdie and Dixon ed.), December 1, 1774. For more on celebratory toasts as a method of unity, see Richard J. Hooker, "The American Revolution Seen Through a Wine Glass," *William and Mary Quarterly* 11, no. 1 (1954):52–77.

34. *Essex and Merrimack Packet*, October 26, 1774.

35. *Connecticut Journal*, October 24, 1774; *Massachusetts Gazette and Weekly News-Letter*, November 3, 1774.

36. *Pennsylvania Packet*, October 31, 1774; *Rivington's New York Gazetteer*, November 3, 1774, November 17, 1774; *Virginia Gazette* (Purdie and Dixon ed.), November 3, 1774; *Pennsylvania Gazette*, November 2, 1774; *Massachusetts Gazette and Weekly News-Letter*, November 10, 1774, December 8, 1774. For owning copies as tokens of inclusion, see "Extract from a Letter from a Gentleman in New York to His Correspondent in London, 7 November 1774," Force, *American Archives*, 1:969.

37. *The Wonderful Appearance of an Angel, Devil, and Ghost to a Gentleman in the Town of Boston, in the Nights of the 14th, 15th, and 16th, of October, 1774* (Boston, MA: John Boyle, 1774). For advertisements for this pamphlet see *Massachusetts Gazette and Weekly News-Letter*, December 16, 1774, December 22, 1774, December 29, 1774.

38. "Bob Jingle," *The Association &c. of the Delegates of the Colonies, at the Grand Congress, Held at Philadelphia, Sept. 1, 1774, Versified, and Adapted to Music, Calculated for Grave and Gay Dispositions* (1774).

39. "Bob Jingle," *The Association &c. of the Delegates of the Colonies, at the Grand Congress.* Some advertisements for this pamphlet can be found in *Massachusetts Gazette and Boston Weekly News-Letter*, December 22, 1774, December 29, 1774.

40. Tim Fulford, "Britannia's Heart of Oak: Thompson, Garrick, and the Language of Eighteenth-Century Patriotism," in *James Thompson: Essays for the Tercentenary*, ed. Richard Terry, (Liverpool: Liverpool University Press, 2000), 191–215.

41. "Poet's Corner," in *Massachusetts Spy*, September 1, 1774.

42. "Poet's Corner," in *Massachusetts Spy*, September 15, 1774, September 22, 1774.

43. "Poet's Corner," in *Massachusetts Spy*, October 6, 1774.

44. *Pennsylvania Packet*, November 21, 1774.

45. Brigadier General Timothy Ruggles, "To the Printers of the Boston Newspapers, 22 December 1774," in Force, *America Archives*, 1:1057.

46. "To the People of New Jersey," *Rivington's New York Gazetteer*, December 1, 1774.

47. Thomas Bradbury Chandler, *What Think Ye of the Congress Now? or, An Inquiry, How Far Americans are Bound to Abide by and Execute the Decisions of, the Late Congress* (New York: James Rivington, 1775), 41–42.

48. Samuel Seabury ["A Westchester Farmer," pseud.], *The Congress Canvassed: Or, An Examination into the Conduct of the Delegates at their Grand Convention, Held in Philadelphia, September 1, 1774. Addressed to the Merchants of New-York* (New York: 1775), 14–16, 25.

49. "A Freeholder of Essex," "Message to Stephen Crane, John De Hart, William Livingston, W. P. Smith, Elias Boudinot, & co., December 1775," in Force, *American Archives*, 1:1094–96.

50. *Massachusetts Gazette and Boston Weekly News-Letter*, December 29, 1774.

51. Memorandum of the King, [1773?], in *The Correspondence of King George III*, ed. Sir John Fortescue, 6 vols. (London: MacMillan and Company, 1927–1928), 3:47–48. Fortescue misdated this note, as colonists did not have a Congress in 1773. W. Baring Pemberton, a biographer of Lord Frederick North, also commented on this minor but consequential error in his *Lord North* (London: Longmans, Green, and Company, 1938), 276, n398. George III likely drafted this memorandum in late 1774 or early 1775, after Congress sent the *Journals of the Proceedings of the Congress* to multiple agents in England to present to the king.

52. *Pennsylvania Gazette*, February 4, 1775.

53. *Boston News-Letter*, December 29, 1774.

54. *Providence Gazette*, December 24, 1774.

55. Richard Henry Lee to Samuel Adams, February 4, 1775, in *The Letters of Richard Henry Lee*, 2 vols. (New York: MacMillan Company, 1911–1914), 1:129.

56. *Rivington's New York Gazetteer*, October 13, 1774.

57. *New York Gazette and Weekly Mercury*, February 20, 1775.

58. *Essex Journal and Merrimack Packet*, October 12, 1774.

59. *Rivington's New York Gazetteer*, October 20, 1774.

60. *Pennsylvania Packet*, December 26, 1774.

61. "To the Farmers of Berks County, 16 January 1775," in Force, *American Archives*, 1:1144.

62. "Association Signed by the Ladies Association of Edenton, North Carolina," in Force, *American Archives*, 1:1050–51.

63. *Boston Evening Post*, November 28, 1774.

64. *Pennsylvania Packet*, December 12, 1774.

65. William L. Saunders, ed., *Colonial and State Records of North Carolina*, 26 vols. (Raleigh, NC: P. M. Hale, 1890), 9:1091.

66. *South Carolina Gazette*, November 21, 1774.

67. *Maryland Gazette*, April 15, 1775, as quoted in Ammerman, *In Common Cause*, 116.

68. Saunders, *Records of North Carolina*, 9:1091.

69. *Boston Gazette*, December 26, 1774.

70. *Pennsylvania Gazette*, November 9, 1774, November 18, 1774.

71. *New York Journal*, December 1, 1774.

72. *Boston Gazette*, December 12, 1774. A shorter version of this event appears in the *Boston Evening-Post*, December 12, 1774.

73. *Providence Gazette*, December 3, 1774.

74. *Boston Gazette*, December 26, 1774.

75. *Connecticut Journal*, November 18, 1774; *Boston Gazette*, November 21, 1774; *Essex Journal*, December 28, 1774, February 15, 1775; *New Hampshire Gazette*, January 13, 1775; *New York Gazette*, January 30, 1775; *Boston Evening Post*, March 13, 1775.

76. For more obituaries that attach virtue to funereal frugality, see *New-York Journal*, December 1, 1774; *Boston Gazette*, November 21, 1774, November 28, 1774; *Massachusetts Gazette and Boston Weekly News-Letter*, November 17, 1774.

77. *Essex Journal*, December 28, 1774.

78. Ann Fairfax Withington, *Toward a More Perfect Union: Virtue and the Formation of American Republics* (New York: Oxford University Press, 1991), 92–143.

79. Ford et al., *Journals of Congress*, 1:102.

80. For Peyton Randolph's health, see Thomas Jefferson's *Biography of Peyton Randolph*, July 26, 1816, in *The Papers of Thomas Jefferson*, eds. Julian P. Boyd et al., 44 vols. (Princeton, NJ: Princeton University Press, 1950–present), 10:268–71. For Randolph's value to Congress's efforts, see George Washington to John Hancock, November 2, 1775, in *The Papers of George Washington: Revolutionary War Series*, eds. Philander D. Chase et al., 26 vols., (Charlottesville: University of Virginia Press, 1985–2018), 2:288–89; John Adams to James Warren, October 23, 1775, in Taylor et al., *Adams Papers*, 3:229–30; *Pennsylvania Packet*, October 30, 1775.

81. Richard Henry Lee to George Washington, October 22–23, 1775, in Chase et al., *Washington Papers*, 2:217–18.

82. John Adams to James Warren, October 23, 1775, in Taylor et al., *Adams Papers*, 3:229–30.

83. Ford et al., *Journals of Congress*, 3:303–4; Samuel Ward to Henry Ward, October 24, 1775, in *Letters of the Members of the Continental Congress*, eds. Edmund C. Burnett et al., 24 vols. (Washington, DC: Carnegie Institution of Washington, 1921-36), 1:240.

84. Solomon Drowne to Sally Drowne, November 12, 1775, in *Pennsylvania Magazine of History and Biography* 5 (1881), 112.

85. *Virginia Gazette* (Dixon and Hunter ed.), November 10, 1775.

86. *Virginia Gazette* (Dixon and Hunter ed.), November 29, 1776.

87. Anderson, *Imagined Communities*; Warner, *Republic of Letters*.

88. Some examples of these advertisements can be found in the *Boston Gazette*, June 16, 1760, September 1, 1760, March 30, 1760; *Pennsylvania Gazette*, October 2, 1760, February 12, 1761.

89. Odia Johnson and William J. Burling, eds., *The Colonial American Stage, 1665–1774: A Documentary Calendar* (Madison, NJ: Fairleigh Dickinson University Press, 2002).

90. Mark Evans Bryan, "'Slideing into Monarchical Extravagance': Cato at Valley Forge and the Testimony of William Bradford Jr.," *William and Mary Quarterly* 67, no. 1 (2010):123–44.

91. Jason Shaffer, "'An Excellent Die': Death, Mourning, and Patriotism in the Propaganda Plays of the American Revolution," *Early American Literature* 41, no. 1 (2006):1–27.

92. See Paul A. Rahe, *Republics Ancient and Modern*, 3 vols. (Chapel Hill: University of North Carolina Press, 1994), 1:129–39; Peter Arnott, "Greek Drama as Education," *Educational Theater Journal* 22, vol. 1 (1970):35–42; Richard McKeon, ed., *An Introduction to Aristotle* (Chicago: University of Chicago Press, 1970), 1448–51.

93. Joy Connolly, "Antigone and Addison's Cato: Redeeming Exemplarity in Political Thought," *International Journal of the Classical Tradition* 21, vol. 3 (2014):317–25; Hannah Filipowicz, "School for Patriots?: The Foundational Dramas of the American and Polish Revolutions Revisited," *Canadian Slavonic Papers* 52, no.1/2 (2010):19–45; Bernard Bailyn, *The Ideological Origins of the American Revolution* (Cambridge, MA: Belknap Press of Harvard University Press, 1967), 44.

94. Shaffer, "Excellent Die," 3–7.

95. Christine Dunn Henderson and Mark E. Yellin, "'Those Stubborn Principles': From Stoicism to Sociability in Joseph Addison's 'Cato,'" *Review of Politics* 76, no. 2 (2014):223–41; Filipowicz, "School for Patriots," 21.

96. Anderson, *Imagined Communities*; Warner, *Republic of Letters*; Pasley, *Tyranny of Printers*; Shaffer, "Excellent Die," 3; Bailyn, *Ideological Origins*, 44.

97. For the print availability and general popularity of *Cato*, as well as the message colonists received from the work, see Forrest McDonald, "Foreword," in

Joseph Addison, *Cato: A Tragedy and Other Selected Essays*, eds. Christine Dunn Henderson and Mark E. Yellin (Indianapolis, IN: Liberty Fund, 2004), ix; See also Bailyn, *Ideological Origins*, 44.

98. Peter R. Henriques, *Realistic Visionary: A Portrait of George Washington* (Charlottesville: University of Virginia Press, 2006), 53, 81–82, 172, 181, 209–10; Gordon S. Wood, *Revolutionary Characters: What Made the Founders Different* (New York: Penguin Books, 2006), 36; John Ferling, *The Ascent of George Washington: The Hidden Political Genius of an American Icon* (New York: Bloomsbury Press, 2009), 11–12; Joseph J. Ellis, *His Excellency: George Washington* (New York: Alfred A. Knopf, 2004), 229; H. C. Montgomery, 'Washington the Stoic," *Classical Journal* 31, no. 6 (1936):371–73.

99. Wellenreuther, "Associations," in Wellenreuther, *Revolution of the People*, 28.

100. *Boston Post-Boy*, 16 January 1775.

101. *Boston Post-Boy*, 16 January 1775.

102. *Essex Journal*, February 15, 1775.

103. *Massachusetts Spy*, March 6, 1775.

104. "New York, 6 November 1774" in Force, *American Archives*, 1:963; *Virginia Gazette* (Dixon and Hunter ed.), November 24, 1774.

105. "Extract from a Letter from Governor Wentworth to William Legge, 2nd Earl of Dartmouth, 2 December 1774" in Force, *American Archives*, 1:1013.

106. *Massachusetts Gazette and Boston Weekly News-Letter*, December 8, 1774.

107. "Committee of Newport, Rhode Island, to the Committee of Philadelphia, 5 January 1775," in Force, *American Archives.*, 1:1098–99.

108. *Virginia Gazette* (Dixon and Hunter ed.), November 24, 1774.

109. Georgetown Committee to St. James Santee Committee, December 28, 1775, in *The Papers of Henry Laurens*, eds. David R. Chestnut, et al., 16 vols. (Columbia: University of South Carolina Press, 1981–2003), 10:594–95.

110. St. James Santee Committee to Georgetown Committee, December 30, 1775, in Chestnut, *The Papers of Henry Laurens*, 10:599–600.

111. For some examples of these auctions and the range of merchandise made available, see *Boston Gazette*, December 19, 1774, December 26, 1774; *Essex Journal*, December 28, 1774, December 28, 1774; "Fairfax County, Virginia Committee, 19 December 1774," and "Charles County, Virginia Committee, 4 January 1775," in Force, *American Archives*, 1:1051, 1091–92.

112. Henry Laurens to John Laurens, February 18, 1775, in *Papers of Laurens*, Chestnut et al., 10:70–73.

113. *South Carolina Gazette*, December 26, 1774.

114. George Washington to Robert McMickan, January 7, 1775, in Abbot and Twohig, *Papers of Washington: Colonial Series*, 10:225–26.

115. Thomas Jefferson to Archibald Cary and Benjamin Harrison, December 9, 1774, in Boyd et al., *Papers of Jefferson*, 1:154–56.

116. *Essex Journal*, February 15, 1775.

117. *Boston Evening Post*, November 28, 1774.

118. "Halifax County, North Carolina Committee, 21 December 1774," in Force, *American Archives*, 1:1055.
119. "Caroline County, Virginia Committee, 16 December 1774," in Force, *American Archives*, 1:1047–48.
120. "By the Committee for Anne Arundel County and the City of Annapolis, 24 December 1774," in Force, *American Archives*, 1:1061.
121. *Massachusetts Gazette and Boston Weekly News-Letter*, December 8, 1774.
122. "Epsom, New Hampshire Resolves, 9 January 1775," in Force, *American Archives*, 1:1105.
123. For a survey of tarring and feathering during the imperial crisis period, see Benjamin Irvin, "Tar, Feathers, and the Enemies of American Liberties, 1768–1776," *New England Quarterly* 76, no. 2 (2003): 197–238.
124. Coleman, *Revolution in Georgia*, 65–66.
125. "Middlesex County, New Jersey Resolutions, 3 January 1775," and "Morris County, New Jersey, 9 January 1775," in Force, *American Archives*, 1:1083–85, 1106.
126. "Ulster County, New York, 6 January 1775," in Force, *American Archives*, 1:1100.
127. "A Meeting of the Freeholders of Elizabethtown, New Jersey, 1 December 1774," in Force, *American Archives*, 1:1012.
128. "To the Committee Appointed to See the Measures of the Congress Executed, Philadelphia, 30 November 1774," in Force, *American Archives*, 1:1011.
129. "Woodbridge, New Jersey Committee, 7 January 1774," in Force, *American Archives*, 1:1102–3.
130. "Extract of a Letter from Annapolis to a Gentleman in New York, February 1775," in Force, *American Archives*, 1:1208.
131. "Wethersfield, Connecticut, 14 February 1775," in Force, *American Archives*, 1:1236.
132. Larry Bowman, "The Virginia County Committees of Safety, 1774–1776," *Virginia Magazine of History and Biography* 79, no. 3 (1971):322–37.
133. "Letter from a Gentleman in Westmoreland County, Virginia, to his Friend in Glasgow, 30 June 1774, from the *Glasgow Journal*, 18 August 1774," in Force, *American Archives*, 1:971–72.
134. "Westmoreland County, Virginia Committee, November 8, 1774," in Force, *American Archives*, 1:970.
135. "Letter from Georgia to a Gentleman in New York, 7 September 1774," and "Sir James Wright to the William Legge, 2nd Earl of Dartmouth, 13 December 1774," in Force, *American Archives*, 1:773, 1040; Coleman, *Revolution in Georgia*, 40; Hall, *Revolutionary Georgia*, 20; *Rivington's New York Gazetteer*, October 13, 1774.
136. *Pennsylvania Packet*, November 21, 1774; Hall, *Land and Allegiance*, 21.
137. Ronald G. Killion and Charles T. Waller, *Georgia and the Revolution* (Atlanta, GA: Cherokee Publishing Company, 1975), especially chapter 2.
138. "St. John's Parish, 9 February 1775," in Force, *American Archives*, 1:1161.

139. "St. John's Parish, Georgia, 9 February 1775," in Force, *American Archives*, 1:1161; Killion and Waller, *Georgia and the Revolution*.

140. "Charleston, South Carolina Resolutions, 24 February 1775" in Force, *American Archives*, 1:1163; Killion and Waller, *Georgia and the Revolution*.

141. Council of Safety to Stephen Bull, December 29, 1775, in Chestnut et al., *Papers of Laurens*, 10:597–98.

142. "Charleston, South Carolina Resolutions, 24 February 1775" in Force, *American Archives*, 1:1163.

143. Christopher Gadsden to William and Thomas Bradford, March 28, 1775, in *The Writings of Christopher Gadsden*, ed. Richard Walsh, (Columbia: University of South Carolina Press, 1966), 101–2.

144. Council of Safety to Stephen Bull, December 29, 1775, in Chestnut et al., *Papers of Laurens*, 10:597–98.

145. Diary of Samuel Ward, September 9, 1774, in Burnett et al., *Letters of Members*, 1:27.

146. Samuel Adams to Elbridge Gerry, October 29, 1775, Cushing, *Writings of Adams*, 3:229–31.

147. Samuel Adams to James Warren, November 4, 1775, in Cushing, *Writings of Adams*, 3:233–38.

148. *Massachusetts Spy*, January 12, 1775.

149. *Boston Gazette*, December 26, 1774.

150. Abigail Adams to John Adams, July 16, 1775, in Butterfield, *Adams Papers*, 1:245–51.

151. *Massachusetts Gazette*, March 2, 1775.

152. "To Cato, Cassandra, and all the Writers on the Independent Controversy," *Pennsylvania Ledger*, 6 April 1776.

153. *New York Gazette and Mercury*, February 20, 1775.

154. William Franklin Speech, May 15, 1775. New Jersey Historical Society. MG37, Governor of New Jersey Manuscripts (1756–1813).

155. See John Ferling, *The Loyalist Mind: Joseph Galloway and the American Revolution* (University Park: Pennsylvania State University Press, 1977); Robert Ernst, "Isaac Low and the American Revolution," *New York History* 74, no. 2 (1993):133–57; Kevin J. Dellape, "Jacob Duché: Whig-Loyalist?," *Pennsylvania History: Journal of Mid-Atlantic Studies* 62, no. 3 (1995):293–305.

156. Mercy Otis Warren, *History of the Rise, Progress, and Termination of the American Revolution, Interspersed with Biographical, Political, and Moral Observations*, ed. Lester Cohen, 2 vols. (Indianapolis, IN: Liberty Fund, 1994) 1:86.

157. Robert Middlekauff, *The Glorious Cause: The American Revolution, 1763–1789* (New York: Oxford University Press, 1982), 319–20; John Ferling, *A Leap in the Dark: The Struggle to Create the American Republic* (New York: Oxford, 2003), 145–49.

158. A Declaration by the Representatives of the United Colonies of North-America, now met in Congress at Philadelphia, setting forth the Causes and Necessity of their taking up Arms, in Boyd et al., *Papers of Jefferson*, 1:213–19; Ferling, *Leap in the Dark*, 145. See also Julian P. Boyd, "The Disputed Author-

ship of the Declaration on the Causes and Necessity for Taking Up Arms, 1775," *Pennsylvania Magazine of History and Biography* 74 (1950):51–73.

159. For colonial thoughts on a selfless king, see William D. Liddle, "'A Patriot King, or None': Lord Bolingbroke and the American Renunciation of George III," *Journal of American History* 65, no. 4 (1979):951–70. For George III's speech, see "A Proclamation by the King for Suppressing Rebellion and Sedition, 23 August, 1775," in *Documents of American History*, ed. Henry Steele Commager (New York: Appleton-Century-Crofts, 1968), 96.

160. Ferling, *Leap in the Dark*, 150. For the transcript, see "His Majesty's Most Gracious Speech to Both Houses of Parliament, 27 October 1775," Library of Congress, accessed August 29, 2021, https://www.loc.gov/item/rbpe.10803800/.

161. Thomas Jefferson to John Randolph, November 29, 1775, in Boyd et al., *Papers of Jefferson*, 1:268–70.

162. James Madison to William Bradford, January 20, 1775, in *The Papers of James Madison*, eds. William T. Hutchinson et al., 17 vols. (Chicago: University of Chicago Press, 1962–), 1:134–38.

163. "A Song on Liberty," *Massachusetts Spy*, May 26, 1774.

164. "A Freeman," in *New England Chronicle, or Essex Gazette*, November 16, 1775; *Connecticut Gazette*, December 1, 1775.

165. John Adams, Notes on Debates, September 6, 1774, in Burnett et al., *Letters of Members*, 1:14.

166. Silas Deane to Patrick Henry, January 2, 1775, in *Letters of Delegates to Congress, 1774–1789*, eds. Paul H. Smith et al., 26 vols. (Washington, DC: Library of Congress, 1976–2000), 1:291.

167. Joseph Reed to Dennis De Berdt, February 13, 1775, in *Life and Correspondence of Joseph Reed*, ed. William B. Reed, 2 vols. (Philadelphia, PA: Lindsay and Blakiston, 1847), 1:96.

168. John Adams to Mercy Otis Warren, April 16, 1776, in Taylor et al., *Adams Papers*, 4:123–26.

169. Notes of Proceedings in the Continental Congress, 7 June to 1 August 1776, in Boyd et al., *Papers of Jefferson*, 1:299–329.

170. John Adams to the United States Senate, December 23, 1799, in *The Works of John Adams, Second President of the United States*, ed. Charles Francis Adams, 10 vols. (Boston, MA: Little, Brown and Company, 1850–1856), 9:142–43.

171. David Ramsey, *The History of the American Revolution*, ed. Lester Cohen, 2 vols. (Philadelphia, PA: R. Aitken & Son, 1789), 2:319–20.

CONCLUSION

1. Herbert Friedenwald, "The Continental Congress," *Pennsylvania Magazine of History and Biography* 19, no. 2 (1895):197–207; Worthington Chauncey Ford's prefatory note in *Journals of the Continental Congress*, eds. Ford et al., 34 vols. (Washington, DC: Government Printing Office, 1904–1937), 1:5–6; Edmund Cody Burnett, "The 'More Perfect Union': The Continental Congress Seeks a Formula," *Catholic Historical Review* 24, no. 1 (1938):1–29; Rick K. Wilson and Calvin Jillson, "Leadership Patterns in the Continental Congress:

1774–1789," *Legislative Studies Quarterly* 14, no. 1 (1989):5–37; H. James Henderson, *Party Politics in the First Continental Congress* (New York: Mc-Graw-Hill Book Company, 1974); Jack P. Rakove, *The Beginnings of National Politics: An Interpretive History of the Continental Congress* (Baltimore, MD: Johns Hopkins University, 1979).

2. T. H. Breen, *The Marketplace of Revolution: How Consumer Politics Shaped American Independence* (New York: Oxford University Press, 2004).

3. David Ammerman, *In the Common Cause: American Response to the Coercive Acts of 1774* (New York: W. W. Norton and Company, 1974), 108.

4. Hermann Wellenreuther, ed., *The Revolution of the People: Thoughts and Documents on the Revolutionary Process in North America, 1774–1776* (Göttingen: University of Göttingen, 2006).

5. Edmund Cody Burnett differentiated between the economic and cultural regulations outlined in the Continental Association but did not go beyond making that distinction. See Burnett, *The Continental Congress* (New York: Macmillan Company, 1941), 55–58.

6. Anne Fairfax Withington, *Toward a More Perfect Union: Virtue and the Formation of the American Republics* (New York: Oxford University Press, 1991).

7. Jerrilyn Greene Marston, *King and Congress: The Transfer of Political Legitimacy, 1774–1776* (Princeton, NJ: Princeton University Press, 1987), 43–44; Breen, *Marketplace of Revolution*, 2–4. See also "Proceedings in the Fields, New York, 6 July 1774" and "Committee of Correspondence at Westerly, Rhode Island to the Committee of Boston, 19 May 1774," in *American Archives: Consisting of a Collection of Authentic Records, State Papers, Debates, And Letters And Other Notices of Publick Affairs, the Whole Forming a Documentary History of the Origins and Progress of the North American Colonies; of the Causes and Accomplishments of the American Revolution; and of the Constitution of Government for the United States, to the Final Ratification Thereof: Fourth Series*, Peter Force, ed., 6 vols. (Washington, DC, 1837–1853), 1:312, 336–37.

8. Judith Nisse Shklar, "Politics and Friendship," *Proceedings of the American Philosophical Society* 137, no. 2 (1993):207–12; Peter Thompson, *Rum Punch and Revolution: Taverngoing and Public Life in Eighteenth-Century Philadelphia* (Philadelphia: University of Pennsylvania Press, 1999); David W. Conroy, *In Public Houses: Drink and the Revolution of Authority in Colonial Massachusetts* (Chapel Hill: University of North Carolina Press, 1995); Robert Earle Graham, "The Taverns of Colonial Philadelphia," *Transactions of the American Philosophical Society* 43, no. 1 (1953):318–25. See also Silas Deane to Mrs. Deane, September 6, 1774, Edmund C. Burnett et al., eds., *Letters of the Members of the Continental Congress*, 24 vols. (Washington, DC: Carnegie Institution of Washington, 1921–1936), 1:11; "Joseph Reed to Josiah Quincy, 25 October 1774," in *Life and Correspondence of Joseph Reed: Military Secretary of Washington, at Cambridge; Adjutant General of the Continental Army; Member of the Congress of the United States; and President of the Executive Council of the State of Pennsylvania*, ed. William B. Reed, 2 vols. (Philadelphia, PA: Lindsay and Blakiston, 1847), 1:85.

9. For some examples, see John Adams, Diary, September 3, 1774, in *Diary and*

Autobiography of John Adams, ed. L. H. Butterfield, 4 vols. (Cambridge, MA: Harvard University Press, 1961), 2:119–20; *Pennsylvania Packet*, September 19, 1774.

10. For the selection of Carpenters' Hall, see Caroline Robbins, "Rights and Grievances at Carpenters' Hall, September 5–October 26, 1774," *Pennsylvania History: A Journal of Mid-Atlantic Studies* 43, no. 2 (1976):100–18; Silas Deane to Mrs. Deane, September 5, 1774, in Burnett et al., *Letters to Members*, 1:11. For Charles Thomson's election, see "Joseph Galloway to William Franklin, 5 September 1774," in *Archives of the State of New Jersey: First Series, Documents Relating to the Colonial History of the State of New Jersey*, eds. Frederick W. Ricord and William Nelson, 10 vols. (Newark, NJ: Daily Advertiser Printing House, 1880–1886), 10:475–76.

11. For the moment that inspired Charles Thomson to record Congress's minutes in this fashion, see John Sanderson, "Biography of the Signers of the Declaration of Independence," *American Quarterly Review*, vol. 1 (1827); 30–31. See also Ford et al., *Journals of Congress*.

12. For the floor debate on locating American liberties, see John Adams, Diary, September 8, 1774, in Butterfield, *Adams Diary*, 2:128.

13. Joseph Galloway, *The Historical and Political Reflections on the Rise and Progress of the American Rebellion* (London: G. Wilkie, 1780), 66; John Adams, Diary, September 8, 1774, in Butterfield, *Adams Diary*, 2:129–30.

14. For the Suffolk Resolves, see Worthington Chauncy Ford et al., eds., *Journals of the Continental Congress*, 34 vols. (Washington, DC: Government Printing Office, 1904–1937), 1:31–37.

15. For Congress's letter to Thomas Gage, Address to the people of Great Britain, Memorial to the Inhabitants of North American, and Petition to the King, see Ford et al., *Journals of Congress*, 1:60–61, 82–90, 90–101, 115–22.

16. John Ferling, *Leap in the Dark: The Struggle to Create the American Republic* (New York: Oxford University Press, 2003), 121; Robert Middlekauff, *Glorious Cause: The American Revolution, 1763–1789* (New York: Oxford University Press, 1982), 251–52; Maier, *Resistance to Revolution: Colonial Radicals and the Development of American Opposition to Britain, 1765–1776* (New York: W. W. Norton & Company, 1972), 251–52.

17. For some examples, see *Pennsylvania Gazette*, November 2, 1774; *Pennsylvania Packet*, November 7, 1774; *Rivington's New York Gazetteer*, November 10, 1774; *Connecticut Journal*, November 18, 1774; *Virginia Gazette* (Purdie and Dixon ed.), December 1, 1774.

18. Anne Fairfax Withington, *Toward a More Perfect Union: Virtue and the Formation of the American Republics* (New York: Oxford University Press, 1991).

19. *Connecticut Journal*, November 18, 1774; *Boston Gazette*, November 21, 1774; *Boston Post-Boy*, January 16, 1775; *Essex Journal*, February 15, 1775.

20. "To the People of New Jersey," *Rivington's New York Gazetteer*, December 1, 1774; "A Freeholder of Essex," "Message to Stephen Crane, John De Hart, William Livingston, W. P. Smith, Elias Boudinot, & co., December 1775," and

"A Meeting of the Freeholders of Elizabethtown, New Jersey, 1 December 1774," in Force, *American Archives*, 1:1094–96, 1012.

21. Ford et al., *Journals of Congress*, 2:184–85; Barbara Clark Smith, *The Freedoms We Lost: Consent and Resistance in Revolutionary America* (New York: The New Press, 2010), 138.

22. John Adams to John Jay, August 6, 1785, in Lint et al., *Adams Papers*, 17:304–6.

23. Withington, *More Perfect Union*, 247–48.

24. Samuel Adams to Samuel Cooper, July 20, 1776, in *The Writings of Samuel Adams*, ed. Harry Alonzo Cushing, 4 vols. (New York: Knickerbocker Press, 1904–1907), 3:301–2.

25. Samuel Adams, to Benjamin Kent, July 27, 1776, in Cushing, *The Writings of Samuel Adams*, 3:303–4.

26. Thomas Jefferson to Benjamin Franklin, August 3, 1777, in Boyd et al., *Papers of Jefferson*, 2:26.

27. Thomas Jefferson to Benjamin Franklin, August 3, 1777, in Boyd et al., *Papers of Jefferson*, 2:26.

28. John Adams to a Friend in London, January 21, 1775, in Taylor et al., *Adams Papers*, 2:214–16.

SELECTED BIBLIOGRAPHY

The following selections represent the literature that proved fundamentally informative to the preceding pages.

PRIMARY SOURCES

PUBLISHED PRIMARY SOURCES

Abbot, W. W., and Dorothy Twohig, eds. *The Papers of George Washington: Colonial Series.* 10 vols. Charlottesville: University of Virginia Press, 1983–1995.

Adams, Charles Francis, ed. *The Works of John Adams: Second President of the United States with A Life of the Author.* 10 vols. Boston, MA: Charles C. Little and James Brown, 1851–1856.

Ballagh, Curtis James, ed. *The Letters of Richard Henry Lee.* 2 vols. New York: MacMillan and Company, 1911–1914.

Boyd, Julian P., et al., eds. *The Papers of Thomas Jefferson.* 43 vols. Princeton, NJ: Princeton University Press, 1950–2018.

Burnett, Edmund Cody et al., eds. *Letters of the Members of the Continental Congress.* 24 vols. Washington, DC: Carnegie Institution of Washington, 1921–1936.

Butterfield, L. H., ed. *Diary and Autobiography of John Adams,* 4 vols. Cambridge, MA: Harvard University Press, 1961.

Butterfield, L. H. et al., eds. *Adams Family Correspondence,* 13 vols. Cambridge, MA: Harvard University Press, 1963–present.

Carter, Clarence Edwin, ed. *The Correspondence of General Thomas Gage with Secretaries of State, and with the War Office and the Treasury, 1763–1775.* 2 vols. New Haven, CT: Yale University Press, 1931–1933.

Chase, Philander D. et al., eds. *The Papers of George Washington: Revolutionary War Series.* 26 vols. Charlottesville: University of Virginia Press, 1985–2018.

Chestnut, David R. et al., eds. *The Papers of Henry Laurens*. 16 vols. Columbia: University of South Carolina Press, 1981–2003.

Cresswell, Nicholas. *The Journal of Nicholas Cresswell*. New York: Dial Press, 1924.

Cushing, Harry Alonzo, ed. *The Papers of Samuel Adams*. 4 vols. New York: Knickerbocker Press, 1904–1907.

Drowne, Solomon. *Selected Letters of Dr. Solomon Drowne. Pennsylvania Magazine History and Biography* 48 (June 1924): 227–50.

Force, Peter, ed. *American Archives: Consisting of a Collection of Authentic Records, State Papers, Debates, And Letters And Other Notices of Publick Affairs, the Whole Forming a Documentary History of the Origins and Progress of the North American Colonies; of the Causes and Accomplishments of the American Revolution; and of the Constitution of Government for the United States, to the Final Ratification Thereof: Fourth Series*. 6 vols. (Washington, DC: 1837–1853).

Ford, Worthington Chauncy et al., eds. *Journals of the Continental Congress, 1774–1789*. 34 vols. Washington, DC: Washington Printing Office, 1904–1937.

Fortescue, Sir John, ed. *The Correspondence of King George III*. 6 vols. London: MacMillan and Company, 1927–1928.

Hutchinson, William T. et al., eds. *The Papers of James Madison: Congressional Series*. 17 vols. Chicago: University of Chicago Press, 1962–1991.

Wroth, L. Kinvin and Hiller B. Zobel, eds. *The Adams Papers: The Legal Papers of John Adams*. 3 vols. Cambridge, MA: Harvard University Press, 1965.

Labaree, Leonard et al., eds. *The Papers of Benjamin Franklin*. 42 vols. New Haven, CT: Yale University Press, 1959–present.

Looney, J. Jefferson, ed. *The Papers of Thomas Jefferson: Retirement Series*. 14 vols. Princeton, NJ: Princeton University Press, 2004–2017.

Mays, David John, ed. *The Letters and Papers of Edmund Pendleton*. 2 vols. Charlottesville: University Press of Virginia, 1967.

Reed, William B., ed. *Life and Correspondence of Joseph Reed: Military Secretary of Washington, at Cambridge; Adjutant General of* the Continental Army; Member of the Congress of the United States; and President of the Executive Council of the State of Pennsylvania, 2 vols. Philadelphia, PA: Lindsay and Blakiston, 1847.

Riley, Stephen T. and Edward W. Hanson, eds. *The Papers of Robert Treat Paine*. 5 vols. Charlottesville: University of Virginia Press, 2012–2020.

Ryden, George Herbert, ed. *Letters to and from Caesar Rodney: Member of the Stamp Act Congress and the First and Second Continental Congresses; Speaker of the Delaware Colonial Assembly*. Philadelphia: University of Pennsylvania Press, 2017.

Smith, Paul H. et al., eds. *Letters of Delegates to Congress, 1774–1789*. 26 vols. Washington, DC: Library of Congress, 1976–2000.

Taylor, Robert J. et al., eds. *The Papers of John Adams*. 18 vols. Cambridge, MA: Harvard University Press, 1977–present.

Walsh, Richard, ed. *The Writings of Christopher Gadsden*. Columbia: University of South Carolina Press, 1966.

Ward, Samuel. *Diary of Governor Samuel Ward, Delegate from Rhode Island. Magazine of American History with Notes and Queries* 1 (1877): 439–42.

Wirt, Henry. *Patrick Henry, Life, Correspondence and Speeches*. 3 vols. New York: Charles Scribner's Sons, 1891.

NEWSPAPERS

Boston Chronicle
Boston Evening-Post
Boston Gazette
Boston Newsletter
Boston Post-Boy
Connecticut Courant
Connecticut Gazette
Connecticut Journal
Essex Gazette
Essex Journal and Merrimack Packet
Georgia Gazette
Independent Reflector
Maryland Gazette
Massachusetts and Boston Weekly News-Letter

Massachusetts Gazette
Massachusetts Spy
New England Chronicle, or Essex Gazette
New Hampshire Gazette
Newport Mercury
New York Gazette and Weekly Mercury
New York Mercury
Pennsylvania Chronicle
Pennsylvania Gazette
Pennsylvania Ledger
Pennsylvania Packet
Providence Gazette
Rivington's New York Gazetteer
Virginia Gazette (Dixon and Hunter ed.)
Virginia Gazette (Purdie and Dixon ed.)

PAMPHLETS AND BOOKS

Chandler, Thomas Bradbury. *A Friendly Address to All Reasonable Americans, on the Subject of Our Political Confusions: In Which the Necessary Consequences of Violently Opposing the King's Troops, and of a General Non-Importation Are Fairly Stated.* New York: James Rivington, 1774.

———. *What Think Ye of the Congress Now? or, An Inquiry, How Far Americans are Bound to Abide by and Execute the Decisions of, the Late Congress.* New York: James Rivington, 1775.

Galloway, Joseph. *A Candid Examination of the Mutual Claims of Great-Britain, and the Colonies: With a Plan of Accommodation, on Constitutional Principles.* In *The American Revolution: Writings from the Pamphlet Debate, 1764–1776*, ed. Gordon S. Wood, 2 vols. 2:411–57. New York: Library of America, 2015.

———. *The Historical and Political Reflections on the Rise and Progress of the American Rebellion.* London: G. Wilkie, 1780.

"Bob Jingle." *The Association &c. of the Delegates of the Colonies, at the Grand Congress, Held at Philadelphia, Sept. 1, 1774, Versified, and Adapted to Music, Calculated for Grave and Gay Dispositions.* New York: James Rivington, 1774.

Mayhew, Jonathan. *A Discourse Concerning Unlimited Submission and Non Resistance to the Higher Powers.* Boston, MA: Daniel Fowle, 1750.

———. *The Snare Broken, a Thanksgiving-Discourse, Preached at the Desire of the West Church, in Boston.* Boston, MA: Richard and Samuel Draper, Edes, and Gill, 1766.

Oliver, Peter. *Origin and Progress of the American Rebellion.* Edited by Douglass Adair and John A. Shutz. San Marino, CA: The Huntington Library, 1961.

Ramsay, David. *The History of the American Revolution.* Edited by Lester H. Cohen. 2 vols. Indianapolis, IN: Liberty Fund, 1990.

Warren, Mercy Otis. *History of the Rise, Progress and Termination of the American Revolution, Interspersed with Biographical, Political, and Moral Observations.* Edited by Lester H. Cohen. 2 vols. Indianapolis, IN: Liberty Fund, 1994.

Seabury, Samuel. *The Congress Canvassed: Or, An Examination into the Conduct of the Delegates at their Grand Convention, Held in Philadelphia, September 1, 1774. Addressed to the Merchants of New-York.* New York: James Rivington, 1775.

The Wonderful Appearance of an Angel, Devil, and Ghost to a Gentleman in the Town of Boston, in the Nights of the 14th, 15th, and 16th, of October, 1774. Boston, MA: John Boyle, 1774.

SECONDARY SOURCES

BOOKS

Abbot, W. W. *The Royal Governors of Georgia, 1754–1775.* Chapel Hill: University of North Carolina Press, 1959.

Ammerman, David. *In the Common Cause: American Response to the Coercive Acts of 1774.* New York: W.W. Norton & Company, 1974.

Anderson, Benedict. *Imagined Communities: Reflections on the Origins and Spread of Nationalism.* London: Verso, 1983.

Bailyn, Bernard. *The Ideological Origins of the American Revolution.* Cambridge, MA: Harvard University Press, 1967.

Boyd, Julian P. *Anglo-American Union: Joseph Galloway's Plans to Preserve the British Empire, 1774–1788.* Philadelphia: University of Pennsylvania Press, 1941.

Breen, T. H. *The Marketplace of Revolution: How Consumer Politics Shaped American Independence.* New York: Oxford University Press, 2004.

Burnett, Edmund Cody. *The Continental Congress.* New York: Macmillan Company, 1941.

Carp, Benjamin. *Defiance of the Patriots: The Boston Tea Party and the Making of America.* New Haven, CT: Yale University Press, 2011.

Clark, Peter. "Games and Sports in the Long Eighteenth Century: Failures in Transmission." In *Leisure Cultures in Urban Europe, 1700-1870: A Transitional Perspective,* eds. Peter Borsay and Jan Hein Furnée, 72–90. Manchester: Manchester University Press, 2015.

Cohen, Lester H. *The Revolutionary Histories: Contemporary Narratives of the American Revolution.* Ithaca, NY: Cornell University Press, 1980.

Coleman, Kenneth. *The American Revolution in Georgia, 1763–1789.* Athens: University of Georgia Press, 1958.

Conroy, David W. *In Public Houses: Drink and the Revolution of Authority in Colonial Massachusetts.* Chapel Hill: University of North Carolina Press, 1995.

Dickinson, Harry T. "Magna Carta in the American Revolution." In *Magna Carta: History, Context, and Influence,* ed. Lawrence Goldman, 70, 100. London: University of London Press, 2018.

Ellis, Joseph J. *His Excellency: George Washington.* New York: Alfred A. Knopf, 2004.

———. *The Quartet: Orchestrating the Second American Revolution, 1783–1789.* New York: Vintage Books, 2015.

Ferling, John. *The Loyalist Mind: Joseph Galloway and the American Revolution.* University Park: Pennsylvania State University Press, 1977.

———. *Setting the World Ablaze: Washington, Adams, Jefferson, and the American Revolution.* New York: Oxford University Press, 2000.

———. *A Leap in the Dark: The Struggle to Create the American Republic.* New York: Oxford University Press, 2003.

———. *The Ascent of George Washington: The Hidden Political Genius of an American Icon.* New York: Bloomsbury Press, 2009.

Fischer, David Hackett. *Paul Revere's Ride*. New York: Oxford University Press, 1994.

Frazer, Gregg L. *God against the Revolution: The Loyalist Clergy's Case against the American Revolution*. Lawrence: University Press of Kansas, 2018.

Fulford, Tim. "Britannia's Heart of Oak: Thompson, Garrick, and the Language of Eighteenth-Century Patriotism." In *James Thompson: Essays for the Tercentenary*, ed. Richard Terry, 191–215. Liverpool: Liverpool University Press, 2000.

Gerlach, Larry. *Prologue to Independence: New Jersey and the Coming of the Revolution*. New Brunswick, NJ: Rutgers University Press, 1976.

Greven, Philip J. Jr. "Family Structure in Seventeenth-Century Andover, Massachusetts." In *Colonial America: Essays in Politics and Social Development*, eds. Stanley N. Katz, John M. Murrin, and Douglas Greenburg, 137–44. New York: McGraw Hill, 1983.

Griffin, Patrick. *America's Revolution*. New York: Oxford University Press, 2013.

Habermas, Jürgen. *The Structural Transformation of the Public Sphere*. Cambridge, MA: MIT Press, 1991.

Hall, Leslie. *Land and Allegiance in Revolutionary Georgia*. Athens: University Press of Georgia, 2001.

Harley, Lewis R. *The Life of Charles Thomson: Secretary of the Continental Congress and Translator of the Bible from the Greek*. Philadelphia, PA: George W. Jacobs & Company, 1900.

Henderson, H. James. *Party Politics in the First Continental Congress*. New York: McGraw-Hill Book Company, 1974.

Henriques, Peter R. *Realistic Visionary: A Portrait of George Washington*. Charlottesville: University of Virginia Press, 2006.

Hoeder, Dirk. *Crowd Action in Revolutionary Massachusetts, 1765–1780*. New York: Academic Press, 1977.

Howard, A. E. Dick. *The Road from Runnymede: Magna Carta and Constitutionalism in America*. Charlottesville: University of Virginia Press, 1968.

Isaac, Rhys. *The Transformation of Virginia, 1740–1790*. Chapel Hill: University of North Carolina Press, 1982.

Jillson, Calvin and Rick K. Wilson. *Congressional Dynamics: Structure, Coordination, and Choice in the First American Congress, 1774-1789*. Stanford, CA: Stanford University Press, 1994.

Johnson, Odia and William J. Burling, eds. *The Colonial American Stage, 1665–1774: A Documentary Calendar*. Madison, NJ: Fairleigh Dickinson University Press, 2002.

Kelly, Gordon P. *A History of Exile in the Roman Republic*. Cambridge: Cambridge University Press, 2009.

Killion, Ronald G. and Charles T. Waller. *Georgia and the Revolution*. Atlanta, GA: Cherokee Publishing Company, 1975.

Labaree, Leonard Woods. *Conservatism in Early America*. Ithaca, NY: Cornell University Press, 1948.

Maier, Pauline. *From Resistance to Revolution: Colonial Radicals and the Development of American Opposition to Britain, 1765–1776*. New York: W. W. Norton & Company, 1972.

Marston, Jerrilyn Greene. *King and Congress: The Transfer of Political Legitimacy, 1774–1776*. Princeton, NJ: Princeton University Press, 1987.

McCoy, Drew. *The Elusive Republic: Political Economy in Jeffersonian America*. New York: W. W. Norton & Company, 1980.

McDonald, Forrest. "Foreword." In Joseph Addison, *Cato: A Tragedy and Other Selected Essays*, eds. Christine Dunn Henderson and Mark E. Yellin. Indianapolis, IN: Liberty Fund, 2004.

Middlekauff, Robert. *The Glorious Cause: The American Revolution, 1763–1789*. New York: Oxford University Press, 1982.

Morgan, Edmund S. and Helen M. Morgan. *The Stamp Act Crisis: Prologue to Revolution*. Chapel Hill: University of North Carolina Press, 1962.

Morgan, Edmund S. *Inventing the People: The Rise of Popular Sovereignty in England and America*. New York: W. W. Norton & Company, 1988.

Mullins, Patrick. *Father of Liberty: Jonathan Mayhew and the Principles of the American Revolution*. Lawrence: University Press of Kansas, 2017.

Nelson, Eric. *The Greek Tradition in Republican Thought*. Cambridge: Cambridge University Press, 2004.

Newman, Simon P. *Parades and the Politics of the Street: Festive Culture in the Early American Republic*. Philadelphia, PA: University of Pennsylvania Press, 1997.

Onuf, Peter S. and Nicholas Cole. *Thomas Jefferson, the Classical World, and Early America*. Charlottesville: University of Virginia Press, 2011.

Pasley, Jeffrey L. *The Tyranny of Printers: Newspaper Politics in the Early Republic*. Charlottesville: University of Virginia Press, 2001.

Pasley, Jeffrey L., Andrew W. Robertson, and David Waldstreicher, eds. *Beyond the Founders: New Approaches to the Political History of the Early American Republic*. Chapel Hill: University of North Carolina Press, 2004.

Pemberton, W. Baring. *Lord North*. London: Longmans, Green, and Company, 1938.

Pocock, J. G. A. *The Machiavellian Moment: Florentine Thought and the Atlantic Republican Tradition*. Princeton, NJ: Princeton University Press, 1975.

Rahe, Paul. *Republics Ancient and Modern*, 3 vols. Chapel Hill: University of North Carolina Press, 1994.

Rakove, Jack N. *The Beginnings of National Politics: An Interpretive History of the Continental Congress*. Baltimore, MD: Johns Hopkins University Press, 1979.

Rice, Kym S. *Early American Taverns: For the Entertainment of Friends and Strangers*. New York: Regnery Gateway, 1983.

Richard, Carl J. *The Founders and the Classics: Greece, Rome, and the American Enlightenment* Cambridge, MA: Harvard University Press, 1994.

Shafir, Gershon, ed. *The Citizen Debates*. Minneapolis: University of Minnesota Press, 1998.

Shalev, Eran. *Rome Reborn on Western Shores: Historical Imagination and the Creation of the American Republic*. Charlottesville: University of Virginia Press, 2009.

Smith, Barbara Clark. *The Freedoms We Lost: Consent and Resistance in Revolutionary America*. New York: The New Press, 2010.

Struna, N. L. *People of Prowess: Leisure and Labor in Early Anglo-America*. Urbana: University of Illinois Press, 1996.

Thompson, Peter. *Rum Punch and Revolution: Taverngoing and Public Life in Eighteenth Century Philadelphia*. Philadelphia: University of Pennsylvania Press, 1999.

Vincent, Nicholas. "Magna Carta: From King John to Western Liberty." In *Magna Carta: History, Context, and Influence*, ed. Lawrence Goldman, 25–40. London: University of London Press, 2018.

Waldstreicher, David. *In the Midst of Perpetual Fetes: The Making of American Nationalism*. Chapel Hill: University of North Carolina Press, 1997.

Warner, Michael. *The Letters of the Republic: Publication and the Public Sphere in Eighteenth Century America*. Cambridge, MA: Harvard University Press, 1990.

Wellenreuther, Hermann, ed. *The Revolution of the People: Thoughts and Documents on the Revolutionary Process in North America, 1774–1776*. Göttingen: University of Göttingen, 2006.

Withington, Ann Fairfax. *Toward a More Perfect Union: Virtue and the Formation of American Republics*. New York: Oxford University Press, 1991.

Wood, Gordon S. *The Creation of the American Republic, 1776–1787*. Chapel Hill: University of North Carolina Press, 1969.

———. *The Radicalism of the American Revolution*. New York: Vintage Books, 1991.

———. *Revolutionary Characters: What Made the Founders Different*. New York: Penguin Books, 2006.

———, ed. *The Idea of America: Reflections on the Birth of the United States*. New York: Penguin, 2011.

ARTICLES

Aitken, Robert and Marilyn. "Magna Carta." *Litigation* 35 (Spring 2009): 59–62.

Arnott, Peter. "Greek Drama as Education." *Educational Theater Journal* 22 (March 1970): 35–42.

Beeman, Richard R. "The Democratic Faith of Patrick Henry." *Virginia Magazine of History and Biography* 95 (July 1987): 301–16.

Botein, Stephen. "Cicero as Role Model for Early American Lawyers: A Case Study in Classical Influence." *Classical Journal* 73 (April–May 1978): 313–22.

Bowman, "The Virginia County Committees of Safety, 1774–1776." *Virginia Magazine of History and Biography* 79 (July 1971): 322–37.

Boyd, Julian P. "The Disputed Authorship of the Declaration on the Causes and Necessity for Taking Up Arms, 1775." *Pennsylvania Magazine of History and Biography* 74 (January 1950): 51–73.

Breen, T. H. "Horses and Gentlemen: The Cultural Significance of Gambling Among the Gentry of Virginia." *William and Mary Quarterly* 34 (April 1977): 239–57.

———. "The Baubles of Britain: The American and Consumer Revolutions of the Eighteenth Century." *Past and Present* 119 (May 1988): 73–104.

Brown, David C. "The Keys to the Kingdom: Excommunication in Colonial Massachusetts." *New England Quarterly* 67 (December 1994); 531–66.

Bryan, Mark Evans. "'Slideing into Monarchical Extravagance': Cato at Valley Forge and the Testimony of William Bradford Jr." *William and Mary Quarterly* 67 (January 2010): 123–44.

Bullock, Steven C. and Sheila McIntyre. "The Handsome Tokens of a Funeral: Glove Giving and the Large Funeral in Eighteenth-Century New England." *William and Mary Quarterly* 69 (April 2012): 305–46.

Burnett, Edmund Cody. "The 'More Perfect Union': The Continental Congress Seeks a Formula." *Catholic Historical* Review 24 (April 1938): 1–29.

Calhoun, Robert M. "'I Have Deduced Your Rights': Joseph Galloway's Concept of his Role, 1774–1775." *Pennsylvania History: A Journal of Mid-Atlantic Studie*s 35 (October 1968): 356–78.

Chroust, Anton-Hermann. "The Lawyers of New Jersey and the Stamp Act." *American Journal of Legal History* 6 (July 1962): 286–97.

Cohen, Kenneth. "'The Entreaties and Perswasions of our Acquaintance': Gambling and Networks in Early America." *Journal of the Early Republic* 31 (Winter 2011): 599–638.

Creviston, Vernon P. "'No King Unless it be a Constitutional King': Rethinking the Place of the Quebec Act in the Coming of the American Revolution." *Historian* 73 (Fall 2011): 463–79.

Dellape, Kevin J. "Jacob Duché: Whig-Loyalist?" *Pennsylvania History: A Journal of Mid Atlantic Studies* 62 (Summer 1995): 293–305.

Ernst, Robert. "Isaac Low and the American Revolution." *New York History* 74 (April 1993): 133–57.

Ferling, John. "Joseph Galloway: A Reassessment of the Motivations of a Pennsylvania Loyalist." *Pennsylvania History: A Journal of Mid-Atlantic Studies* 39 (April 1972): 163–86.

————. "Compromise or Conflict: The Rejection of the Galloway Alternative to Rebellion." *Pennsylvania History: A Journal of Mid-Atlantic Studies* 43 (January 1976): 4–20.

Finkelberg, Margalit. "Virtue and Circumstances: On the City-State Concept of Arete." *American Journal of Philology* 123 (Spring 2002): 35–49.

Friedenwald, Herbert. "The Continental Congress." *Pennsylvania Magazine of History and Biography* 19 (1895): 197–207.

————. "The Journals and Papers of the Continental Congress." *Pennsylvania Magazine of History and Biography* 21. (1897): 161–84.

Graham, Robert Earle. "The Taverns of Colonial Philadelphia." *Transactions of the American Philosophical Society* 43 (1953): 318–25.

Grebe, Sabine. "Why Did Ovid Associate His Exile with a Living Death?" *Classical World* 103 (Summer 2009): 491–509.

Henderson, Christine Dunn and Mark E. Yellin. "'Those Stubborn Principles': From Stoicism to Sociability in Joseph Addison's 'Cato.'" *Review of Politics* 76 (Spring 2014): 23–41.

Henriques, Peter R. "An Uneven Friendship: The Relationship Between George Washington and George Mason." *Virginia Magazine of History and Biography* 97 (April 1989): 185–206.

Hooker, Richard J. "The American Revolution Seen Through a Wine Glass." *William and Mary Quarterly* 11 (January 1954): 52–77.

Irvin, Benjamin. "Tar, Feathers, and the Enemies of American Liberties, 1768–1776." *New England Quarterly* 76 (June 2003): 197–238.

Jackson, Harvey H. 'Factional Politics in Revolutionary Georgia, 1774–1777." *Georgia Historical Quarterly* 59 (Winter 1975): 388–401.

Klein, Milton M. "The Rise of the New York Bar: The Legal Career of William Livingston." *William and Mary Quarterly* 15 (July 1958): 334–58.

Knoll, Mark A. "The American Revolution and Protestant Evangelicalism." *Journal of Interdisciplinary History* 23 (Winter 1993): 615–38.

Langston, Paul. "'Tyrant and Oppressor!': Colonial Press Response to the Quebec Act." *Historical Journal of Massachusetts* 34 (Winter 2006): 1–17.

Liddle, William D. "'A Patriot King, or None': Lord Bolingbroke and the American Renunciation of George III." *Journal of American History* 65 (March 1979): 951–70.

Medhurst, Martin J. "From Duché to Provoost: The Birth of Inaugural Prayer." *Journal of Church and State* 24 (Autumn 1982): 573–88.

Morgan, Edmund S. "The Puritan Ethic and the American Revolution." *William and Mary Quarterly* 24 (January 1967): 3–43.

Montgomery, H. C. "Washington the Stoic." *Classical Journal* 31 (March 1936): 371–73.

Neill, Edward and John Hancock. "Jacob Duché, the First Chaplain of Congress." *Pennsylvania Magazine of History and Biography* 2 (1878): 58–73.

Peterson, Charles E. "Carpenters' Hall." *Transactions of the American Philosophical Society* 43 (1953): 96–128.

Riley, Edward M. "The Independence Hall Group." *Transactions of the American Philosophical Society* 43 (1953): 7–42.

Rhoades, Matthew L. "Blood and Boundaries: Virginia Backcountry Violence and the Origins of the Quebec Act, 1758–1775." *West Virginia History* 3 (Fall 2009): 1–22.

Robbins, Caroline. "Rights and Grievances at Carpenters' Hall, September 5–October 26, 1774." *Pennsylvania History: A Journal of Mid-Atlantic Studies* 43 (April 1976): 100–18.

Sanderson, Lewis R. "Biography of the Signers of the Declaration of Independence." *American Quarterly Review* (1827): 30–31.

Schlesinger, Arthur Meier. "Political Mobs and the American Revolution, 1765–1776." *Proceedings of the American Philosophical Society* 99 (August 1955): 244–50.

Shaffer, Jason. "'An Excellent Die': Death, Mourning, and Patriotism in the Propaganda Plays of the American Revolution." *Early American Literature* 41 (2006): 1–27.

Shankman, Andrew. "Liberty and Dignity in America." *Remnant Review* 1 (2005): 67–112.

Shklar, Judith Nisse. "Politics and Friendship." *Proceedings of the American Philosophical Society* 137 (June 1993).

Shuffelton, Frank. "'Philosophic Solitude' and the Pastoral Politics of William Livingston." *Early American Literature* 17 (Spring 1982): 43–53.

Stoudt, John Joseph. "The German Press in Pennsylvania and the American Revolution." *Pennsylvania Magazine of History and Biography* 59 (1935): 74–90.

Velema, Wyger R. E. "Conversations with the Classics: Ancient Political Virtue and Two Modern Revolutions." *Early American Studies* 10 (Spring 2012): 415–38.

Wiener, Frederick Bernays. "The Rhode Island Merchants and the Sugar Act." *New England Quarterly* 3 (July 1930): 464–500.

White, Cyril M. "Charles Thomson: The Irish-Born Secretary of the Continental Congress, 1774–1789." *Studies: An Irish Quarterly Review* 68 (Spring/Summer 1979): 33–45.

Wilson, Rick K. and Calvin Jillson. "Leadership Patterns in the Continental Congress: 1774-1789." *Legislative Studies Quarterly* 14 (February 1989): 5–37.

Wolf, Edwin. "The Authorship of the 1774 Address to the King Restudied." *William and Mary Quarterly* 22 (April 1965): 189–224.

York, Neil L. "Imperial Impotence: Treason in 1774 Massachusetts." *Law and History Review* 29 (August 2011): 657–701.

ACKNOWLEDGMENTS

THIS PRESENT WORK IS THE RESULT OF INSPIRATION I DREW FROM the discovery of a quote. While researching a paper on the American Revolution as a graduate student at Rutgers University, Camden, I stumbled upon a letter Thomas Jefferson had written to Benjamin Franklin in 1777. Within its lines, Jefferson described Americans' shift from monarchy to republicanism as a process no more troubling than changing clothes. I did not realize the gravity of this description at the time, as I had not given much thought to the emotional trauma some colonists experienced during those heady days of violent revolution. The quote stuck with me though, and I found myself repeating it in classrooms and lecture halls each academic year. While attending to doctoral studies at Temple University, I had several ideas for a dissertation but did not have the confidence that these earliest inquiries could sustain or even merit the length of a manuscript. I began paging through Peter Force's *American Archives*. I found in the first volume a collection of county- and parish-level resistance resolutions local Whigs had drafted in response to Parliament's Coercive Acts. I saw in these resolutions a grassroots call for colonists to join in self-denial and stand in solidarity with the suffering seaport of Boston. The continued adherence to this sacrifice, as far as I could tell, represented the process that Jefferson had drawn Franklin's attention to. After I completed my doctoral studies, my adviser, Gregory J.W. Urwin, pushed me to revise my dissertation before presenting it to get published. I spent about six months editing, re-thinking, and re-writing that manuscript. I am deeply grateful to Professor Urwin for his insights. I could not have been more fortunate in having such a seasoned scholar guide me on this journey.

Completing this book required many hearts, heads, and hands. Andrew Shankman of Rutgers University, Camden, read the draft and offered both valuable advice for improvement as well as some much-needed enthusiasm. Rick Demirjian invited me to present the first chapter at the Third Annual Conference on American Political History at the Lebanon Valley College Center for Political History and I gained critical insight for potential additions and suggestions for other avenues to explore. I received valuable critiques on the second chapter from participants attending a Temple Early Atlantic Seminar. I am also indebted to Susan Kern, Executive Director at William and Mary Historic Campus, who graciously took the time to help me navigate through the digital archives at Colonial Williamsburg. James Amemasor from the New Jersey Historical Society kindly took the time to assist me with the Shippen family papers. My colleagues at Cinnaminson High School (and beyond) helped out as well, reading early drafts of each chapter. I remain sincerely appreciative of Sean Wilson, Robert Becker, Daniel Matz, Laurie Hyland, and Chip Witte for taking the time to read and comment on my work. They patiently allowed themselves to be held as intellectual captives as I imposed upon their time. I am honored that Bruce H. Franklin and Don N. Hagist selected this present manuscript for inclusion in the Journal of the American Revolution book series.

Finally, a house does not make a home; the social environment within its walls, however, does. To that end, I can only say thank you to my wife, Jacquelyn, whose patience and willingness to take on more while I hunted for elusive evidence, made researching and writing this book possible. She also displayed remarkable fortitude as I no doubt bored her on countless occasions with any findings, theories, or odd anecdotes I discovered along the way. Incredibly, this publication synchronizes with our twentieth wedding anniversary. My young children, River, Dakota, and Kai, three demanding and curious little creatures, offered me a constant reminder of the tremendous cost of this pursuit. They reinforced how much I value what unfolds within the walls of our home. Thank you for your unconditional support, needed distractions, and the (more than) occasional dose of madness.

INDEX